£2-25

C000090383

THE ASSAULT ON THE RAND

24 June 2014

— Amazon.co.uk —

THE ASSAULT ON THE RAND

KEVIN WAKEFORD AND THE BATTLE
TO SAVE A CURRENCY

Barry Sergeant

This is for Mark, the GudMan, for always being there.

Published by Zebra Press
an imprint of Random House Struik (Pty) Ltd
Reg. No. 1966/003153/07
Wembley Square, First Floor, Solan Road, Gardens, Cape Town, 8001
PO Box 1144, Cape Town, 8000, South Africa

www.zebrapress.co.za

First published 2013

1 3 5 7 9 10 8 6 4 2

Publication © Zebra Press 2013
Text © Barry Sergeant 2013

Cover photographs © Kevin Wakeford: Raymond Preston/Times Media Syndication;
Thabo Mbeki: Keystone/FeatureNET/PictureNet;
Tito Mboweni: Shaun Harris/PictureNET Africa;
Jürgen Schrempp: AP Photo/Christof Stache/PictureNet
Author photo: Thys Dullaart

PUBLISHER: Marlene Fryer
MANAGING EDITOR: Robert Plummer
EDITOR: Mark Ronan
PROOFREADER: Lisa Compton
COVER AND TEXT DESIGNER: Jacques Kaiser
TYPESETTER: Monique van den Berg
INDEXER: Sanet le Roux

Set in 10.5 pt on 14 pt Minion

Printed and bound by Ultra-Litho, Johannesburg

ISBN 978 1 77022 554 1 (print)
ISBN 978 1 77022 555 8 (ePub)
ISBN 978 1 77022 556 5 (PDF)

Contents

Preface

Comme je descendais des Fleuves impassibles,
Je ne me sentis plus guidé par les haleurs ...

As I descended impassable rivers,
I no longer felt guided by the ferrymen ...
— Arthur Rimbaud

There are many events in a country's affairs that easily slip by or through the daily cacophony of the media – 'through the cracks'. This now includes social media, a force that has heavily democratised the news process and made it more difficult for news to remain suppressed. Yet whether today or centuries ago, there is another process that plays out by linking an array of events in a way that finds a lasting significance. How many of us are aware of this process?

Take the year 2001, one of the biggest ever in terms of hard news. Above all else, on 11 September, the World Trade Center in New York City was attacked, changing the course of world history. It was also the year that Enron, a darling of the US investment and media establishment, filed for bankruptcy, on 30 November. This was close to a global event. Certainly, it permanently changed the course of US corporate history.

The Enron debacle led to the promulgation of new laws, not least the so-called Sarbanes–Oxley Act of 2002, also known as the Public Company Accounting Reform and Investor Protection Act. This federal legislation set new or enhanced standards for all US-registered public company boards, management and public accounting firms.

Here in South Africa, 2001 was the year that would mark the country's greatest financial crisis. Seen in context and with great hindsight, the crisis was over so quickly that it almost seemed unbelievable. This was the year in which South Africa's currency, the rand, collapsed, when every-thing – including the 'fundamentals' so loved by economists and analysts – indicated that, if anything, the rand should have appreciated during 2001. Instead, when measured from its highest to lowest levels against the dollar during the year, the rand collapsed by as much as 45 per cent.

The South African government did not appear to have the vaguest idea of what was going on; if it did, it wasn't letting on. The Reserve Bank, the country's central bank, which is especially charged by the Constitution to defend the value of the rand, was, as it turned out, doing the opposite. It seemed bizarre that the charge to defend the currency would eventually come from a single person working in the private sector.

Late in 2001, Kevin Wakeford, the then CEO of the South African Chamber of Business, blew the whistle on the rand. Immediately, the currency started to appreciate and would do so for years. One of the most perplexing issues of the saga is that Wakeford was attacked from the start by the establishment – big (but not small) corporates, the big banks and various strategically placed persons in the political establishment.

Wakeford was, however, heavily supported by the man – more correctly today, the *person* – in the street. As the months went by during 2002, and the Rand Commission came and went, it was increasingly clear that Wakeford's short career as a whistle-blower was going to explode in his face. The narrative of this book examines the reasons for the rand's collapse, and the reasons for its recovery. Much of this discussion takes place – since there is no real choice – within an international context. Currencies, and especially free-floaters such as the rand, operate in the opposite of a vacuum.

But the narrative of this book is far more focused on the human elements of the rand's collapse, on the human consequences of being a whistle-blower. From early 2001, I developed a special affinity with Wakeford. As a human being and as a journalist, I found the collapse of the rand during 2001 irresistible. It caught the attention of a nation, and it really had my attention.

There were daily, sometimes hourly, sensational headlines and sound bites. But there was something else – something far larger, something elusive. There was a sense, to me at least, that the collapse of the rand was anything but random. Financial markets have perplexed us for centuries, and there was no reason to expect that there was much, if any, rationality behind the rand market during 2001. There were, however, people. It was a matter of finding out who was involved – behind the masks of the banks, the corporates and the various government institutions.

I also had a high degree of affinity with Wakeford's instincts as a whistle-blower. If I had been in his position at the time, I would have done exactly the same thing as he did, and faced the same consequences. As it turned out, I exposed the names of corporates and the bank that Wakeford named when he appeared under oath at the Rand Commission. Technically, I named the names before he did. In that sense, at least, I joined the ranks of whistle-blowers.

I have been blowing various whistles for many years, an activity for which I have been punished and persecuted time and again. Perhaps the most extreme of these was the cancellation of my UK passport in 2008. The British High Commission in Pretoria forced some artificial pretext on me, and after more than three decades of holding a UK passport, I was rendered stateless. I was an international refugee.

Two of my sisters, who decades ago had been granted UK passports under identical circumstances, continue to hold them to this day. I took formal opinions from specialist lawyers in Johannesburg and London, and was told that I simply had no recourse or right of appeal. I had noted that the British High Commissioner to South Africa from March 2005 to May 2009, Paul Boateng, was a man known overtly to be close to Thabo Mbeki, president of South Africa from June 1999 to September 2008.

The narrative of this book makes it clear that Mbeki viewed Wakeford's talents, and Wakeford's progressive, if not revolutionary, ideas for South African business, as a major threat. Even after Wakeford was wiped off South Africa's face during the latter part of 2002, there is evidence that Mbeki remained on his case.

It would be fruitless to speculate that Mbeki prevailed on Boateng to destroy my identity, but the thought has crossed my mind. Post-democratic South Africa can be a cruel and savage place, and I am more than happy to still be alive. But that, thankfully, is not what this book is about. Compared to my experiences, Wakeford took serious punishment for standing up for his beliefs.

Wakeford took on a global bank, some overstuffed fat-cat corporates and, as he was to find out, the power brokers behind the South African government. What emerges is the overwhelming impression that South Africa's elites are stricken with nerves and paranoia, and terrified of their own shadows. If there is any lesson to be learnt from this, it would be something along the lines of 'don't even think of taking on the fearful and the nervous'. So raw are these nerves that it is difficult not to think of the metaphor of the dog in the manger.

This book emerged from the friendship that Kevin Wakeford and I built up from early 2002, which has continued to grow over the years. For reasons that will become apparent in the book, Wakeford has been reluctant to flesh out the full version of his story for the best part of a decade. Although this ages the story, it also more than improves it, in the sense that, as the storyteller, I have been able to refer to valuable allied material and information that have become available over the past decade.

I have spent hundreds, if not thousands, of hours interviewing Wakeford. I have also made the best possible attempt to obtain 'the other side of the story' from a number of parties, as indicated in detail in the narrative. It has been exceptionally difficult to obtain the other side of the story, mainly because what happened to the rand in 2001 was heavily covered up and has remained a cover-up.

What we heard during and around the Rand Commission was a cacophony of gibberish from a series of representatives of Big Money. To be fair, there were exceptions; there were individuals who gave testimony that was absolutely straight up and straight down, and which has stood through the years. At the time, useful testimony was rapidly shot down by the vested interests that had never wanted the commission to be held in the first place.

Do not expect this book to lead you to a smoking gun. Much of the world is grey and what happened to the rand during 2001 remains firmly in that category. At the same time, the narrative of the book leaves the reader in little doubt as to what happened to the currency, certainly in the sense that there was delinquency in the markets and that, as ever, there were people pushing all the buttons.

What I have presented is a comprehensive account of circumstantial evidence. I hope, however, that the narrative is less about trying to prove anything than about examining the role of certain people in events that, like the rand's collapse in 2001, will always seem to have been bigger than life. Perhaps the rand's roller-coaster ride of 2001 was truly bigger than life.

BARRY SERGEANT
MAY 2013

Acronyms and abbreviations

AMSA: ArcelorMittal South Africa
ANC: African National Congress
BEE: black economic empowerment
CEO: chief executive officer
CFC: client foreign currency
CFTC: Commodity Futures Trading Commission
CIA: Central Intelligence Agency
CoAL: Coal of Africa
COSATU: Congress of South African Trade Unions
DMR: Department of Mineral Resources
FBI: Federal Bureau of Investigation
forex: foreign exchange
FSB: Financial Services Board
IBUK: Investec Bank UK
Idasa: Institute for a Democratic Alternative for South Africa
IDC: Industrial Development Corporation
IMF: International Monetary Fund
IPO: initial public offering
JSE: Johannesburg Stock Exchange
LIBOR: London inter-bank offered rate
LTCM: Long-Term Capital Management
MD: managing director
NAFCOC: National African Federated Chamber of Commerce and Industry
NGO: non-governmental organisation
NOFP: net open forward position
NPA: National Prosecuting Authority
NUSAS: National Union of South African Students
NYSE: New York Stock Exchange
OWS: Occupy Wall Street
PCJF: Partnership for Civil Justice Fund
RRH: Randgold Resources Holdings
SAA: South African Airways
SABC: South African Broadcasting Corporation

SACOB: South African Chamber of Business
SEC: Securities and Exchange Commission
SIOC: Sishen Iron Ore Company
TMT: technology-media-telecoms

Introduction

'*The most effective way to destroy people is to deny and obliterate their own understanding of their history.*' – *George Orwell*

During 2001, South Africa's currency weakened by an astonishing 45 per cent from its strongest to its weakest point against the dollar. A sense of deep panic gripped the nation. Nobody had a ready answer to what had rapidly developed into the country's greatest financial crisis. At one end of the socio-economic scale, the poorest of the poor were facing an explosion in basic prices – for food, fuel and transport. At the other end, people were aghast as the value of so many of their investments crashed. Their long-booked overseas Christmas holidays were summarily cancelled; imported caviar and champagne were out of range for all but the very wealthy.

Exporters were reaping heavy benefits in the short term, but these would not be sustainable in the face of imminent hyperinflation and widespread economic, social and political collapse. A deep sense of confusion descended over the country.

The Reserve Bank, South Africa's central bank, had no ready explanation for what was going on. This seemed surprising, given that South Africa's Constitution, so often touted as the best in the world, provides that the bank's 'primary object … is to protect the value of the currency in the interest of balanced and sustainable economic growth in the Republic'. The Constitution further states that the Reserve Bank 'must perform its functions independently and without fear, favour or prejudice'. It somehow seemed that the Reserve Bank, the Treasury and the Ministry of Finance had been caught napping at the wheel.

Kevin Wakeford, CEO of the South African Chamber of Business (SACOB), blew the whistle on the rand during the opening days of 2002. Within months, a judicial commission of inquiry would start hearing evidence. Sadly, the commission's terms of reference were highly limited. The commission published two reports, after being split 2:1. Overall, the commission left more questions unanswered than resolved.

This book examines the broader context of the 2001 meltdown of the rand. With the benefit of more than a decade now passed, it is possible to shine more light on the rand currency market than ever before. Currencies form one of the world's major markets, alongside equities, bonds, commodities and properties. Free-floating currencies such as the rand are vulnerable to many forces, both domestic and international. This narrative examines such factors, both in South Africa and abroad, in an attempt to articulate more fully the causes of the crisis and its aftermath.

This book traces for the first time Wakeford's dramatic experiences as one of the first whistle-blowers to take on a global bank. This would develop into a trend that has only intensified over time. We have seen one global bank after another being held up for transgressions that now range from mean, nasty and gigantic misrepresentations to money laundering on behalf of rogue states and consorting with major drug traffickers.

At the time, Wakeford could not possibly have realised that he had lit a fuse that would in due course flash out across the global banking system.

For their part, banks have developed a system of admitting no liability, although they pay massive fines for their violations, and then literally move on to the next killing ground.

In 2001 politicians and officials in power in South Africa had no real appetite to take on the people and forces that had so craftily worked to wreck the rand. Instead, the choice was to deal with the matter within a few months, albeit under the aegis of a judicial commission of inquiry. The 'guilty' were slapped on their wrists and held to account for little more than technical infringements.

South Africa's elites had once again conquered the masses. Yet there was evidence, including sworn testimony that the commission had heard in public, that pointed directly to very serious transgressions in the rand market. There were irrefutable indications that there had been serious delinquency in the markets. The commission was protected, so to speak, not only by its narrow terms of reference, but also by the vested interests breathing like dragons ready for war.

And so the commission chose to gloss over powerful material that in ordinary circumstances would have seen a heavy redirection of the commission's investigations and interrogations. Therefore, the commission's work was incomplete, which satisfied a number of vested interests. The delinquency so patently exposed at the commission could have been investigated by relevant law-enforcement, and related, agencies.

The press – more correctly 'the media' in the modern context – played a controversial and regrettable role during and after the rand crisis. It seems hard to comprehend that I was the only journalist who broke ranks, and named the global bank before its name was made public at the commission. It was incandescently clear that the press had no appetite to dig into the story, once again suiting a number of vested interests. It is a sad indictment of the South African press that, barring an exception here and there, its 'traditional' role has been largely subsumed by NGOs and other civil organisations. In recent years, the press has been used as the tool of various warring political factions, by means of leaks to various high-circulation newspapers. These stories are presented as 'scoops', and involve little active participation or skill on the part of the journalist or the newspaper.

Filthy lucre continues to rule the press, raising the dull cliché of 'he who pays the piper calls the tune'. In practice, many of the dynamics in and around the rand crisis were either ignored or buried. Most of these, hopefully, have finally been bought to life in the narrative of this book.

There were a number of separate agendas at work. Chief among these, perhaps, was President Thabo Mbeki's fear of many things, not least the influential voice of business, as articulated by Wakeford. Mbeki responded to Wakeford's calls for a commission by later announcing, as mentioned, its highly limited terms of reference. As the weeks went by, it became increasingly clear, to Wakeford at least, that he was going to be hauled in front of the commission as a sacrificial lamb. One of the main strategies at the time was a witch-hunt for Wakeford's source. None of the witch-hunters, including the commission, explained how identifying that person or persons would help explain what had happened to the rand.

This was a strange little tactic, but a treacherous one: if the source could be identified, then, no doubt, an appropriate pretext would have been established to derail the commission. The easiest example would have been that a 'competitor' had jealously ratted out the global bank, and that, therefore, what had happened to the rand was a red herring. Nothing, of course, could have been further from the truth. What happened to the rand was measurable, absolute and real: by very definition there were competitors in the market.

And it was not only Mbeki who wanted Wakeford to keep quiet. Wakeford made no new friends when he probed a global bank and a number of big corporates. Various negative forces coalesced, and Wakeford was removed from the scene in October 2002. A number of people expressed the hope that he would never again find employment. However, these negative forces were unable to resist or influence the positive forces that merged to underpin the appreciation of the rand-dollar exchange rate by more than 100 per cent over the three years after Wakeford blew the whistle.

If it was correct to say that Mbeki wanted to weaken, if not emasculate, the voice of business, he largely succeeded. After Wakeford's departure from SACOB, the voice of business in South Africa has successively faded to little more than a dull chatter on the horizon. If it can be said that Mbeki favoured a policy of divide and rule, he succeeded insofar as business is concerned. Sadly, there is circumstantial evidence that Mbeki was not finished with Wakeford, even after he left SACOB.

Mbeki had long shown, mainly by his choice of cabinet members, that he preferred acquiescent, sycophantic weaklings, and although Wakeford had served in a completely different capacity, he represented a threat to Mbeki's style of 'quiet diplomacy' on matters of public interest – a modus operandi that also created unease among a good number of South African corporates. For example, Wakeford's public stand relating to property rights in Zimbabwe and his questioning of inflation targeting as part of monetary policy in early 2000 had incensed Mbeki and his team.

As we have long known, it was Mbeki who initiated, intentionally or otherwise, the process of weakening South Africa's democratic institutions. It was Mbeki who drove rusty nails into the national justice cluster, which has continued to degenerate to the point where civil society widely disrespects law enforcement and widely suspects that prosecutions are inevitably part of unseen political agendas. More to the point, perhaps, are those prosecutions that are 'omitted', and more so, prosecutions that simply never materialise, even when there are cases that are patently sound on a prima facie basis.

It is also important to note that, like Richard Nixon, Mbeki didn't like smart people. Yes, Mbeki has a university degree, but Wakeford has that and a whole lot more: in November 2000 he was appointed as professor extraordinaire by the Port Elizabeth Technikon (now the Nelson Mandela Metropolitan University) in managerial economics.

There was little in Mbeki's conduct to suggest that he was seeking elevation from the humdrum of presidency to the legacy of greatness. Compare that with Wakeford, who was doing nothing more than what came naturally to him. It is fair to ask how one man, whom later so many wanted wiped off the face of the earth, could have influenced the rand's value in such a dramatic way. How could one man, in effect, have acted to restore hundreds of billions of rands to South Africa's national balance sheet? It took courage and resolution and, above all else, the innate knowledge of, and disrespect for, the evil forces that had been at work during 2001. Those forces were defeated – and deeply embittered.

Wakeford's legacy is a tribute to the successful exercising of civil rights in the face of overwhelming odds characterised by the presence of both public- and private-sector elites bent on preserving power that smacks of illegitimacy. Even today, civil society remembers the man who 'saved the rand'. At the time, Wakeford enjoyed immeasurable support from ordinary South Africans. They, like Wakeford, were crushed.

And so be it.

1
Wild horses in the markets

Wakeford calls for a 'currency commission'... He reflects on his formative years... The workings of South Africa's political and economic elites... Wakeford among the first in the world to take on a global bank ... Foreign banks flock to South Africa's new democracy... A short history of the rand and exchange controls... The age of delinquent capital... Gekko: 'Greed is good'... The wants and wishes of Wall Street, from Merrill Lynch to Goldman Sachs... Eliot Spitzer climbs into Wall Street... SEC director says, 'No product is too complex, and no investor too sophisticated, to avoid a heavy price.'

'But to my mind, though I am native here
And to the manner born, it is a custom
More honour'd in the breach than the observance.'
– Hamlet

When Kevin Wakeford, CEO of the South African Chamber of Business, blew the whistle on the rand, he was motivated primarily by his determination to find answers as to why the currency had melted down over 2001, and especially towards the end of the year. He was resolute in wanting to find out exactly what had happened: he wanted *all* the details. He was equally driven by a deep concern for SACOB's 40 000-odd indirect members, mainly small family businesses, and, ultimately, the South African economy as a whole.

On 4 January 2002, SACOB had released a public call to action, in asking for the appointment of a 'currency commission'.

Wakeford called on the relevant authorities to establish a commission to investigate the current demise of the rand, claiming that certain institutions had utilised 'dubious financial methods and instruments' to manipulate the currency to 'enrich themselves'.[1]

Wakeford wrote a letter to President Thabo Mbeki on 8 January 2002, calling for a commission of inquiry into the rand. It was of note that on this date, the rand traded below 11 units to the dollar. Less than a month before, the currency had traded as low as R13.84, a level not seen before or since. Something, perhaps Wakeford's calls for a national investigation of the rand in the press in mid-December 2001, had already restored tens of billions of rands to South Africa's national balance sheet. It is likely that some of those with delinquent deals were already beginning to unwind their offshore positions, hence the strengthening of the rand.

Wakeford called for the commission in his personal capacity. But even so, he had no personal or ulterior agenda. He bore no malice. He simply wanted the truth and an intervention that would arrest the crisis – and, indeed, reverse the direction of the rand's value to the positive. And truth, as some of us know, is elusive and always slippery, flashing in the shadows and then vaporising. From the start, Wakeford suspected that there had been delinquency in the markets. He had been given specific information by a high-ranking executive about certain corporate deals that had gone through the rand market during 2001: certain named South African companies had been buying offshore assets. The common denominator in each deal was a foreign bank that had set up a branch in Johannesburg in the early 1990s to cash in on South Africa's successful transition to democracy.

On the face of it, the deals would have been negative for the rand, in that rands were sold and foreign currencies bought. In most, if not all, advanced economies, the deals would simply have gone through the markets. South Africa, however, had instituted foreign-currency-exchange controls as early as 1933. The most stringent parts of these controls remain in place to this day.

In some cases, the effect of the controls is that some individuals, some companies and some banks from time to time drum up inspiration to do deals that are designed to remain undetected. Smuggling is part of human nature, and wherever there have been controls, not least currency controls, people have found loopholes, and more. One of the simplest ways to ship capital out of South Africa is to buy Krugerrands, gold coins that rank as legal tender, and then smuggle the loot over the border. This can be bothersome, but it can work. And there are far more sophisticated schemes that have popped up from time to time.

In short, Wakeford suspected there was a lot more to the 2001 rand story than a few corporate deals. As 2001 wore on, he had experienced increasingly anguished calls from an increasing number of SACOB members. During December 2001, the anxious calls approached hysteria. After he went public, Wakeford received hundreds upon hundreds of messages of support: letters, emails, letters to the press and telephone calls. Professor Ben Turok, an ANC MP, was quoted in the press as speaking in Parliament to the effect that Wakeford's actions should be applauded and supported.

The National African Federated Chamber of Commerce and Industry (NAFCOC), which represented a considerable number of micro and small businesses in the townships, had also thrown its weight behind Wakeford. NAFCOC would send a large contingent to the commission on the day Wakeford testified early in April 2002.

But while Wakeford welcomed the support, he was also mindful of the potential backlash against his call to action. He would be naming a global bank that had a very active branch in Johannesburg, and he would be naming some big entities listed on the JSE and other securities exchanges. He would be going up against some powerful vested interests. So far as Wakeford was concerned, there was nothing personal in this, as already mentioned. He had no intention to cause harm – he only wanted everyone to know what had harmed the rand, to redress the ongoing crisis and to establish whether lessons could be learnt in order to defend against another possible attack on the rand.

But the first job was to try to reverse the 2001 crisis.

As the pressure built up, Wakeford realised that he was putting everything on the line, including his career. And he had come a very long way.

***

Wakeford was born in Port Elizabeth. His parents had divorced when he was two, and his mother, Norma, had no choice but to go out to work. She spent her entire career working as a secretary. Her personal economic struggle, self-sacrifice and sturdy determination made an early and lasting impression on her son. Her compassion and generosity, and knowing that she was categorised as a 'poor white', created a consciousness in the young Wakeford that connected him directly with the struggles that women and single mothers faced in society as a result of inequities and exploitation, particularly rife in South Africa. To this day, Norma (now aged 80) has never owned a vehicle. She gets around on the community bus service in Port Elizabeth and from time to time waves down a township taxi. Even at her age, she still calls on the elderly, who are often bed-ridden, and spends quality time with them – often reading to them or slapping up a wholesome meal – as part of her voluntary and self-initiated community outreach work. Wakeford remembers how his mother used to walk him to junior school; unable to afford new shoes, she used cardboard linings.

His father, Ronald, now deceased, had been a warrant officer in the police – the equivalent of a sergeant major in the military. Towards the middle of his career, he was stationed at Swartkops, which fell under the Coega district. Ronald Wakeford's responsibilities included filling in 'influx-control reports'. These, as he discovered, were meant to show that black people were migrating from the urban areas back to rural areas in the Ciskei and Transkei. This suited the apartheid government, which sought to justify its policies on every possible front. In practice, Ronald Wakeford found that the influx was in fact an outflow – away from the rural areas towards the growing urban areas in so-called white South Africa.

He was visited by superiors and given instructions that he had to amend his reports to state that the opposite was taking place. But he refused and soon enough he was told that he would be transferred to the police station at Carlisle Bridge, a remote Karoo town in the Eastern Cape on the Fish River, between Grahamstown and Bedford. This was a classic downwards promotion. Ronald Wakeford found that the facility comprised two rondavels. There was a single black policeman at the station, and in the charge office a big jabbering baboon, chained to the counter. Who in their right mind would try to lay charges or lodge a complaint at this police station?

Ronald Wakeford had no intention of relocating to an obscure outpost in the middle of nowhere, far from his new wife, two sons and stepdaughter, no matter how beautiful the scenery. He drew a trump card and reminded the police that he had been badly injured while on duty, years before, as a passenger in a police vehicle. He demanded to be medically boarded and to be retired on a full pension. He threatened to go to the press on the issue of deceiving the public on influx control. The police capitulated, and Ronald Wakeford found himself retired at the age of 47, on full pension and with free medical treatment for the rest of his life. His stance on refusing to falsify influx-control reports for the benefit of his political masters had a profound influence on his son. Kevin Wakeford wondered whether his whistle-blowing instincts were inherited from his father and deeply embedded in his stubborn and impetuous Irish DNA.

During his earliest school years as a day scholar, when he used to walk to school, Wakeford looked forward to weekends, when he could spend time with Theo Qabaka, the son of Norma Wakeford's domestic servant, Francis Qabaka. Theo, who attended a township school, was two years Wakeford's senior. He was blessed with extraordinary intellectual talent, especially in maths and science, so much so that the little boy was soon giving Wakeford 'extra lessons'. Qabaka also taught Wakeford how to marshal his boxing skills. He was Wakeford's best friend during his primary-school years. Because of this friendship, Wakeford earned the infamous nickname of Kaffir at Grey Junior School. The young Wakeford often lamented the clear disadvantages and alienation that Theo had to experience, even though Theo was more talented intellectually and physically than Wakeford – and probably more than most of Wakeford's Grey Junior schoolmates. Qabaka, who excelled in matric in 1978, would eventually attend the University of the Witwatersrand, in Johannesburg. He graduated with a master of science in metallurgy, and during his subsequent career worked for De Beers, Anglo American and AngloGold Ashanti.

The two have remained friends over the years. Qabaka was one of the speakers at Wakeford's 40th birthday celebrations, where he reminisced about how he and Wakeford had played 'spin the bottle' with white girls.

Qabaka's role and place in society have informed a number of decisions that Wakeford has made. Qabaka contributed in no small way to Wakeford's deep sense of humanity and natural sense of non-racialism when interacting with others. The friendship also inculcated in Wakeford an acute awareness of the struggle that black people had to endure in a society that at that time was patently unequal, unfair and, simply put, racist. This was a society that would ultimately constrain the ability of the two youngsters to interact as normal friends. When Wakeford went from Port Elizabeth to boarding school in Grahamstown in 1976, opportunities to rub shoulders with his boyhood friend diminished considerably. It was as if a formative era had suddenly skidded to a halt.

Following those early years, Wakeford was sent off to boarding school at the very tender age of six, in 1969. He was a boarder for the rest of his school days, and has fond memories: 'Boarding school teaches you to share; it teaches you to be accountable; it also teaches you to stand your ground if you need to. I had some rough and tumbles. I was rebellious at certain stages of my early teenage years.'

After school Wakeford was called up for National Service and joined the infantry. He was called up to Grahamstown and then went to 'JLs', or junior leaders, at Oudtshoorn. He became a 'one-pip lieutenant', trained troops, went to the dreaded border and returned. Without really thinking, he had agreed to doing his National Service, as he was only 19 and, in his own words, his 'political astuteness had not been developed to the extent of opting out and emigrating'.

His Damascene experience would follow the nasty two-year stint of National Service. He couldn't afford tertiary studies, so he found a job as a surgical rep through his business mentor, Gerald John. This lasted for 18 months, allowing him to save up and study at the University of Port Elizabeth, where he majored in politics, public administration, anthropology and, in his honours year, political economics and conflict resolution.

Wakeford was awarded university colours for academic performance: a BA *cum laude* and a BA honours *cum laude*. His political interests were further awakened when at university he became increasingly involved with Idasa (the Institute for a Democratic Alternative for South Africa), headed by Frederik Van Zyl Slabbert, whom Wakeford ranked as a man of 'high intellect'. Wakeford clashed with Van Zyl Slabbert and his cronies on governance matters at Idasa in 1987, in connection with how management was accounting for and utilising donor funds. And, in 1987, Wakeford's early whistle-blowing hit the front page of *Business Day*.

During these years, Wakeford wasn't a typical political activist: 'I think by virtue of being drawn into Idasa as a part-time coordinator, I was placed into the middleman role of facilitator; Van Zyl Slabbert was trying to engender a debate around non-racialism versus racism and multiracialism.' Wakeford felt that a lot of people failed to make the distinction between non-racialism and multiracialism, an issue that he feels has prevailed to this day. Multiracialism distinctly recognises different races but promotes cooperation between races and ethnic groups. This is a far cry from the prejudicial ideology of racism – but does not go far enough.

Non-racialism embraces people on the basis of their humanity, and refuses to acknowledge race or ethnicity as a factor in human relations. To this very day, Wakeford believes that group identity and multiracialism are at the heart of many of our sociological constraints in business, sport and society at large in South Africa. This phenomenon impedes the country's progress at every level of our society, says Wakeford – even in organised business.

He found that at university, he became 'sensitised and perhaps even conscientised' when he interacted with people from the political underground and the liberation movements. His early experiences and social consciousness, forged by his friendship with Theo Qabaka, were aroused again.

While at university, Wakeford encountered white activists, including the extraordinary Watson family. Daniel 'Cheeky' Watson was trying to deracialise rugby by playing in the townships – and getting arrested for his efforts. Cheeky had been publicly repudiated by the then president of the South African Rugby Board, Danie Craven, and had forfeited the opportunity to play for the Springbok team. Craven was quoted as saying that Cheeky Watson would never have the honour of wearing the Springbok blazer.

Cheeky has three brothers, Valence, Ronald and Gavin, all raised in a family that was closely connected to the Pentecostal Church. The family lived a simple but wholesome life, and were strongly influenced by their father, a lay preacher. The brothers were keen sportsmen. At the age of 21, Cheeky played for the Gazelles (the equivalent of the junior Bok team today), which acquitted itself fairly well in a brutal match in Port Elizabeth in 1976 against the All Blacks, the most accomplished international side in the history of the game.

Wakeford, who had followed in his father's footsteps and attended Graeme College in 1976, remembers the indelible mark that the Watsons had made on the small and humbly resourced school: 'While they were at Graeme, the first rugby team was invincible.' They whipped almost every Eastern Cape school team in 1973, including those from the revered St Andrews, Selborne, Dale, Queens and Grey.

Theo Qabaka had told Wakeford about his white rugby heroes – the Watsons, whom the young Wakeford had not had the privilege of watching in the KwaZakhele and Zwide townships. Even Kevin's father, Ronald, an Old Graemian, who was a policeman in the area at the time, had spoken highly of Cheeky's rugby prowess even though he was playing non-racial rugby in the townships. Cheeky was asked by Mona Badela, a journalist and president of the KwaZakhele Rugby Union – known as Kwaru – to assist in the development of township rugby. The trouble, so to speak, started when Watson invited the Kwaru rugby team to train at the St George's sports ground B field in Port Elizabeth, which happened to be out of public view.

Cheeky Watson had played wing for the Gazelles in the winter of 1976 and was generally recognised as one of the best up-and-coming talents in international rugby. Some commentators said that Watson as a wing was on par with All Blacks Bryan Williams and Grant Batty, and indeed every great wing who has worn colours since then. In Wakeford's humble opinion – which assumes different proportions in sporting matters – Cheeky Watson was, and still is, the greatest wing of all time. Later in 1976, Cheeky and his brothers were visited at their clothing shop in Port Elizabeth by none other than Ian Kirkpatrick, the Springbok coach, who indicated that Cheeky would be selected for the Springbok team, which was planning to tour France in 1977. There was one simple condition: 'Don't continue with your plans to play the first non-racial match in the townships.'

Cheeky did not so much as ponder the matter. He turned down the offer and announced that from that point forward he would play non-racial rugby in the townships. That, in effect, was the beginning and the end of his career as an international test player. On 10 October 1976, Cheeky Watson and his older brother Valence played in a match that achieved notoriety with 13 black players from Kwaru against the South Eastern Districts Rugby Union at the Dan Qeqe Stadium in Zwide. At the time, non-racial sports meetings were banned. The stadium was surrounded by armoured vehicles; the two Watson brothers exited from a taxi meant to carry black passengers.

The marginalisation of the Watsons continued apace: they were ostracised, mobbed in public, shot at and in 1986 their house was burnt to the ground, an act many progressive South Africans believe was planned and implemented by the South African government's covert operations. Wakeford felt that 'it was a time of great learning for me and discovering that perhaps we don't hold the cudgels of truth … your truth might be different to my truth, and when you meet people, particularly in the townships and people such as the Watson family, you discover that there's humanity that is way beyond yours in terms of sharing, in terms of sacrificing for each other. That had a huge impact on my life.'

The Watsons had sacrificed everything. Yet they did not represent the typology of left-wing politics: their response to apartheid was faith-based. This approach to South Africa's dilemma was appealing to Wakeford, who felt awkward around some of the toffee-nosed and privileged left-wing whites, who failed to impress him. At times he got the distinct impression that the white left had long betrayed whatever convictions they had once, if ever, held. It seemed to him that they were acting out of a sense of guilt stemming from exorbitant wealth and conspicuous privilege.

This was also a time of fear. The National Union of South African Students (NUSAS) was exposed at the time for harbouring numerous government spies. And this was even more reason for Wakeford to link up with the Watsons, who were in his view authentic members of the ANC underground – dedicated and credible political and sports activists who were 'on the bones of their arses' when he met them. They had lost everything but never failed to inspire their fellow activists.

There may have been a climate of fear, but people were doing things and going places, and Wakeford was no exception. At times as a student he was somewhat vocal. The University of Port Elizabeth was an extremely conservative university and, as a freshman, Wakeford was convinced by his seniors that by joining the National Party Youth he could contribute by reforming the system from within the party. In his first year, he rose to the esteemed position of youth leader in the province. He resigned from the party the same year.

He was involved in founding the Concerned Students' Movement, given that starting a NUSAS branch was out of the question, as NUSAS was banned at the university. The Concerned Students' Movement was not only vocal; it also became involved in a great deal of activity in the township areas. Wakeford has fond memories of these times: 'We didn't just talk the talk, we walked the walk. Idasa, too, was a great experience – just meeting people with headspace and a level of activism and self-sacrifice that were way beyond mine at that time.'

His tenure at the Consultative Business Movement in 1990 and 1991 helped him grasp the need to transform the South African economy. It was paramount, in his view, to avoid throwing the baby out with the bath water, as he has always believed in the free-enterprise system while remaining convinced that unbridled monopolistic capitalism and excessive concentration of wealth based on inequity and exploitation could simply not be sustained.

For the 27-year-old Wakeford, deracialising the economy at a grass-roots level was an absolute non-negotiable tenet of a future South African economy. Wakeford ploughed his energy into other activities as well, and became deeply involved in the development phase of the first micro-lending entity in South Africa. This was an NGO, a non-profit, Section 21 company called the Group Credit Company. It was run by, in Wakeford's words, 'a very, very committed lady, Christine Glover, who also came out of the NGO sector and who understood the Western Cape townships: Khayelitsha and Gugulethu, places like that'.

The idea was based on the Grameen Bank model, developed in Bangladesh, whereby lending was fostered among savings groups. In Xhosa these are known as *umgalelos*: groups, usually women, usually entrepreneurs who didn't have formal jobs. If the group had, say, six members, they would save for six months to build up a deposit and then the first two members would borrow. Four months later, the next two would borrow and, say, six months later, the next two. The concept was a rotating savings and borrowing club, smaller than the *stokvel* units, which were big in those days, with, at times, 100 people or more. Wakeford discovered that the Grameen Bank model was based on group sociology, specifically the notion that 'when you're very poor, you borrow and you are accountable to your peers in the group'. Wakeford found that the Xhosa people at the time were far more modernised than people in Bangladesh, where the Grameen model originated. They were far more individualistic and they didn't want to be accountable. 'Let's call it,' says Wakeford, 'the delinquency in the borrowing markets for others.'

They were keener on being responsible for their own loans. So Wakeford started talking to the trade union movement and to pension funds, and soon enough he started what are known as employer lending schemes. For housing purposes, these were partly secured by pension funds. The employer implemented a payroll deduction facility; the trade unions endorsed the credit criteria and the methodologies used to assess a client. The schemes did not use the typical credit-bureau evaluation materials and methodologies, which are evergreen and ever controversial. Instead, people would be 'eyeballed' in the workplace and, where appropriate, lending would be more liberally authorised.

This all proved to be so successful that the micro-lending NGO morphed over time into a private entity, Cash Bank, owned today by Nedbank. Wakeford also assisted the IDT Finance Corporation, which then transformed itself and became very much part of the African Bank, another successful financial-services player. It should be noted that Wakeford does not necessarily agree with the current modus operandi of these institutions. Today, years later, micro-lending is a huge sector in South Africa.

Wakeford also stepped into a commercial job, at Firestone South Africa. The CEO, Bill Taylor, had taken note of Wakeford in the Port Elizabeth region after he had contested the Newton Park constituency seat for the Democratic Party in 1989, as one of the youngest candidates fielded by the party. This was after Wakeford had received the blessing of the ANC underground to participate.

Wakeford did not win the seat but seriously dented one of the National Party's most secure strongholds in the city. Suddenly, it seemed that the youngish Wakeford was everywhere. In the same year, he was elected leader of the Democratic Party Youth Wing in the Eastern Cape. Once the ANC was unbanned, he officially joined the ranks of the party in the Eastern Cape, and soon after that he hosted Nelson Mandela at a welcoming function on behalf of the business community. Due to the nature of Wakeford's newfound and future work in organised business, he did not renew his party membership, fearing that his employers would consider him conflicted when dealing with government and other social formations.

So Wakeford's formative years were influenced by a selection of special people and events that left him with a distinct distaste for inequality, inequity, racism and exploitative behaviour. Wakeford was passionate about many things. And now here he was, blowing the whistle on the rand.

Looking at the broader context, there was no particular reason for the rand to have taken such a severe beating in 2001. Despite the magnitude of the gigantic meltdown, the origins of the event remained mysterious.

Wakeford considered his options. He was irrevocably convinced that the specific information he had been given was too sensitive to be disgorged at the SACOB level. Instead, adamant that the issue, or issues, were of national consequence, he publicly called for a commission of inquiry and was immediately approached by the Presidency.

No matter who was listening, and it took a lot of listening, Wakeford was worth hearing out. He was like some kind of lighthouse. Somehow, it seemed that he had been preparing for decades to tackle an issue of national, and possibly international, importance.

When you examine Wakeford's comments in the press during his tenure as CEO of SACOB and later in his *Business Day* column, he can be characterised as an outspoken economic patriot, a devoted promoter of fairness, a warrior for small business, both black and white, and a courageous defender of the downtrodden.

***

'By this means [fractional reserve banking] government may
secretly and unobserved, confiscate the wealth of the people and not
one man in a million will detect the theft.' – *John Maynard Keynes*,
The Economic Consequences of the Peace *(1920)*

It is impossible to fully comprehend Wakeford's rand journey without considering events in the global markets, specifically in the Western world, where the markets, as we know them, were developed. By comparing the domestic and global markets, such as this may be possible, a better understanding can be gained of what Wakeford did, and why he did it.

At the domestic level, the roots of South Africa's 2001 currency crisis can be traced to the country's much-vaunted democratic conversion, which had the afterbirth wiped off its dirty face in 1994. Since then, as Shakespeare may have written, democratic values have often been more honoured in the breach than in the observance. Nowhere is this more prevalent than in the conduct – or misconduct – of the country's ruling elites. The structure of the elite is ever changing, but for periods certain leading players, and their parasitic (in old language, sycophantic) followers, can easily be identified. These short-lived elites rule the country, hunting down short-term gains before a new elite barges in, wrecks the party and takes over, replicating all over again the pursuit of short-term gains. Over-all, it is a moving violation, a recipe for the ongoing wreckage of a country.

There is little, if any, continuity between the administration of one president and the next, as seen in the transition between Mbeki and Zuma, which took effect at the infamous Polokwane ANC elective conference in December 2007. South Africa's ANC politics are about personality cults, rather than about leaders who can quietly deliver on promises in basic areas such as health, education and municipal service delivery. The country is now legendary for its dysfunctional health system, its ruined state edu-cation system, its emphasis on consumption rather than capital formation, its unemployment rate, which is among the highest in the world, its divi-siveness at almost every level and its appetite for respecting anything that's big, bent and twisted. Only the values of Nelson Mandela have endured, and he has been out of executive government since 1999. It may be coinci-dental, but it seems disturbing that the attack on the rand happened less than two years after Mandela had retired.

Offering here an academic treatise on the structure of South Africa's elites would be circumspect, generalised and pretty much good for noth-ing. Instead, it could be useful to refer to a fine take on it, delivered by someone who almost worked the system into a giant piece of hamburger meat, the late Brett Kebble, a man of extraordinary talent and ambition, and with a strong taste for the dark side of life:

> On our first black economic empowerment deal, I went with the big names of the empowerment game to Whiskey Creek. I realised then and there that this had fuck all to do with development; it was all about wealth and rivalry. I tried to deny what I was seeing, at the time. I'm sorry I did. This was a black royalty. Royalty have been my enemies … I knew why the old-order thinkers were scared of what we're doing. What we're doing eats their lunch. Now I realised that much of what the public perceived as the new order was merely the old order with black faces.[2]

The narrative of this book deals with some of the people who constitute South Africa's economic and political elite, which include, from time to time, certain high-end politicians, certain big financial institutions, certain top-level bureaucrats and certain others who have joined the elite by hook, crook or even by marriage.

South Africa's economic elite are loosely knit, but when any kind of threat is discerned, their ranks do the clichéd thing and close in, inevitably with devastating effect. In practice, the elite regard themselves as above anything – especially criticism. Much the same can be said of the political elite, although survival in the political domain is far less assured than with vested business, financial and property interests. In practice, however, the political and economic elites gorge at the same trough, and the two sets of wingless vampires are symbiotic in the most indigestible ways imaginable.

This all means that we have a country with only a veneer of confidence. One day, South Africa is a nation of unshaved and panicked sheep. The next day, it is a nation of disturbed and unwashed swine. Then it goes back to being a nation of panicked sheep, and so on. There are brief moments when the country somehow shows a vague indication that it could be a great country – if only because of a day of perfect weather.

Kebble took on the entire system, for specific reasons. There are very few people who have taken on the entire system, and Kevin Wakeford is one of them. His reasons and motives were completely different from Kebble's, but ironically, he found himself hunting in the same grounds. Both Kebble and Wakeford shook the cages of the elites. The system closed its botulism-riddled jaws on both men.

***

> *'The problem with fiat money*[3] *is that it rewards the*
> *minority that can handle money, but fools the generation*
> *that has worked and saved money.' – Adam Smith*

This roller-coaster narrative has benefited heavily from the more than a decade that has elapsed since the drama during 2001. So often, one can only start to understand history many years after the events, and even then questions may well remain.

Looking beyond the domestic arena, it is important to note that Wakeford was one of the first people in the world to take on a global bank. Since his efforts, the conduct of global banks has deteriorated further, and in many cases degenerated to the level of sub-Mafia activities. It took years before the system itself finally decided to take on the global banks.

The damage wrought by the 2008 global credit-markets crisis continues to be felt to this day. During the modern era, there has been no market failure or financial foulness that even vaguely matches the magnitude of the 2008 credit-markets crisis. It began with a vengeance in October 2007, when events in US markets started unfolding around the so-called subprime mortgage crisis. The roots of the crisis can be traced to the early 2000s, when the Federal Reserve, the US central bank, had implemented a policy of extreme accommodation, allowing official interest rates to fall to the lowest levels in decades, if not ever. At the same time, the US government promoted a policy, logical to anyone who listened to it, of encouraging the granting of mortgages to the widest possible franchise.

In due course, financial institutions started offering mortgage bonds to customers who fell under the classification of 'subprime', a euphemism for making credit available to people who would not ordinarily have qualified for it. These were people who did not qualify as 'prime' clients, hence 'subprime'. In no time, the brains trusts on Wall Street were bundling subprime bonds with higher-quality bonds, and selling the resulting hybrid products in what is generally known as 'securitisation' of underlying securities, in this case, mortgages.

The trick was that genuinely top-grade bonds were mixed, inside the same products, with toxic subprime bonds. These hybrid securities would never have seen the light of day without appropriately acceptable credit ratings from rating agencies such as Standard & Poor's, which earned very fancy fees for their activities. By now it is well known that the credit-rating agencies were either conned into overrating these securities, or too stupid to have known that all such hybrid securities were doomed from the outset.

It is important to note that in the rating of securities by so-called independent agencies, only products falling in the category of 'investment' grade count. Anything less than that is essentially junk, and therefore 'untouchable'. The apparent beauty of the mortgage-cocktail products was that if an individual hybrid security was somehow lacking, it could be adjusted by taking some subprime products out and replacing them with higher-grade bonds.

The hybrid securitised products with investment-level classifications from the credit-rating agencies were sold across the US, and in many other countries, mainly to institutional investors. Few, if any, of these investors read the fine print. Starting around October 2007, the meltdown in the hybrid products set in as many thousands of holders of subprime mortgages started to default. By this time, hundreds of billions of dollars were involved.

Regulators, bureaucrats and law-enforcement authorities were forced into action, but it soon became evident that the crisis was out of control. The scandal snowballed during 2008, plunging the world into recession. The federal government in the US was forced to step in, authorising bailouts of banks deemed too big to fail. However, the rot was systemic to the extent that other kinds of financial institutions were also bailed out. But the main failure during 2008 was not in the credit markets: it was confidence, a very human emotion, which vanished. Despite the extent of the bailouts and the Federal Reserve's practically unlimited efforts to stimulate economic activity, the credit markets remained in freeze mode: no bank of any size would lend to any other bank, never mind to corporations or individuals.

For very different reasons, confidence likewise evaporated in South Africa in 2001, intensifying as the months went by. The rand fell, fell further and then collapsed. Those who were around then will no doubt recollect that it was a terrifying time. There is little question that had the 2001 meltdown continued, staple foods such as mielie meal would have doubled in price within months; fuel prices would have skyrocketed; hyperinflation would have set in; and the economy as a whole would have been forced into deep and vicious recession, with no clear way out. There would have been panic at a national level because the country had failed. It is correct to say that exporters benefited from a collapsed rand – certainly in the short term. But in the medium and long term, the benefits to exporters would have become illusory, as domestic costs exploded and the national mood continued to fail.

The full extent of what happened during 2001 will never be truly known, mainly because so much of it has been covered up. It was not only the banks that were involved – let's say certain banks, to be fair – but also those who depend on banks for significant income. This includes auditors – let's say certain auditors, to be fair – and also lawyers – to be fair, let's say 'not all of them' – and various support artists, not least those in the spin-doctor business. The South African government also benefited significantly from the cover-up.

Governments have been taken down by bank failures, and although the 2001 rand currency crisis was a massively profitable period for certain banks, the South African government was not in a position to handle the fallout. Politically, it had no choice but to cover the crisis up. If the full extent of the rand crisis had been allowed to unravel, confidence in South Africa's banking system would have taken many years to recover. The root-stock of banking may be money, but the trunk and branches are made of confidence.

The enduring attraction of banks to nation builders is that banks supply an economy's lifeblood – money. Without filthy lucre, there would be no transactions, no trade and no real development. Through history, banks have become increasingly woven into the tapestry of humankind. A company, even a very big one, may fail, but that is normally accepted as part of supply and demand, in the same way that weeds, no matter how large, have to be uprooted to allow the growth of healthy young plants. But banks are somehow more important than companies and are seen as part of society, almost like a member of the family that is simultaneously loved and hated.

Banks evoke emotions, as anyone finds out when they apply for their first loan, only to be rejected, and even more so when a loan is eventually granted, or when a repayment has to be skipped due to circumstances beyond the individual's control. Beyond stirring deep feelings, banks enjoy privileges available to no other kind of enterprise. Indeed, some cynics may say that banks are the oldest confidence trick of all. Put simplistically, if a bank accepts deposits of, say, $10 million, 'the law' permits the bank to loan a multiple of that amount – say, in a modest system, $20 million. Banks lend money that they simply don't have. In reality, banks can lend $100 million for every $10 million taken in by way of deposits. Banks literally lend thin air, which, if commoditised, would be recognised as confidence.

Banks need to pay the rent. So in the time-honoured tradition, all else being equal, the bank pays depositors a lower interest rate than the lending rate charged to borrowers. This spread, as it is known, generates the bank's profits. If trust in the bank fails, confidence can evaporate overnight. A run on the bank would render it insolvent. If fear about the bank becomes systemic, the country's entire banking system could crash. The economy would grind to a halt and remain frozen. The ruling political party or parties would be threatened to the roots, if not pushed out of power.

However, South Africa's currency crisis was *not* about a run on any bank or banks. It was about the inexplicable collapse of the rand, which, like a systemic failure of the banking system, severely undermined public confidence. The rand crisis was about what certain banks were doing in the currency – and related – markets. If the nature of these activities had been fully disseminated in the public domain, there would have been widespread revulsion. This, in turn, would have undermined confidence. More important, however, is that foreign investors would have been seriously turned off.

Unlike with the rand crisis, there was no way of stopping the details of the 2008 global credit-markets crisis going public. The meltdown had provided unprecedented insight into the consequences of a failure in confidence. During 2008, the Federal Reserve was authorised to bail out certain banks, at costs running into hundreds of billions of dollars. The damage was not restricted to the banking sector either – there was collateral damage in other kinds of financial institutions, such as insurance firms, and many more billions were spent on further bailouts. The US feared a systemic meltdown, and sensed that it would spread across the global economy, literally bringing the economic world to a halt.

The US government authorised the Federal Reserve to implement bailout packages of a size and nature unheard of in history. Even so, as mentioned, the credit markets remained frozen to the point where banks would not even lend to each other. The Federal Reserve was forced to continually drop interest rates to levels unknown in US history in an attempt to stimulate economic activity.

For its part, South Africa has done whatever it takes to ensure the maintenance of a stable banking system. Above all else, South Africa permits banks to make extraordinary profits. This allows modestly talented management to prosper, but, more important, it effectively protects any of the big players from potential insolvency, or anything close to it. As a rule, the more that banks profit, the more banks revert to the mean: mediocrity. The perverse advantage of this system is that South African banks tend to toe the line, unlike their US counterparts, where competitiveness fosters increasingly risky behaviour aimed at unearthing new areas of profits.

Given this, it is hardly surprising that in South Africa it was foreign banks – not all of them, to be sure – that were at the epicentre of the 2001 rand currency crisis. A number of these 'prestigious names' had flocked into South Africa like vultures early in the 1990s, when it seemed clear that the country would somehow be able to pull off a peaceful transition to democracy. Certain members of the global banking community identified South Africa as a potentially lucrative source of profits. It may be noted, with some cynicism, that the opening of the country's borders was also regarded as highly significant by a number of international narcotics networks. Since the transition to democracy, South Africa has become a major transit point for the global narcotics trade. The country's borders are porous and law enforcement has never been quite what it should be – and in some cases, simply nowhere near what it could or should be.

It may seem unfair to discuss banks and drug traffickers in the same paragraph, but this book will show that it should come as no surprise at all. The difference is that drug traffickers do not regard themselves as respectable, no matter how much wealth they may amass.

***

'Man is born free, and everywhere he is in debt.' – Paul Mills

During South Africa's transition to democracy, the foreign banks that set up shop in the country assured the country's policy-makers that the presence of foreign banks would ensure South Africa easier access to global capital markets for bonds, stocks and commodities. The quid pro quo was that the domestic branches of big foreign banks expected to generate very good returns from their South African activities: big fat profits. On Wall Street, this is captured by the descriptor 'bulge-bracket banks'.

During the 1990s, it was thought that the domestic branches of certain foreign banks would indeed generate enormous returns from the country's much-vaunted privatisation programme. The problem was, the programme never saw the light of day. The opposite happened. The ANC, the ruling party since 1994, has found it all but impossible to take its hands off the levers of power. If anything, it has taken policy decisions aimed at further intervention in the economy. The party's political progress – assuming that it has made progress, which it vows it has – has been inversely related to the country's unemployment rate, which has steadily increased to among the highest in the world. Put another way, the ANC's progress in the economic sphere has been predominantly in a reverse direction. South Africa's economic annual growth rate has been among the meekest of any emerging nation.

One of the many levers of power that the ANC refused to deal with, in principle, was foreign-currency-exchange controls. These controls have been around in South Africa since 1933, when they were aimed at preserving domestic capital, restricting the quantum that could be expatriated. It is the aim of most, if not all, countries to maintain a stable currency; this way elites in the business and political arenas have one less thing to worry about.

A volatile currency, particularly one that is crashing, as in the case of the rand in 2001, creates a sense of panic, and can easily become catastrophic for the ruling political party and deeply damage the interests of business. South Africa's white governments had for a long time been wide awake to the possibility of capital flight; hence their imposition of currency controls 80 years ago. As the decades went by and the country was targeted for foreign sanctions in a bid to force the termination of apartheid, foreign-exchange controls were tightened. Government policy on foreign-currency-exchange controls was increasingly strict: penalties for contraventions were draconian.

Investigations of violations in the field, such as they were, were protected by omnipotent secrecy laws. As is well known, during the apartheid era, so-called sanctions busters organised all kinds of nefarious deals in everything from oil to arms. The deals required hard currency, and utmost secrecy. Sadly, the new South African government, amid all its promises of delivering to the world the best Constitution ever, hung on to exchange controls like a dog with an old bone that refused to yield its marrow. After the transition to democracy, South Africa introduced lightweight relaxations to exchange-control policy, mainly for individuals. Foreign travel allowances were increased and a limited amount of capital could be legally shipped offshore. In the main, however, the controls remained very much in place, suggesting that South Africa was nervous about the advent, and the aftermath, of democracy.

The country's exchange controls have forever been administered, in practice, by the Reserve Bank on behalf of the Treasury, the operating arm of the Department of Finance, the domain of the finance minister. Since the transition to democracy in 1994, South Africa's administration of exchange controls had become increasingly patchy: it was hard work, most of it deadly boring. During the 1990s, the domestic branches of various newly arrived foreign banks quickly found out that only 1 per cent of foreign-exchange transactions were monitored by the Reserve Bank. The other 99 per cent were 'self-administered' by authorised currency dealers. Such authorised dealers included several banks, which testified at the Rand Commission. These were ABSA, Standard Bank, Board of Executors, Citibank, J.P. Morgan, FirstRand, NIB Bank, Investec and Deutsche Bank.

The administration of South Africa's foreign-exchange controls depended on trust. This is the only feasible conclusion, considering that the Reserve Bank could only see 1 per cent of the picture. In a nutshell, the rand market was largely unregulated, with little, if any, oversight. And there were other weaknesses. The rand may rank as the world's second most traded emerging-market currency, but it comprises less than 1 per cent of trade in global currencies. The world system is dominated by the world's only reserve currency, the dollar, the almighty greenback, which accounts for around 90 per cent of all currency trade. This meant that by international standards, the rand was relatively illiquid: a smallish market, rendering it vulnerable to speculators.

Besides its relative illiquidity, the rand has always been vulnerable to changes in commodity prices. For decades, the vast majority of global commodities have been quoted and traded in dollars. South Africa has long been an open economy, with a relatively high level of both exports and imports. Exports have forever been dominated by commodities, and the rand is known as one of a number of so-called commodity currencies. It is of note that since around 1995, the dollar has exhibited an inverse correlation with the dollar gold-bullion price to the tune of at least 90 per cent. In other words, if the dollar weakens, the gold price is highly likely to increase – and vice versa. The same principle applies to most other commodities, though to a lesser degree. As such, currencies tend to move broadly in line with dollar commodity price trends.

For many decades, South Africa dominated world gold production. This peaked, however, in 1970, at about 1 000 tonnes of gold a year. In recent years, South Africa's production has been below 200 tonnes a year, and may be as little as 100 tonnes in 2013. While other mineral exports, such as platinum, chrome, coal and iron ore, have increased, the rand's value benefited for decades from South Africa's significant, world-leading gold production. In an informal sense, South Africa possessed its own 'gold standard'.

***

> 'In the absence of the gold standard, there is no way to protect savings from confiscation through inflation ... Deficit spending is simply a scheme for the "hidden" confiscation of wealth. Gold stands in the way of this insidious process. It stands as a protector of property rights.'
> – Alan Greenspan, Gold and Economic Freedom (1966)

The term 'gold standard' should not be used loosely, given the small but fanatical gold-bullion club, whose members are scattered across the globe. During the modern era, gold has been referred to by some in negative terms, such as a 'barbarous relic', but there is no question that the metal has long had a historical, and ongoing, role in money systems. Before the modern era, in the wake of World War II, a system described as similar to the gold standard was established by the major powers in the form of a gold-exchange standard under the Bretton Woods Agreements.

Many countries' currencies were pegged, by agreement, to the dollar. In return, the US promised to fix the price of gold at around $35 an ounce. As such, all currencies pegged to the dollar had a fixed value in gold. However, from the time of the administration of French president Charles de Gaulle and up to 1970, France slimmed its dollar reserves, swapping the dollars for gold bullion from the US government. This setback for the system was deepened by heavy US spending on the Vietnam War, and a swelling US trade deficit. In the final blow for the system, President Richard Nixon announced on 15 August 1971 that direct convertibility of the dollar to gold would be terminated.

It may seem strange today, but for decades the rand cost more than the dollar. From the inception of the rand in 1961 right through to 1982, a rand cost a princely $1.40. The exchange rate was not influenced in any way by the termination of the Bretton Woods system. For decades, the rand was one of the world's strongest currencies, backed by domestic gold production and unmined reserves. But on the back of more than a decade of declining gold production, and under growing political pressure, the rand broke parity with the dollar in March 1982. It soon cost more than R1.00 to buy a dollar. By February 1985, a dollar cost R2.00. After P.W. Botha made his infamous Rubicon speech on 15 August 1985, the rand weakened significantly to R2.40 to the dollar. It then strengthened in the following years to R2.00 and better, but then started to depreciate again out of fear of impending majority rule.

By November 1992, a dollar cost R3.00. The rate depreciated to R3.60 after the country's first democratic elections in 1994. For a period of 11 months after the abolition of the dual exchange-rate system on 10 March 1995, the unified rand was stable at around R3.60 to the dollar. During 1996, there was a 'sell-off' of the rand: the currency lost 20 per cent of its value, falling to R4.50 to the dollar by June 1996. During and around September and October 1997, when the so-called Asian contagion gripped global markets, the rand lost more than 20 per cent of its value. The rand strengthened again in 1999, trading in a broad band between R5.50 and R6.40 to the dollar.

When Thabo Mbeki was inaugurated as president in 1999, the rand broke through R6.00 to the dollar. The currency lost further ground when Tito Mboweni was appointed governor of the Reserve Bank. The currency started the new millennium at around R6.12 to the dollar. During 2001, the rand was absolutely punished and in December of that year fell to a record low – not seen since – of R13.84 to the dollar.

After Wakeford blew the whistle and the Rand Commission was appointed, the rand appreciated rapidly. Within months of the commission's report in 2002, the rand was again trading below R9.00 to the dollar. By the end of 2004, a dollar cost a more modest R5.70.

A negative run on any country's currency, if sustained, can take a country down into the pits of hell – economically speaking, at the very least. Zimbabwe is a case in point. In 2009 Zimbabwe unilaterally instated the US dollar as its local currency to prevent any further economic fall-out. The country's economy has been improving ever since.

When reviewing the long-term performance of the rand, it is crucial to note that the dollar itself terminated a bull market early in 2002. The greenback has remained in a broad bear market ever since, reflecting the US's poor terms of trade. At the same time, in early 2002, dollar commodity prices commenced a long-term bull market, which in some quarters has been described as a 'supercycle'. Commodity prices experienced a double whammy: not only had the dollar started up a bear market, but China's economic expansion was also taking root.

Commodity currencies were expected to benefit from rising commodity prices, on the back of rising physical demand, and further boosted by the weakness of the dollar. The list included the rand; the Australian, New Zealand and Canadian dollars; Brazil's real; the krone of Norway; and the krona of Sweden.

China's presence in foreign-exchange markets has loomed ever larger for the past two decades. China's currency, the yuan,[4] has long been pegged to the dollar. As the dollar weakened, the yuan followed. From early 2002, this meant that Chinese exports were increasingly cheaper in foreign-currency terms. Along with relatively cheap labour costs, this made China's output increasingly competitive around the world. For China, this was also a double whammy: China was essentially exporting its super-competitiveness to the rest of the world, to such an extent, indeed, that global inflation started to fall. This exerted downward pressure on interest rates in most countries and contributed, no matter how indirectly, to the precipitation of the global credit-markets crisis, centred on the US.

China also rapidly progressed to become the biggest consumer of virtually every raw material in the world, and would soon become the biggest producer of a number of commodities, such as steel, aluminium and gold. The overall impact on dollar commodity prices was significant. Using the dollar gold-bullion price as a measure, from lows of around $250 an ounce shortly before the new millennium, prices rose incessantly and during 2011 threatened to reach $2 000 an ounce.

There is no question that since Wakeford blew the whistle, the rand has benefited both from the dollar bear market and the commodities super-cycle. During the infamy of 2001, the rand kicked off the year at around

R7.60 to the dollar and slowly collapsed at one point in December 2001 to R13.84, as mentioned. The rapid appreciation of the rand over the next three years to as high as R5.70 to the dollar can be explained in part by the behaviour of the bear dollar and by bull commodity prices. But even so, there is little doubt that the rand was trashed to way below its intrinsic value in 2001.

There have also been crucially important dynamics at the global macro-economic level in respect of interest rates. Following the 9/11 attacks, interest rates in the large developed economies, from the US to Japan, fell to around zero and have remained pegged there. This resulted in relative currency strength in a number of emerging-market economies where interest rates remained high. This includes, of course, South Africa. From 2002 to 2012, the rand strengthened against the dollar at a compound annual growth rate of 2 per cent a year. Over the previous two decades, the rand had *depreciated* against the dollar at a compound annual growth rate of more than 10 per cent a year.

Seen from this perspective, the rand bear raiders who trashed the currency during 2001 attacked during a perfect storm: the dollar was in the final months of a multi-year bull market; dollar commodities were at the end of an even longer bear market; and the rand's long-term depreciation against the dollar was in its dying stages.

Although both domestic and global macroeconomic factors played a role in the pricing of the rand during 2001, there's no question that Wakeford's whistle-blowing had profound consequences for South Africa as a whole. If this sounds like hyperbole, consider again the reality that South Africa does not exist in a vacuum, as most aptly illustrated by the rand's status as a free-floating currency in the global money pool.

Markets are nothing without people; and, as such, markets can sometimes be used for ulterior motives. On this score, it is worth examining the inextricable linkages between money, a tangible (or fungible, if the lawyers are given a say), and humans, who run markets, for good or for ill. It is said that money has no language, but it may be useful to ask if there is anything more international than money, of which currency is the chief exchange mechanism.

There are some human qualities that may be even more universal than money: greed, envy and all the other deadly sins. If there is anything delightful about markets at all, it is the presence of people. In the Oliver Stone film *Wall Street*, protagonist Gordon Gekko (Michael Douglas) immortalised some of mankind's quaint delicacies: 'The point is, ladies and gentlemen, that greed, for lack of a better word, is good. Greed is right. Greed works.'

It is widely conceded that there is no such thing as a perfect market. Sooner or later there will be an imperfection in supply or demand: a flood will disrupt supplies, or a sudden craze will push demand through the roof. During 2001 the rand wasn't trashed by markets, it was trashed by people – certain people, to be more polite. What did these people do, and why did they do it?

Part of the answer is to be found in people's boundless energy in inventing new types of enterprises. When, for example, is a bank a bank? Traders and bankers may have been around since time immemorial, but the modern-day investment banker is a recent concept. Banks have always played the role of accepting deposits, making loans and earning an income on the spread. The investment banker went a step further – by using the bank's balance sheet to make direct investments that carried risk. In effect, he shifted the risk from his own jugular to the shareholders of the bank and, more to the point, to the trusting people and companies that had placed their hard-earned cash with the bank for safekeeping.

Given that banks were allowed to deploy in investments a higher ratio of the cash than they held as deposits, investment bankers have been massively advantaged, or, to use the jargon, they are 'leveraged' like no other. The world would never be the same. From the start, apart from the ability to leverage investments by using something close to thin air, it was apparent that investment bankers stood to benefit from inside knowledge.

Investment bankers would be operating on both sides of the fence. Detailed knowledge was acquired from debtors – as anyone who has filled in a loan application knows – and from that knowledge, investment bankers would learn about potential low-hanging fruit. Where a profit, especially a quick one, was sensed, the investment bankers would quickly reach for their investor hats.

'Trust me, I'm your banker.'

Investment bankers, like investors and speculators, are motivated primarily by greed, and inspired mainly by fear. However, at a higher – or, better put, lower – level, investment bankers are motivated by being the best: the 'biggest swinging dick on Wall Street', or in less profane terms, a 'master of the universe' (from a wildly popular toy for boys). History has shown that opportunistic investment bankers cannot resist being human – that is, operating outside the client's line of sight but, if need be, against the client's interests. Investment bankers love gorging at the trough. History also shows that if investment bankers are caught with their hands in the cookie jar, scandals, and even imprisonment, only seem to provide inspiration.

Various attempts were made over the decades, mainly in the US, to erect 'Chinese walls' – impenetrable barriers – between traditional banking activities and investment-banking endeavours. But little real success has been achieved, even after massive and systemic events have rattled the world's biggest economy, and the world. Take the example of Long-Term Capital Management (LTCM), founded in 1994 by John Meriwether, Wall Street's once-fabled Salomon Brothers bond trader. LTCM hired the best of the best, including Nobel Prize–winning economists Myron Scholes and Robert Merton, and David Mullins, a former vice chairman of the Federal Reserve.

Apparently smart investors, including the inevitable investment banks, charged like bulls to invest, pumping $1.3 billion into LTCM up front. Most hedge funds try to exploit the leverage concept and try to identify unique opportunities in the markets. LTCM took a fancy to Russian debt. During the summer of 1998, Russia defaulted on its domestic debt, and decreed a moratorium on bank payments. Hedge funds that had been long of (i.e. buyers of) high-yielding Russian domestic debt had simultaneously hedged such positions by shorting (i.e. selling) Russian foreign debt, and at the same time shorted forward sales of rubles to Russian banks.

LTCM was up to its eyeballs on the wrong side of *both* the Russian bets. It was long on Russia's domestic debt and short on Russia's foreign debt. Fair enough, it was unprecedented for an emerging country such as Russia to default on domestic debt but not on foreign debt – it had almost always happened the other way round. Domestic debt defaults were easier to avoid. LTCM's gamble depended on forecasts that turned out to be horribly wrong: human error. Less than four years after its launch, LTCM was technically bust. To avoid a possible systemic crisis in the global financial system, the Federal Reserve unleashed a $3.5 billion rescue package, raised from leading Wall Street investment and commercial banks. Back in those good old days, bankers were expected to bail out bankers. That is truly a bygone era.

Taxpayer bailouts for various fallen angels in the financial-services sector have now become the norm. For the bankers, this is like taking candy from kids – it's something that seems to fall out of thin air. It's doubtful that the US, or any country, learnt anything from the LTCM failure.

The next big surprise was Enron. For many years, this decade's wave of money scandals were benchmarked against the December 2001 implosion of a company that once ranked among the top 10 in the US. This, and many contemporaneous and subsequent scandals, involved most leading investment banks on Wall Street, and followed the bursting of the biggest stock-market bubble ever, in March 2000. This was when the technology-media-telecoms (TMT) bubble burst explosively. The TMT era precipitated the corruption of investment-banking research staff and the wanton demolition of Chinese walls, which had supposedly separated research analysts from investment bankers: the two sets of professionals, the world was told, operated completely independently of each other, and did not communicate in any way.

The scandals triggered deep-level investigations led by Eliot Spitzer, 63rd New York State Attorney General. From January 1999 to December 2006, Spitzer and his team won major prosecutions over white-collar crime, securities fraud, internet fraud, environmental-protection fraud, computer-chip price fixing and the 2003 mutual fund scandal.

Spitzer's attack on conflicts of interest was vitriolic. The gist of it was that companies had published positive research reports on various stocks despite poor underlying fundamentals. The 'official' research was used by brokers in the firm to promote the stocks, creating an environment of 'pump and dump' – for the firms, that is. Investors and speculators had their faces ripped off. Responding to subpoenas, Merrill Lynch handed over 30 boxes of printed emails. In an indictment issued by the Washington-based Securities and Exchange Commission (SEC) on 28 April 2003, Merrill Lynch investment analyst Henry Blodget faced allegations that

> during the relevant period [he had] issued research reports on one
> internet company, GoTo.com, that violated antifraud provisions of

the federal securities laws, and issued research reports on six other internet companies that expressed views inconsistent with privately expressed negative views as discussed below. These reports violated NASD and NYSE rules that require, among other things, that published research reports have a reasonable basis, present a fair picture of the investment risks and benefits, and not make exaggerated or unwarranted claims.[5]

Publicly, Blodget was wont to describe certain companies as 'an attractive investment'; privately, he would sometimes express a different view, and was not unknown to use colourful language, not least the well-known 'POS' (piece of shit). In response to civil fraud charges levelled by the SEC, Blodget agreed to a permanent ban from the securities industry. He also paid a $2 million fine, plus a $2 million disgorgement.

Spitzer eventually reached a settlement with the major Wall Street investment banks: the so-called Global Settlement, an enforcement deal signed on 23 April 2003 between the US's key financial regulators and 10 of the US's biggest investment firms, which declined to admit wrongdoing. New rules were passed to break the ties between investment banking and stock-analyst compensation. A total fine of $1.4 billion was paid up by Merrill Lynch, Bear Stearns, Credit Suisse First Boston, Deutsche Bank, Goldman Sachs, J.P. Morgan Chase, Lehman Brothers, Morgan Stanley, Salomon Smith Barney and UBS Warburg – in a nutshell, the biggest names on Wall Street, the centre of the world's capital markets.

The disgraces, arrests, convictions and sentencing continued for a long time. Frank Quattrone, once one of Wall Street's biggest individual names, was probed, and in August 2006 made a deferred prosecution agreement in terms of which he was not required to serve jail time. Quattrone, once head of technology banking at Credit Suisse First Boston investment bank, made billions for clients and then lost billions, and was finally caught. At the peak of his time at the firm, in the mid-1980s, he was earning around $120 million a year. These evil geniuses were starting to get serious airtime, and even made it into popular entertainment. People like Quattrone inspired motion pictures such as *Wall Street* and countless writings.

The swagger of investment bankers had already been laid bare in the 1987 classic *The Bonfire of the Vanities*, in which journalist-turned-author

Tom Wolfe distilled the essence of Wall Street in Sherman McCoy, an arrogant investment banker, truly a 'master of the universe'. *Bonfire* was the bestselling fiction debut of the decade. Alongside the master of the universe, its characters include a vicious mistress, wives like 'social X-rays', scumbag politicians, tabloid hacks, burlesque and silent giants ruminating in the justice system, and cops – Jewish, Italian, black and Irish. This was a cauldron of infamy, circulating around a bonfire of burning money, replenished in fresh crispy wads arriving by the hour.

In gaining knowledge of what happens in markets – as opposed to listening to the spin wound out by the likes of a Blodget – some of the non-fiction can be very useful. In his book *F.I.A.S.C.O.: Blood in the Water on Wall Street*, Frank Portnoy profiles the deal that earned Morgan Stanley one of the swankiest fees in Wall Street history: a $74.5 million profit for inventing a derivative that magically 'disappeared' zillions in losses off a Japanese company's balance sheet. These were the earlier days of derivatives. Portnoy's book covers the early and mid-1990s, the setting for some of the biggest derivatives wipeouts ever known: the Orange County, California, bankruptcy; the demise of Barings Bank; agonising losses at Procter & Gamble, Dell Computers and Gibson Greetings; and the Mexican peso swamp monster. Derivatives, at the centre of each these scandals, have been described by iconic US investor Warren Buffett as 'financial weapons of mass destruction'.

In *F.I.A.S.C.O.*, Portnoy reveals the bloodlust that has long consumed investment banking, a place where the siren blares: 'There's blood in the water. Let's go kill someone.' Derivatives traders, egged on by virtual steroids pumped into them by management, and galvanised by gun-toting senior salesmen, traded in financial war zones while drooling over *Soldier of Fortune*. They would swagger around the trading room (complete with pizza-gorged bellies and sweat-drenched faces) when they had pulled off a deal that 'ripped off' a client's face. If this was free enterprise, who could have wished for better?

Earlier, another of Wall Street's own, Michael Lewis, described in vivid detail the skulduggery at Salomon Brothers between 1984 and the crash of October 1987. However, the best part of his book happens just outside the trading war zone. In *Liar's Poker*, Lewis describes a single spectacular bet in the eponymous game that rewards trickery and deceit. The ultra-wealthy chairman of Salomon Brothers, John Gutfreund (pronounced 'good friend'), challenged his legendary chief trader, John Meriwether: 'One hand, one million dollars, no tears.' A million dollars was a lot of money back then, money that even the chief trader possibly did not have available. A true master of the universe, Meriwether replied: 'No, John, if we're going to play for those kinds of numbers, I'd rather play for real money. Ten million dollars. No tears.' Gutfreund's reaction is history.

As it turned out, Spitzer's attempts to reform Wall Street – and with it, the financial-services sector across the Western world – were in vain. As mentioned, in October 2007, the US subprime crisis started to emerge. This would plunge global credit markets into a hellfroth, precipitating the 2008 world recession.

One commentator put it this way from the US, the heart of the 2008 financial crisis: 'The old walls of crony capitalism are held together by self-serving, self-policing and self-destructive regulatory bodies. The inability of the present system of regulation to deal with the complexities of expanding capitalism and protect us from inordinate concentrations of systemic risk has been tragically demonstrated.'[6]

The brains trusts on Wall Street had gone too far, and some of Wall Street's biggest names were in trouble, a kind of trouble that had not been seen for decades, if ever. In March 2008, Bear Stearns collapsed, and in September that year, Lehman Brothers, which had traded on Wall Street since 1887, went bust. As it turned out, a complete failure of global proportions was avoided, but politicians, regulators and law enforcers floundered in response to one of the greatest collective failures ever seen in the markets. And the very investment banks that had ripped the guts out of the system were among those chosen to be bailed out using taxpayers' money, and government debt – a delayed form of tax.

This time the public were outraged: no matter how complex the gobble-degook concocted by the brains trusts on Wall Street, the consequences were clear to all but tiny infants and the insane. This time, people were suffering; foreclosures on homes rose to levels not seen for decades and the rate of home defaults accelerated under the stubborn refusal of the US economy to revive from below-trend growth. The average US citizen knew that the brains trusts on Wall Street had gone too far. The smell of blood was in the air.

But even within such a sleazy and contaminated environment, there was no shortage of lone-wolf lurkers. One of them, Bernard Madoff, a New Yorker, admitted Ponzi-toasting billions of dollars in investor funds. On 29 June 2009, Madoff was sentenced to 150 years in prison, the maximum allowed. He had pleaded guilty to 11 federal felonies and admitted his involvement in a Ponzi scheme, ranked as the biggest in US history and, no doubt, the world. It seemed, however, that one Jeffry M. Picower was the biggest beneficiary of Madoff's mischief. On 25 October 2009, Picower was found dead at the bottom of a pool at his home in Palm Beach. His estate settled claims against it of $7.2 billion. Madoff's Ponzi scheme involved around $65 billion.

The bigger picture remains as big as ever – and who can speak bigger than a politician? Economists … perhaps. Given a market, there are people who will peddle anything. In his book *The Fortune Sellers: The Big Business of Buying and Selling Predictions*, William Sherden reviews leading research conducted since the 1970s concerning the accuracy of economic forecasts. He found that economists cannot do anything, really. They cannot predict turning points; their ability to forecast is neither better nor worse than guessing; there is no evidence that forecasters' skills have increased since the 1970s (if anything, they have deteriorated over time); 'consensus' forecasts are of no special help; and so on. Even so, economists continue to flog their snake oil, flanked by all kinds of other white-collar beasts intent on making a personal billion.

Wall Street remains the global benchmark for everything that is good about money and, increasingly, everything that is bad about money. Wall Street is the most mimicked market in the world – a number of its murky practices have been exported, with variations, around the world. Politicians make little headway in their efforts to reform Wall Street. President Barack Obama made many promises during his first term, which included – naturally, it would seem, after the disaster of 2008 – reforms for Wall Street. If anything, Obama has been criticised for allowing Wall Street to reform in the wrong direction.

And then along came a case that everyone said would never happen: the SEC threw the book at Goldman Sachs, Wall Street's great survivor. Goldman Sachs started out with a single office in New York in 1869, and for decades has been talked of as housing Wall Street's bluest blood. Today Goldman is a little different. Its CEO, Lloyd Blankfein, has sometimes been described as a strutting peacock. Amid the general public outrage following the unveiling of the SEC's case, the wise ones at Goldman Sachs opted for a settlement, thus avoiding the fuller gory details of the case against it unfolding in a courtroom.

On 15 July 2010, the SEC boldly announced that 'Goldman, Sachs & Co. will pay $550 million and reform its business practices to settle SEC charges that Goldman misled investors in a subprime mortgage product just as the US housing market was starting to collapse'. According to the SEC, Goldman Sachs 'acknowledged that its marketing materials for the subprime product contained incomplete information'.[7]

In its initial filing, the SEC had complained that Goldman Sachs 'misstated and omitted key facts regarding a synthetic collateralized debt obligation (CDO) it marketed that hinged on the performance of subprime residential mortgage-backed securities'.[8]

In this alarming case, Goldman failed to disclose to investors, according to the SEC, vital information about the CDO, particularly the role that hedge fund Paulson & Co. Inc. had played in the portfolio-selection process, and the fact that Paulson had taken a short position against the CDO.

In plain terms, Paulson & Co. had played a part in setting up a product that was designed to fail, and had immediately bet that it would indeed fail. Put another way, Paulson & Co., with intimate early knowledge of the product, invested millions of dollars on the product failing. The product failed. Paulson & Co. banked hundreds of millions of dollars; Goldman Sachs also made *very* good money on the deal. In its public admission, Goldman Sachs acknowledged that 'in particular, it was a mistake for the Goldman marketing materials to state that the reference portfolio was "selected by" ACA Management LLC without disclosing the role of Paulson & Co. in the portfolio selection process and that Paulson's economic interests were adverse to CDO investors'.[9]

Robert Khuzami, director of the SEC's division of enforcement, crowed that

half a billion dollars is the largest penalty ever assessed against a financial services firm in the history of the SEC. This settlement is a stark lesson to Wall Street firms that no product is too complex, and no investor too sophisticated, to avoid a heavy price if a firm violates the fundamental principles of honest treatment and fair dealing.

In the fine print, Goldman Sachs agreed to settle the SEC's charges 'without admitting or denying the allegations by consenting to the entry of a final judgment that provides for a permanent injunction from violations of the antifraud provisions of the Securities Act of 1933'.[10]

Despite its various concessions, Goldman Sachs had secured its 'non-admission' as part of the settlement with the SEC. In its own mind at least, Goldman Sachs had not violated any laws, and the SEC had signed to that effect. The almighty Goldman spin machine had long cranked into action: the reason given for the settlement was that a full court case on the dispute would take the firm's best out of circulation for far too long. At the same time, suspicions were raised by the Goldman machine that lawmakers had become overzealous, and had honoured the tradition created by Spitzer of forcing opponents into no-win court cases that were far easier to settle.

It is evident, and this will be further explored in the narrative, that the banking sector in the Western world today thrives on a culture of non-admission. Latter-day developments, particularly in the US, go a long way to contextualising Wakeford's decision to take on a global bank back in 2002, along with a number of corporates with substantial clout. It was only after Wakeford had blown the whistle that law-enforcement agents and regulators, mainly in the US, finally realised that banks – those with a global footprint or practising as a 'bulge bracket' investment bank – had become a huge and irreversible problem. The evidence is that these banks were somehow classified in a special category by law-enforcement agents and regulators.

The resounding 'too big to fail' descriptor that was informally attached to certain banks out of fear that the failure of a single such bank could trigger the collapse of an economy, and even the global economy, went further. This special place in society carried another privilege: diluted treatment at the hands of law-enforcement agents and regulators. Yes, Goldman had settled with the SEC for $550 million in 2010, but relative to Goldman's profits, the damage was more like a speeding fine for a super-car than something that really hurt. Goldman declared pre-tax profits of

$12.9 billion in 2010, after the spectacular $19.8 billion that had been posted for 2009. It was also telling that the SEC made an attempt to go after certain individuals at Goldman, but lost its appetite. In more recent years, US law-enforcement agents have finally admitted that big banks and big investment banks really are special.

The situation was no different in South Africa. Here there were further difficulties, stemming mainly from the structures of the elites in banking, business and politics. What Wakeford didn't know when he blew the whistle in 2002 was that SACOB's chairman, Christoph Köpke, answered to a person who had significant influence at the global bank that Wakeford fingered, plus one of the big corporates, and he also sat on President Mbeki's investment advisory council. As Wakeford would find out, these conflicts of interest were going to create all kinds of heavy-duty problems. Wakeford says that had he known at the time, it would have had no influence on his decision to blow the whistle.

All Kevin Wakeford wanted to be assured of was that the rand currency market had been a market of 'honest treatment and fair dealing', to use Khuzami's words during the Goldman case. He always knew that no such finding would be made, never mind mentioned.

2
Horse-trading

Currency, the most important price in an economy ... The power of
the dollar and the rise of the yuan ... Anonymous markets immune to
the whims of politicians ... The South-East Asian currency crisis ... Crucial
role of trade accounts ... The rand as a commodity currency ... Influences
on the rand in 2001, from delinquent capital to Zimbabwe ... Bar-room
theories ... The 'us' and 'them' syndrome ... Intrepid bankers: HSBC's
mind-boggling romance with Mexican drug traffickers.

*'The Bank is responsible, on behalf of the Minister of Finance,
for the day-to-day administration of exchange controls in South Africa.
Exchange Control Regulations are the legal provisions that limit
the extent to which South African residents and companies
may transfer funds abroad.' – South African Reserve Bank*

The term 'horse-trading' can be traced to the notion that a horse can be
very difficult to evaluate. This keeps doors open for unscrupulous dealers
and agents. Other assets – not least securities such as currencies – are likewise difficult, if not impossible, to accurately evaluate at any particular
time. What's worse is that predicting an asset's value at some time in the
future is a mug's game. The only real certainty is that the value of an asset
will change over time.

The valuation of securities is an elusive concept. Mainstream markets
have long been established for stocks, bonds, commodities, property – and,
of course, currencies. If the forward values of an asset could be predicted
with ease, anybody and everybody could easily become a millionaire. But
investing and speculating are both notoriously dangerous activities. Even
an investor who puts money into so-called blue-chip investments faces all
kinds of dangers. Especially after the fees of money managers are factored
in, the reality is that it's difficult for the average investor to come out on top.

A particular horse may be very important to a particular person, but there are few assets that affect people as much as currency. Currency transactions have an impact on everyone. The poor may never own stocks, bonds, commodities or property, but they touch currency all the time. The economic health, or otherwise, of a nation, and of the world in general, is signalled by the prices of goods and services. Currency is the common denominator, the yardstick and the benchmark.

A wise person once said that the price of a currency is the most important price of all. In a model country, currency policy would focus on maintaining a stable currency. If this is attained, then the value of the currency becomes a background factor in the functioning of the economy as a whole. Yet the record of even the almighty dollar shows that the notion of a stable currency is an elusive, if not impossible, goal.

There is nothing investors fear more than uncertainty. In the case of currencies, the greatest fears are over volatility and, worst of all, collapse. A depreciating currency may be 'good' for exporters, but a currency that is going to hell will ultimately result in ruination – in every sense – and even the exporters will eventually be found on the road to hell. From uncertainty flows disturbance, from disturbance flows fear and from fear flows speculation – rational and otherwise. When there is a radical change in price, as was the case with the rand's collapse in 2001, any number of theories are given. It seems that anyone who had thought about the subject for more than a few minutes would happily venture an interpretation.

The rand became a household talking point during 2001, and especially in the fourth quarter of the year, when the currency took a catastrophic beating – one that could have pushed South Africa over the edge into financial chaos, instantly fomenting unprecedented social and political unrest.

Despite the jargon surrounding exclusive trading in high-end markets, be it stocks, bonds, commodities or currencies, the pricing of these securities is ultimately determined by the point where supply and demand intersect. However, price changes in the physical markets are also driven by market psychology, which can be influenced by a myriad of factors, ranging from rumours about North Korea test-launching a warhead to speculation that the chief executive of a big company may have fallen gravely ill. Markets are also influenced by data, such as a company that posts an above-forecast increase in profits, or a bank that reports bad debts at a higher level than had been expected.

Many markets have grown to gigantic proportions, especially over the past two decades or so as trade has moved towards globalisation. At any given time of the day or night, the markets – some would say the 'amorphous markets' – provide real-time information on the value of traded securities. Where there is a willing buyer and a willing seller, a price of exchange can be established. Whether or not the price has integrity is another issue. Warren Buffett once said that 'price is what you pay, value is what you get'.

Politicians and markets don't mix

As 2001 progressed and the rand's value increasingly contracted, and a real sense of panic set in, interpreting and misinterpreting what was going on were largely left to the press – 'press' referring to both print and electronic media.

In 2001 President Thabo Mbeki, finance minister Trevor Manuel and Tito Mboweni, governor of the Reserve Bank, were unable to shed much light on the rand situation. In any event, little was ventured. Markets have long perplexed, and even downright confused, politicians, and most other people, in every corner of the earth. In a perfect world, the price of any freely traded security – be it a stock (more commonly known as a 'share' in South Africa, referring to a listed company), bond, commodity or currency – reflects everything known about that particular security at a particular point in time.

For example, the stock price of a well-established and seemingly dominant company may suddenly come under pressure in the face of a market rumour that the chief executive may have done, or been aware of, something untoward, or even illegal. The company issues an outright denial of the rumour. Despite that, the market may disbelieve the denials and continue to take a 'bearish' view on the value of the stock – for the meantime, anyway. For anyone not right at the coalface of the market, this kind of price action can be very confusing. If anything in the world tops the ranking for ambivalence, it would probably be markets: the money equivalent of marriage – you can't do with them, and you can't do without them.

Most chief executives sound like amateurs when discussing markets. Writing in the UK's *Financial Times* on 18 July 2010, John Kay commented that 'politicians and chief executives of all political colours become angry when anonymous markets do not take their assertions at face value. The anonymous market cannot be dictated to or defeated in debate. Leaders cannot shout down, fire or arrest the non-existent Mr Market.'

The term 'Mr Market' is attributed to Benjamin Graham, partner of legendary US investor Warren Buffett. Graham coined an imaginary investor, 'Mr Market', to demonstrate his point that a wise investor chooses investments based on fundamental (also known as 'intrinsic' or 'underlying') value, as opposed to the opinions of others or the direction of the markets. This school of thought leans heavily on objectivity, which is often ignored in markets, where subjectivity and rumours tend to prevail.

There would be little, if any, surprise if South African politicians were immune to the 'Mr Market' condition of objectivity. There is nothing quite like a politician flexing muscles – muscles that did not change in size after the person was appointed as minister. One of the best examples, which may well have haunted Trevor Manuel for years, is when he said in 1996: 'I insist on the right to govern ... I insist on the right not to be stampeded into a panic decision by some amorphous entity ... called the market.'[1]

Markets may seem amorphous – lacking specific shape – at times, but there is no question that markets have played a dominant role in humankind's development for many centuries. Markets are fundamentally governed by supply and demand. In the perfect market – which, to reiterate, does not exist – the two forces at any particular point in time determine the value of the underlying security – be it a stock, bond, commodity or currency.

Markets are subject to innumerable imperfections. One of these is size: a small market is generally described as 'illiquid', and the price of the underlying security may change in a jagged and illogical way. In a highly liquid market, such as that of the dollar, price changes tend to be smoother and more logical, certainly when seen in hindsight. Individual securities with a high degree of liquidity are described as exhibiting 'price integrity', which means the market is seen as sufficiently large to resist the influence of speculators or other interventionists, real or imagined.

Where there are interventions, the agents involved are normally meticulously careful to flag the markets so as to avoid accusations of underhand conduct and the possibility of being accused of using insider information in an underhand way. A good example may be found in the US Federal Reserve, which for much of this decade, and specifically during and after the 2008 credits-market crisis, has embarked on a number of massive monetary exercises aimed at stimulating economic activity in the US. The Federal Reserve has been scrupulously careful in warning the markets well before the event, allowing the market to prepare its reaction long before the actual event. Savvy speculators try to be ahead of it all ('buy on the rumour, sell on the facts').

Illiquid markets and selling short

An illiquid market can be regarded as vulnerable to speculative intervention. A player with a big balance sheet may decide, for whatever reason, that the value of a certain illiquid security is likely to rise. A big player can sustain this belief for quite some time, and bring undue influence to bear on the price of the security.

The flip side of this is when the value of a security is seen or perceived as overvalued, for whatever reason. This kind of security may suddenly find itself in a 'bear' market, which may or may not be part of a broader trend. Investors and speculators who buy into this theme sell the security. The action is more generally known in markets as 'shorting'. Given a bearish undertone, investors and speculators prefer to be 'short' of a security.

Then there is the case of a speculator who senses that a particular security will come under price pressure, but does not own the particular security, and cannot, therefore, benefit by going short. In stock markets, few jurisdictions in the world permit what is known as 'naked' shorting. If a player wants to short a particular stock, but owns no such stock and goes into the market and sells the stock, the action is described as 'naked shorting'. The speculator has sold fictional shares. The motive is to sell fictional shares of a particular stock at, say, R10 a share, and to buy it back later at, say, R5 a share.

The speculator will then deliver the stock bought at half price to the buyer who bought for R10. The speculator makes a fortune. The window of opportunity is that there is a permitted delivery time after the initial sale of the shares by the speculator – historically, seven days. This means that the speculator is working in very short-term territory. He or she sells today at R10 a share, hoping within days to buy the shares at R5 a share, for delivery to the hapless buyer who transacted at R10 a share.

Today, speculators in stock markets are required to either own, or borrow, stock before selling it. In the majority of shorting cases, however, the speculator does not own the stock: borrowed stock is used. The speculator who is looking to short at R10 a share must borrow as many shares as are going to be sold. The speculator must identify an investor, typically an institution, holding, say, 10 million of the shares in question. Provided the speculator possesses sufficient standing in the market, the institution should in theory be prepared to lend the 10 million shares to the speculator, who then sells the borrowed stock. If the stock can later be bought back for R5 a share, the speculator will be more than able to make good on the shares borrowed at R10 a share. The speculator pockets a tidy profit of R5 a share. This process means that speculators are unable to sell 'fictional' shares into the market. If that were allowed, a bear run on a stock could extend to insanely low levels, undermining confidence in the stock market as a whole.

In the US, the prearrangement of borrowing a security prior to a short sale is known in market jargon as a 'locate'. In 2005 the SEC instituted Regulation SHO to address the widespread failure to deliver securities, aimed at preventing naked selling. More stringent regulations were established in September 2008, and made permanent in 2009.

In practice, it may be permissible, given that certain conditions have been fulfilled, to short not only stocks, but also bonds, futures, currencies and commodities. In global markets, however, speculators tend to hedge short positions within the markets, as such. As mentioned in Chapter 1, LTCM took a long position on Russia's domestic debt to hedge its short position on Russia's foreign debt. As it turned out, LTCM was wrong on both counts: a double whammy pushed LTCM into insolvency.

Any market of any size can crash – and most probably will, sooner or later. Argentina defaulted on part of its foreign debt early in 2002. There have been similar events in the private-bond market, seen most recently in the 2008 subprime mortgage-bond crisis in the US. There have also been apocalyptic events in currency markets. Among the most contagious was the 1997 Asian currency crisis, which at the time inflamed fears of a global economic meltdown. The crisis started in Thailand, which had allowed its foreign debt to grow to dangerous levels. Technically, the country was 'insolvent' before the currency crisis even started. The country had also fallen victim to a property bubble; interest rates were high, attracting 'hot money'; and it was also subject to the whims of 'crony capitalists'. Crony capitalism, characterised as a close relationship between certain individuals in government and certain individuals in private enterprise, has been well documented, and includes the *keiretsu* in post-war Japan, the powerful families controlling enormous wealth in Latin America and the *chaebol* in South Korea.

The roots of the Asian currency crisis can be traced to the mid-1990s, when the US started to raise interest rates as it continued recovering from recession. This created yet another negative factor for the South-East Asian subregion, which had been attracting heavy speculative inflows by offering relatively high interest rates. Rates in the US were increasingly attractive and had the effect of eroding the quantum of capital flowing into South-East Asia, weakening currencies in the region. The currency contagion spread across the region, affecting Indonesia, South Korea, Hong Kong, Malaysia, Laos and the Philippines. China, Taiwan, Singapore and Vietnam were also hurt. A number of theories have been developed to explain the Asian currency crisis. The most convincing, it would seem, is that a herd mentality developed, not unlike the psychology that precedes a run on a bank, and remains in place afterwards until extraordinary measures are taken, typically by government.

The Asian currency crisis devastated the region. The extent of the meltdown can be illustrated by referring to the Indonesian currency, which traded at around 2 600 rupiah to the dollar before the crisis. The rate collapsed to over 11 000 rupiah to the dollar early in January 1998, with spot rates rising to more than 14 000 later in the month and again to around those levels during mid-1998. By this stage, short-term interest rates in Indonesia had risen to 65 per cent a year, in an effort to at least stem the crisis. Economies ground to a virtual halt and millions of jobs were lost across the subregion. South Korea and Thailand suffered the most. Then, within months, the crisis was over. Economists and other experts have offered many explanations for why the crisis exploded into life so quickly, and then died so quickly. The effects of the crisis, however, lingered for many years.

Commodity prices took a severe beating during and after the crisis. The reduction in oil revenue, in particular, triggered the 1998 Russian financial crisis, and likewise in Brazil and Argentina. There was any amount of collateral damage. The Russian crisis triggered the collapse of US hedge fund LTCM, and the Federal Reserve was forced to lead a bailout programme of $3.6 billion. Argentina experienced a crisis that lasted from 1999 to 2003. In early 2002, as noted, it defaulted on part of its external sovereign debt. Foreign investment had fled the country. The currency exchange rate – formerly a fixed 1-to-1 parity between the peso and the dollar – was floated and quickly descended to chaotic levels, triggering galloping inflation and attracting, in turn, high interest rates, which further choked economic activity.

Seen in broader terms, the Asian currency crisis was linked to the global backlash against the Washington Consensus and institutions such as the International Monetary Fund (IMF) and the World Bank, which have continued, and so far failed, to seek consensus on globalisation as a whole.

Policy-makers around the world studied the Asian currency crisis intensely and tried to learn from it. In some countries, measures were implemented to at least avoid the terrible processes that could ruin a currency, and a state. The main policy response, especially in South-East Asia, was to build up foreign-exchange reserves as a bulwark against currency attacks. This required major commitment at the national level: Asian countries scrambled to increase manufactured exports, and at the same time focused on minimising imports. This boosted the competitiveness of the region, which within a decade would grow to rank as an economic powerhouse. Being called to arms is one thing; being called to improving one's lot can be far more beneficial.

Trade accounts are central to measuring country health

The level of a country's foreign-exchange reserves is a function of its balance of payments, which has two main components: services and trade. Services are sometimes described as 'invisible'; trade refers to tangible goods. Leaving aside services, which are relatively smaller in emerging-market economies, a country's trade balance is determined, over time, by netting exports and imports.

A country that exports more than it imports boasts a trade surplus; the inverse produces a trade deficit. For emerging economies, the quickest way to boost exports is to focus on manufactured goods, requiring optimal inputs from labour, capital and technology, and necessary support from government.

Some economists argue that a country's trade balance is largely fictional, since a trade account does not exist, as such. This is true. The trade account refers to the net surpluses – or deficits – produced by the country's enterprises in aggregate. A country's trade account can, therefore, be calculated by means of statistics. The point is that if the country as an entity exports more than it imports, its enterprises are sitting, on a net basis, with more foreign currency than domestic currency. This means that 'the country' is better able to defend against attacks, such as may materialise, on its domestic currency. Where a country as a whole enjoys a surplus of foreign-currency holdings, or reserves, policy-makers provide strong guidance on where such holdings should be parked.

For example, in response to the Asian currency crisis, Japan, a developed economy, implemented policies specifically aimed at building up its foreign-exchange reserves. This lead was followed by other Asian countries, not least China. The example was likewise followed in other emerging-market countries, notably Brazil, Russia and India. In the vast majority of cases, dollar holdings are the number-one choice. In late 2012, China held net foreign reserves of $3.3 trillion (including gold), compared to South Africa's $51 billion.[2]

The US Treasury bill – a bond – has long been the first choice for dollar holdings, serving the US in many ways. The dollar had entered a bear market early in 2002 mainly on the back of the US's twin deficits: the country was running deficits – and still does – on its federal budget (government was spending more than it was raising via the tax system) and also on its current account. The US had become a net importer. Many of its services and goods had become uncompetitive on global markets, and needed a boost from a weaker dollar.

Given that China's yuan was riding on the dollar's weaker coat-tails, stimulating both US and Chinese exports, many other countries started 'competing' for weaker currencies. For many decades, it has been taken for granted that the only good currency is a strong currency. From the beginning of the new millennium, this principle has been turned on its head. Countries were now soft-shoe dancing for weaker currencies, aimed at building up trade surpluses and, hence, foreign reserves.

As should be clear by now, the US and China are two special cases. Shortly after the start of the new millennium, China developed to become the epicentre of world economic activity, and rapidly attained the world's biggest trade surplus. At the same time, China had an intrinsic interest in a weaker dollar, given that its yuan is tied to the dollar. At the same time, again, the US is one of China's biggest customers. So large has the Chinese trade surplus become that it literally has no choice but to park its surplus dollars in US Treasury bonds. And here is the irony: it is mainly China that finances the US's trade deficit. The two countries are joined at the head, shoulders and indeed the nether regions. In more economic and financial senses than the normal mind could probably comprehend, the US and China are one giant country.

For many decades, South Africa ran a trade surplus, given its strong exports of commodities and agricultural products, along with a fair showing from the manufacturing sector. Around the turn of the century, this started to change. South Africa has seemingly been attempting the impossible by skipping the process of wide industrialisation as it develops, hopefully, from an emerging economy to a developing one. In reality, the farming sector has shrunk, especially relative to the size of the growing population, and the all-important manufacturing sector has been dealt one blow after another. The financial-services sector (including real estate), which arguably adds little value to the real economy, has become the country's biggest economic component. At the same time, rampant consumerism, underpinned by one of the world's lowest savings rates, has fuelled imports. Policy-makers have done little, if anything, to diversify the real economy – in fact the evidence points to the contrary.

In December 2012, the South African Reserve Bank reported that 'the trade deficit [had] widened further, from R75.7 billion in the second quarter of 2012 to R82.3 billion in the third quarter'.[3] Relative to the size of South Africa's economy, this ranks as one of the biggest trade deficits in the world. This is not good. South Africans pay for this terribly large trade deficit by way of an invisible tax – interest rates that rank among the highest in the world. Compare this to the US, which is able to attract investments in its Treasury bonds due to its status as the world's biggest economy, along with the dollar's status as the world's only international reserve currency. Policy-makers and investors around the world have been undeterred by US interest rates sitting at historic lows for many years. The dollar remains a safe haven, no matter how hysterically the cynics may react.

Commodity currencies are different

For investors, speculators and other players in global markets, currencies have enduring value. In December 2012, Goldman Sachs, the everlasting Wall Street firm, published some of its 'top' investment ideas for 2013.[4] In the currency arena, the top pick was a recommendation to sell the Australian dollar in 2013. This was of note for South Africa because both the Australian dollar and the rand are generally regarded as commodity currencies (as mentioned above).

Goldman's number-one trade idea for 2013 involved two commodity currencies: short (sell) the Australian dollar against (buy) the Norwegian krone. The reasons for Goldman recommending this global macro-trade could have been of interest to any South African interested in the value of the rand.

The rand, indeed, has been depreciating broadly and steadily against the dollar since April 2011, when the dollar cost around R6.70. Towards the end of 2012, it was trading around R8.50 to the dollar, a level not seen since 2008, during the global credit-markets crisis, when most currencies crashed against the dollar. In January 2013, the rand traded above nine to the dollar, a four-year low for the rand. The Australian dollar, compared to the rand, which has faced headwinds from certain political developments, and several credit rating agency downgrades on its foreign debt, has fared better: it was quicker to recover from the 2008 lows than the rand, and over the past two years has to some extent ignored 'reality' – or at least gravity.

Commodity currencies have generally faced softer dollar prices for more than two years. A specific South Africa–Australia overlap has been seen in both countries in their deteriorating trade balances, which traditionally bodes negatively for a currency. It is likely, however, that the enduring attraction of both the Australian dollar and the rand has been the countries' high interest rates.

These attract what are known as hot portfolio flows, or global movements of 'overnight' cash, which, above all else, funds trade deficits. In a sense, citizens of Australia and South Africa are paying for the excesses of their countries' imports over exports by paying higher interest rates: this may be regarded as a hidden tax. In the long run, an excess of imports over exports translates into a steadily weaker currency, as seen in the US dollar starting up a long-term bear market early in 2002.

Unlike the US dollar, the rand and the Australian dollar are small fish in a big pond. US interest rates are at historic lows, but South Africa and Australia have no choice but to compete with relatively high interest rates. Towards the end of 2012, while three-month interest rates were around 0.31 per cent in the US and 0.19 per cent in Japan, the comparatives for Australia were 3.45 per cent and a whopping 5.09 per cent for South Africa. This meant that South African rates were 16 times higher than those in the US.[5]

The Reserve Bank of Australia was busy cutting rates, and was expected to continue with the trend. The South African Reserve Bank had been cutting interest rates on a long-term basis, if particularly slowly, in 2011 and 2012. Lower interest rates mean that both currencies become less attractive, all else being equal. Seen another way, Australia and South Africa would be less attractive from the viewpoint of the 'carry' advantage: for years relatively high interest rates in both countries have made it expensive to short (sell) both currencies.

Regarding the Norwegian currency, Goldman Sachs anticipated that Norway might grow more strongly in 2013, fuelling the possibility of higher interest rates.

***

> 'The modern banking process manufactures currency out of nothing.
> The process is perhaps the most astounding piece of slight hand that
> was ever invented … If you want to be slaves of the bankers, and
> pay the cost of your own slavery, then let the banks create currency.'
> – Lord Josiah Stamp, former director of the Bank of England (1937)

In 2001, any number of theories were advanced on the rand, aimed at attempting to explain its plight and the hidden blight behind it. The following factors were cited for the collapse in the value of the rand.

Speculators: For many, including those in financial-services circles, speculators were the usual suspects. At the time, turnover in the global foreign-exchange (forex) markets exceeded $1 trillion – a day, that is. South Africa's daily forex trading was at the most $10 billion, less than 1 per cent of the daily global total. Foreign-exchange trading in South Africa was equivalent to 0.3 per cent of global trade in 1992, rising to 0.5 per cent in 1998 as the country continued to make the transition into the global economy.

The emerging-market currencies combined accounted for just over 5 per cent of global trade in currencies (though this proportion rises every year). The greenback accounted for 90 per cent of all trades. Of the trade in the rand during 2001, about half was conducted by reporting dealers (authorised bank dealers), about a third by other financial institutions such as pension funds and insurers, and about one-sixth by mining houses, multinationals and domestic importers.

Notably, most of the trade in the rand took place in London and New York. An analysis of trade for April 2001 showed that $3.3 billion was traded that month between offshore parties (on an offshore–offshore basis); $3.5 billion was traded onshore–onshore; and $4.5 billion was traded onshore–offshore. As for the $3.3 billion in offshore–offshore trade, there are simply no records of any kind of such transactions, not in South Africa anyway.

As the administrator of South Africa's foreign-exchange markets, the Reserve Bank could no doubt have benefited from some kind of system that analysed market trends. The nature of the Reserve Bank's surveillance is not known.

HIV/AIDS: South Africa had the world's highest absolute infection rate, and treatments for the virus were in their infancy. At the time, the HIV/AIDS issue was a fear factor hovering over South Africa, aggravated by Mbeki's baffling attitude to the infection.

James Cross: This deputy governor of the Reserve Bank was due to retire on 31 December 2001. Given the fear generated by the rand's meltdown, there was speculation about the timing of this event.

Big deals: During 2001, a number of large authorised deals had an impact on the South African foreign-exchange markets, involving De Beers, AngloGold, Dow AgroSciences and Ethos Private Equity.

Exchange controls: Economist Rob Lee had been widely quoted as saying that exchange regulations and laws 'are supposed to stop money moving out of the country. They are much more effective at keeping money out of the country.'[6]

11 September 2001: The attack on New York City's World Trade complex was unlikely to have played any significant role in the collapse of the rand during 2001.

South Africa's current account had moved into deficit. As noted, the main component of the current account, the trade account, had for many years produced surpluses, as mineral and agricultural exports exceeded the level of imports. During 2001, after the 11 September attacks, the global economy weakened and South Africa's exports were expected to fall, to the detriment of the country's current account.

Overseas investment: There was evidence, according to a number of experts, that South Africans preferred to invest abroad rather than in their own country. There was nothing new in this phenomenon.

Direct foreign investment was at the lower end of the longer-term trend line during 2001.

Privatisation: By October 2001, it became clear that South Africa's privatisation programme was not proceeding as had been planned. The listing of Telkom, the state-owned telecommunications company, had been postponed until 2002.

South Africa's bond markets were weak across 2001.

The Reserve Bank did little, if anything, positive for the rand during 2001. It had repeatedly stated that it would not intervene in the markets to protect the rand, strengthening the perception that the rand was a one-way bet. A circular issued by the Reserve Bank on 13 November 2001 authorised South African fund managers to invest a portion of funds under management in offshore markets. The Reserve Bank had also been a net buyer of dollars during 2001, aimed at reducing its exposure to the dollar in the forward markets. The dynamic was exacerbated by the delay in the Telkom listing, which would have produced an inflow of dollars to South Africa.

Cosmetic relaxations of exchange control: Between the announcement in February 2001 of South Africa's 2001/2002 budget and the end of 2002, billions of rands left the country as a result of the increase in certain foreign-exchange allowances, detailed in the budget. In that period, private individuals exported R7 billion; the corporate sector moved R13.5 billion out; and institutional investors transferred R3.8 billion abroad.

Delinquent capital: Definitely a possible cause – not the capital, to be precise, but the individuals and financial institutions that have no 'loyalty' to the rand, and are happy to short (sell) it in the interests of generating profits. Traders, especially those employed by the global players, had shown no mercy during the Asian currency crisis: why should the rand receive special, or different, treatment?

Corporates: It was easier for some of the biggest companies to raise capital in South Africa to finance offshore acquisitions than to raise capital in offshore capital markets, or borrow abroad. Such capital, if exported, would be negative for the rand, as the domestic currency would be sold and foreign currencies purchased.

Zimbabwe: There was a perception that a seemingly never-ending succession of bad news from Robert Mugabe's regime was rubbing off onto South Africa. This assertion may have upset finance minister Trevor Manuel, who was widely quoted in the media as saying that 'we are not South Zimbabwe ... we're South Africa, nor are they "North South Africa", they're an independent country'.

Manuel preferred to look for causes closer to home. For one, he believed that exporters were not following the rule that stipulated a 180-day window to repatriate proceeds of foreign transactions. 'We need a joint effort,' he said. 'The banks need to come to the party. The bulk of those foreign currency accounts are with South African banks, and they need to live strictly by the rule.'

He conceded that the government and leading economists, both locally and internationally, were 'still grappling to find a reason' for the fall in the rand, given South Africa's 'healthy' economy.[7]

The arms deal: South Africa had, infamously, signed a big arms deal in 1999. What had started off at a cost of around R30 billion rapidly ballooned into double that amount, and more and more. Leaving aside the seemingly endless controversies surrounding the arms deal, the simple fact is that it demanded major payments to offshore suppliers: rands had to be sold and converted into hard foreign currencies.

Argentina: This major emerging market was in all kinds of trouble and, as mentioned, defaulted early in 2002 on $132 billion of foreign debt, raising concerns worldwide. Memories of the 1997 South-East Asian currency crisis were still fresh in people's minds. For an evil mastermind hovering over multiple trading screens in, say, London, it was a matter of scouting the global system to identify the next emerging market that would be ripe for the picking. If so, it would be a matter of shorting the target country's currency.

Relocation of big companies: During the second half of the 1990s, a number of South African companies switched their primary domicile from Johannesburg to London. To some cynics, this was self-imposed corporate exile and tantamount to an expression that South Africa was somewhat lacking. This sentiment, some said, rubbed off on the rand.

Companies that moved domicile included Gencor (which acquired Billiton and in 2001 merged with Australian major BHP to create the world's largest diversified resources stock, BHP Billiton), Anglo American, Dimension Data, Old Mutual and South African Breweries (now SAB-Miller). The companies said, with considerable evidence to support their argument, that raising capital in London cost less and was easier to tap. After all, the City had long ranked as one of the world's leading capital markets. There was also no question that inclusion of a stock in London's 100 most valuable listed companies was not only prestigious, but also enhanced investor demand for the stock. This would inevitably place a premium on the stock's rating. For transnational mining companies such as BHP Billiton and Anglo American, there is no question that listings both in London and on the New York Stock Exchange were essential, given the global peer group.

Speaking to various media outlets, economist Nico Czypionka said that by moving their primary listings offshore, South African companies were looking to maximise returns by externalising cash flows offshore. Indeed, the South African Reserve Bank's quarterly bulletins indicated a surge of outflows during 2001. In Czypionka's view, South African corporates were maximising returns by stripping cash flows through various means. This was not unlawful: 'They can't be blamed for it. In fact, it is an imperative for them; their money is at risk. At the moment they can't make money in South Africa, so they pull back and wait.'

He believed that such outflows would last as long as it appeared inevitable that the rand would depreciate further, and that a more robust rand was the only way to reverse the flow. Following the traditions of all great economists, Czypionka soon found himself back where he had started: 'Once there is a strengthening, there could be a gush of return flows, as companies will fear losing out on some of the gains if the rand is seen to become stronger.'[8]

Bar-room talk: Lunatics, jesters and jokers had it that the rand tanked because there was a government conspiracy to keep South Africans from holidaying abroad and spending valuable foreign currency. In hairdressing salons and around the ubiquitous braai, it was said that a weak rand would also mitigate the brain drain. In a sports-mad country, it was standard fare to hear that the rand's crash was a reaction to South Africa's poor showing in rugby internationals in Europe and cricket tests against Australia. The currency's plight was even put down to speculation that the South African government had secretly offered political asylum to Osama bin Laden. And some said it was because China had been selected to host the 2008 Olympic Games.

As it was to turn out, however, the major culprit was completely visible, to prove the epigram that the best place to hide is in plain sight.

Meanwhile, press commentary on the rand was heading off on all kinds of tangents. Sadly, when controversies arise in South Africa, as the debate intensifies, so often the reversion to type spews out: race. On a somewhat sombre note, columnist Khathu Mamaila wrote in the Johannesburg-based *Star* that

> there are people who have no confidence in the ability of blacks to run a country ... There are people who are quick to point out that Africa is a sad story. They point to catastrophes such as those of Angola, Mozambique, the Democratic Republic of the Congo and lately Zimbabwe. They argue that it is just a matter of time before SA follows the rest of the continent, which is on a path to self-destruction.
>
> Can you imagine how strong the rand would be if we were to physically detach South Africa from Africa and make it part of Western Europe? Instead of tailoring everything to appease the faceless investors, perhaps our government should accept that in spite of doing everything in the free market manual, there is nothing they can do to change perceptions based on race.[9]

Investors are faceless in the proverbial sense. But in the real sense, markets are people clutching money, sometimes money as big as mountains. Unlike so many voters, investors vote with their feet – and very quickly.

On a more serious note, economists, politicians and others in the public light mostly prefer to dehumanise the people holding power over money. Put another way, it's easier for those in public positions to speak lots of economic gobbledegook and avoid underlying issues, thereby carefully deflecting attention away from those making the decisions. As the rand crisis developed in 2001, whenever anyone said anything, it was always something about those impossible-to-understand 'markets' or forces that no one understood or could identify. All the while, however, it was *people* who were pushing the buttons.

Given the judicial powers accorded to the Rand Commission, it would have taken a day or two to get to the bottom of the mess. All it needed, in terms of preparation, was a little investigation into who had been the ghosts in the machine during 2001. The Rand Commission was never going to go there.

The choice, instead, was to have the crisis characterised by politicians, bureaucrats and banks holding the high moral ground. Anyone who dared to suggest that any of these parties may have played a part in the rand's collapse was going to be squashed like a bug. This meant, in turn, that politicians, bureaucrats and the big banks had to develop, unofficially or otherwise, a united approach to combating any criticism.

***

'At the end fiat money returns to its inner value – zero.' – Voltaire

The 'us' and 'them' syndrome

In the atavistic sense, the 'us' are in the right, even without knowing the full story, and the 'them' are in the wrong, and may not know anything anyway. The 'us' are the good guys, the 'them' are bad or evil, even if the 'us' do not know exactly who the 'them' are.

This theme can be found across the world; it may or may not be associated with economic well-being. In a joint session of Congress on 20 September 2001, former US president George W. Bush famously said, 'You are either with us, or you are with the terrorists.' Zbigniew Brzezinski, a well-known political scientist and statesman, told Jon Stewart of *The Daily Show* that Bush was expressing 'the notion that he [Bush] is leading the forces of good against the empire of evil'. Indeed.

Bush, however, cannot be said to have originated this concept of divisiveness. It was Jesus who reportedly said, 'Whoever is not with me is against me, and whoever does not gather with me scatters', and 'Whoever is not against us is for us.' Lenin said: 'It is with absolute frankness that we speak of this struggle of the proletariat; each man must choose between joining our side or the other side. Any attempt to avoid taking sides in this issue must end in fiasco.' George Orwell wrote:

> If you hamper the war effort of one side you automatically help that of the other – nor is there any real way of remaining outside such a war, as the present one. In practice, 'he that is not with me is against me'. The idea that you can somehow remain aloof from and superior to the struggle, while living on food which British sailors have to risk their lives to bring you, is a bourgeois illusion bred of money and security.

Mussolini said: '*O con noi o contro di noi*' (You are either with us or against us.) Hilary Clinton said: 'Every nation has to either be with us, or against us. Those who harbour terrorists, or who finance them, are going to pay a price.'[10] Communists, capitalists, fascists, the Son of God, warmongers: all are united by the umbilical human quality of wanting to be heard, and wanting to *win*.

It is long my experience that 'with us' in South Africa so often means that rottenness of every description is to be tolerated, if not favoured. Those who stand for honesty and transparency are to be trampled on. Sometimes, however, someone rises above this. On this score, Oscar Wilde wrote: 'Be yourself, everyone else is taken.'

For the vast majority, being oneself often seems to be so difficult. For any number of reasons, we find ourselves compromised. We may have a family to feed and the economy may be under pressure and unemployment high, triggering conduct that may cross ethical, legal and other lines. A person who is good at heart may be driven into a life of operating in grey areas, or worse, a life of crime. Once the terrible line is crossed, there is no turning back, not in the moral sense. People can be rehabilitated, but their moral conscience can never be restored. As with innocence, there is no regaining.

This book is about the nastiness of the modern era and the horrors of the human ego. It is a story about greed, but it is overwhelmingly a story about delinquent capital and, ultimately, about those who unflinchingly drive at doing literally whatever it takes to achieve certain identified objectives. Over the past decade, in particular, the world has been taken into unknown areas, characterised chiefly by an increasing convergence of the interests, and conduct, of elites in the political, banking and business circles.

No admission and cover-ups

By this point, I would hope that the reader has identified two major themes:

- Most banks are too big to fail. When failure threatens, governments will do whatever it takes to stem and reverse the potential contagion, either remote or otherwise.
- When banks step over the line into illicit conduct, great care will be taken to ensure any necessary or required cover-up. When, however, this conduct is exposed in the public domain, the miscreant bank or banks

will plea-bargain: fines, often running into hundreds of millions of dollars, and perhaps more, will be paid. The bank or banks will then move onto the next kill, as if nothing had happened.

The merry-go-round continues and the ultimate casualties are the ordinary taxpayers – the men, women and children in the street. This has now become part of the human condition. The root of this conduct, ironically, may be less the raw greed to accumulate money than ego boosting. Over the past decade, a number of surveys and analyses have found strong indications that corrupt conduct in the financial markets is more linked to beating a perceived peer group or a specifically identified 'other person' than about making money. If this is true, then the world has become an insufferably cynical place.

What we have learnt, apparently, is that suboptimal conduct in the financial markets is regarded as 'bloodless': why should anyone shoulder the blame, let alone end up in court and be expected to serve time? For the average person, this no longer works: banks, in particular, are close to being stereotyped as hopelessly dodgy.

Banks are doing some real dirt

A common refrain is that competition is always fierce, sometimes forcing banks to stray into grey areas – and sometimes, as increasingly seen, way beyond that. In December 2012, HSBC, 'the worldwide local bank', announced a significant settlement with US authorities. The official announcement was dripping with remorse, or apparently so:

> HSBC has reached agreement with United States authorities in relation to investigations regarding inadequate compliance with anti-money laundering and sanctions laws ... Under these agreements, HSBC will make payments totalling $1.921 billion, continue to cooperate fully with regulatory and law enforcement authorities, and take further action to strengthen its compliance policies and procedures ...
>
> Stuart Gulliver, Group Chief Executive, said: 'We accept responsibility for our past mistakes. We have said we are profoundly sorry for them, and we do so again. The HSBC of today is a fundamentally different organisation from the one that made those mistakes ...'[11]

Reacting to the news of the HSBC settlement, *Forbes* stated: 'For the past five years banks have been at the bottom of all the categories we track (and we track a lot of categories) when it comes to meeting customer expectations.'[12]

HSBC's settlement was prompted by incontrovertible evidence that it had laundered unbelievable amounts of money for some of the biggest players in Mexican drug trafficking.

It was of some interest that on 13 December 2012, the day that HSBC announced its settlement with US authorities, five Deutsche Bank employees were arrested in Frankfurt for money laundering or obstruction of justice. According to reports, it was 'too early' to conclude whether the raids, which involved around 500 tax inspectors, police and prosecutors, 'would yield any new evidence'. A spokesperson for law enforcement said that 'this will take months. I cannot comment about an ongoing investigation.' Prosecutors said they were investigating 25 bank staff 'on suspicion of severe tax evasion, money laundering and obstruction of justice'.[13]

This brings us to the story of how Kevin Wakeford took on the entire system – and, in particular, a global bank. When Wakeford considered blowing the whistle on the rand's collapse during the latter stages of 2001, he started on a perilous journey that, among many other things, would expose ego-drenched conduct in high places. He discovered, very soon, that he was on the wrong side of 'for us or against us'. He was up against at least one big financial-services entity and several corporates. He underestimated the backlash from certain 'leading' members of the press. And on a more serious note, he didn't have the faintest idea of what he would be getting from Tito Mboweni, governor of South Africa's Reserve Bank.

3
The pale horse visits

South Africa's epic 2001 currency crisis ... Gold-mining stocks go into orbit ... The rand plunges by 45 per cent in 2001 ... Wakeford at Keurbooms ... In August 2001, other whistle-blowers had turned up at the Reserve Bank ... The absurdity of South Africa's exchange controls.

'The pale horse's rider was named Death. Hades was following close behind him. They were given power over a fourth of the earth to kill by sword, famine and plague, and by the wild beasts of the earth.' – Revelation 6:8

During 2001 South Africa was hit by a financial crisis of epic proportions: the rand collapsed. At this point, consider that for many decades there had been a universal belief that just as the only good rat is a dead one, the only good currency is a strong one.

This thinking has changed. To recap: the omnipresent dollar entered a bear market early in 2002, and has wobbled along ever since. The main reason for the dollar plunging into a bear market was the US's burgeoning trade deficit, following a prolonged period of rising imports and falling exports, accompanied by a general decline in US competitiveness. As the dollar entered a bear market, Chinese exports became increasingly competitive on international markets. The yuan, pegged to the dollar, fell in tandem and along with relatively cheaper labour costs and rising productivity, China's exports boomed. China was soon producing massive trade surpluses.

The first and only real choice for parking these surpluses was in the world's only international reserve currency, and specifically in US Treasury bonds. These inflows have enabled the US to finance its trade deficit. The US, the world's biggest economy, and China, the epicentre of the world's economy, depend on each other. This is an extraordinary symbiosis that bears no comparison. For practically all other countries, the situation was not so simple. The basic rule still applied: a weaker currency meant increasingly stronger exports and increasingly dearer imports. A weaker currency also meant that tourists were more attracted to holiday in the country.

For South Africa, it specifically meant that its mining exports earned more rands. Almost all commodities are quoted and traded in dollars. In 2001, as the rand increasingly sank, South Africa's mines experienced a boom in revenue – in rand terms. Mines finance local labour and capital in rands, but revenue is derived in dollars. In 2001 a relatively stable gold price of around $275 an ounce and a weakened rand at R13.84 to the dollar made for substantially widening margins. The rand gold price at this exchange rate was R3 806 an ounce; most gold mines were then producing at below $200 an ounce, or R2 768.

Suddenly a very handsome profit of over R1 000 an ounce was being generated, and a gold-mining industry that had been down in the dumps for years suddenly found itself in a vibrant, job-creating and economy-stimulating position. As the dollar entered its bear market early in 2002, the dollar gold-bullion prices started rising. The weakening rand meant that South African gold mines experienced a double whammy – rising dollar gold prices and more domestic currency receipts from a weakening rand. It was a win-win situation for South Africa's mines.

In 2001 Harmony Gold's Ferdi Dippenaar put it thus: 'The old idea of printing money is really happening.'[1] For every 15 per cent of depreciation of the rand, Harmony Gold's operating profit doubled. The company's stock price soared from R37.30 a share on 3 April 2001 to R96.50 a share on 4 February 2002. By 24 May 2002, Harmony's stock price had gone 'truly ballistic', when it traded at R186.80 per share. Nice for Harmony, and especially nice for Harmony shareholders who had happened to buy on the way up, or, better still, at the bottom.

A sustained weaker currency ultimately stimulates fresh home-grown industrial activity. This can eventually produce a virtuous circle, in the form of a booming and growing export sector, and freshly minted import substitution as the domestic economy creates new enterprises and jobs, knocking out certain sectors of imports. But the flip side of a weak currency, as mentioned, is that imports become more expensive. This impacts on a significant part of the economy, ranging from the wholesale-retail sector to capital goods, many of which are imported.

Another significant factor is that prices of South African agricultural produce are based on international benchmarks. For example, the maize price is calculated by taking an international benchmark, such as the prices continually produced out of the Chicago commodity pits. The relevant dollar price is multiplied by the prevailing rand value. All else being equal, farmers benefit from a weaker rand, but consumers end up paying a hefty price. This can be especially detrimental for the poor. South Africa's liquid-fuel prices are also set by reference to international benchmarks. Again, leaving all else equal, a weaker rand can exert considerable negative influence, forcing up rand liquid-fuel prices and rapidly creating cost-push inflation. This affects everyone in the country.

Mining profits boom; consumers suffer under the weight of ballooning food and fuel prices. As such, endless debates continue to rage over whether a strong currency is preferable to a weak one. Without taking sides, a currency that suddenly moves heavily in either direction causes disruption across an entire country. In the capital markets, where companies raise money by issuing new shares or corporate bonds, investors fear uncertainty more than anything else. It is the same in the currency markets. As the days and months went by in 2001, a real sense of panic started to grip South Africa.

During 2001, the rand depreciated from around R7.60 to the dollar at the beginning of the year to over R8.00 for the first time ever during the second quarter. And the pace of depreciation increased:

- R8.52 to the dollar on 11 September;
- R9.03 at the end of September;
- R9.44 at the end of October;
- R10.27 at the end of November; and
- R13.84 on 21 December.

The 21 December rate was an all-time low against the dollar, and the rand has never fallen to that level since.[2]

All told, it hardly takes a genius to work out that the rand's particularly savage beating during the fourth quarter of 2001 was something that had gone overboard. Towards the end of 2012, the dollar was trading at around R8.75 – where it was during early September 2001. The huge period of time that has elapsed, just over 11 years, only serves to increase suspicions that some terrible forces descended on the rand market during 2001.

Note that the rand is inversely quoted against most currencies. At the rand's low of R13.84 to the dollar, one rand would have cost $0.07. This looks embarrassingly cheap. Which it was – in 1980, one rand used to cost $1.40.

Somehow, the rand looks less cheap at R13.84 to the dollar. For purposes of exuding confidence, most currencies are inversely quoted against the dollar – that is, local currency units per dollar. Sterling is one of the few examples where the dollar cost of a pound is the standard quote. Forever, it would seem, one pound has been worth more than one dollar. No doubt, the UK wouldn't dare embarrass the US by choosing an inverse currency quote.

∗∗∗

> *'I will lift up mine eyes unto the mountains:*
> *from whence shall my help come?' – Psalm 121:1*

By mid-December 2001, the rand had lost around 45 per cent of its value from its strongest point, which was at the start of the year. Any currency that nearly halves in value in a year is screaming, but nobody knew quite what the rand was screaming about. Exports were booming all right, but nobody knew if the situation was sustainable. Nothing seemed to make sense. During 2001 the rand depreciated by 43 per cent against the Zimbabwean dollar as well, which was truly unbelievable. And the rand had even lost 37 per cent against the Argentine peso, even though the South American country was facing one of the biggest national financial crises in world history.

Panicking about the rand's decline was one thing; panicking about its relative rate of decline was another thing entirely – something far more desperate. Either way, South African importers increasingly panicked. The overall feedback that Kevin Wakeford received from SACOB members was overwhelmingly negative: uncertainty took grip and fear descended.

It may have been the direction of the rand's movement: a strengthening currency imparts a sense of prosperity, of increasing competitiveness, of perhaps luck. But a weakening currency creates a sense that if the trend line continues, the currency could soon go to hell and be worth next to nothing. As much as the gold mines and others were experiencing a huge expansion in profits, they were also going to ultimately pay the price: imported capital goods would become unaffordable and, far worse, workers would be overwhelmed by exploding basic living costs. The cost of living would become hellish and inevitably unbearable. Sooner or later, hyperinflation would set in, and interest rates would gallop into the stratosphere. In the currency markets, seen from a top-down viewpoint, the rand had spent 2001 as the proverbial sitting duck. Above all, it was characterised by the Reserve Bank's inability to analyse market action and, more so, its inability to adopt a stance, let alone establish a stance at the outset.

The public outcry over the rand built up inversely to the movement in the rand, and the press had at least started asking questions. In mid-December 2001, a spokesperson from the IMF said that the organisation had 'received no official request from South Africa for financial support from the Fund'.[3]

At this point, Argentina was about to renege on its foreign debt. The IMF, however, could see no reason for panic in South Africa: 'The weakness of the rand is not supported by South Africa's macroeconomic fundamentals, which remain solid.' In other words, in the IMF's view, South Africa's economy was in fine fettle.

If that were the case, what on earth *was* the problem with the rand?

***

'If the governments devalue the currency in order to betray all creditors, you politely call this procedure "inflation".' – George Bernard Shaw

In December 2001, Kevin Wakeford was on holiday sitting around a campfire in Keurbooms Caravan Park, not far from Plettenberg Bay, but certainly not part of the area's illustrious villas and sumptuous mansions.

At the time, Wakeford was a young man: just short of 40 years old. In 1999, at the age of 37, he had become the youngest ever CEO of SACOB. He had been interviewed for the job by Mervyn King, a subsequent president of SACOB, Humphrey Khoza, the then president, and Raymond Parsons, the CEO of SACOB at the time.

Wakeford's job was based in the country's commercial capital, although he wasn't part of Johannesburg's 'blue blood' – far from it:

I was an Eastern Caper, a rugger bugger. I'd gone through the political struggle and everything but I wasn't part of this unique Joburg blue-blood system. I think I got in by a fluke because there was an ex-Anglo American guy who'd applied for the job. Business had never felt entirely comfortable with me, but they took me on because of what I'd achieved in the Eastern Cape in building both the Eastern Cape and Port Elizabeth Chambers, the Port Elizabeth Regional Chamber of Commerce and Industry and Business Eastern Cape. We had built it into a formidable force, which in fact got the Coega project going: the deep-water port together with a 13 000-hectare industrial-development zone. In addition, SACOB also desperately needed to reinvent itself and become relevant again. I believe that the selection panel were willing to assume the risk of appointing a young person with good instincts and a solid track record in the chamber movement to adequately and robustly represent them in the broader political economy of South Africa.

The Coega Industrial Development Zone Initiative Company was set up as a multi-stakeholder company in Port Elizabeth by business, government, the parastatal sector, NGOs, trade unions, local corporates and multinational corporations: a broad stakeholder-run initiative company. Wakeford, a non-executive board member of the initiative company, was tasked with raising the initial marketing funds for the company through the private sector. From the corner fish-and-chips shop through to, in those days, Volkswagen Corporation, around R2.5 million was raised within a month. This was used to market and lobby the concept and, as Wakeford puts it, 'the dream of Coega'. National and provincial government then made available R8 million for a strategic environmental assessment, which showed that Coega was the best spot for trans-shipment in the southern hemisphere. Alongside the port was a perfect 13 000-hectare site for both industrial development and trans-shipment activities.

This would include a vehicle-processing centre for the preparation of vehicles for import and export clients. In addition, the industrial-development zone could be used to construct containers, build and repair ships, package and repackage for exports and re-exports, and so on. Says Wakeford:

> We had a huge dream. It's been built … what wasn't achieved was the concessioning of Coega. You have to allow the private sector to be at risk, but also to have the potential rewards. My gut feeling is that it hasn't happened because there's been massive state money involved. This feeds on itself: it becomes a very powerful tool in the hands of bureaucrats. If it is going to fly and attract billions of rand in investment, it must be put out to concession to one of the big operators, as seen at Eilat in Israel, Shannon in Ireland and Jebel Ali in Dubai. There are good operators that turn around containers quickly, that run zones and harbours very efficiently. Coega can work when the private spirit is at work. Today, there is the state fiscus at work: lots of people employed around administering the whole thing but failing to attract sufficient investment.

Wakeford knew of investors keen to invest, but who have walked away because they are unfamiliar with a culture of non-responsiveness. Potential investors also want a low-cost environment and certain industrial-zone-based incentives, which simply don't exist. Wakeford wonders why anyone would invest at Coega when the same investment can be made down the road in Port Elizabeth. He believes a more meaningful form of capitalism is needed in South Africa:

> I believe in stakeholder capitalism, whereas I think at the moment we have private monopoly capitalism and public-sector state capitalism, where opportunities have closed off in certain sectors and competitive behaviour is stifled. If you understand what the private sector wants and needs, and you respond to that on a private-sector basis you will make the project work. You'll fill that zone; in 20 years you won't see a blade of grass. It will be filled with factories, with vehicle-processing centres, with conveyor systems and with plenty of jobs and activity.

Coega seemed very far away during December 2001. Instead, Wakeford sensed that his holiday at Keurbooms was degenerating at a rapid rate. He was being called by members of various chambers of commerce and others – people who were asking: 'Kevin, what on earth is going on?' Wakeford recalls: 'Everyone was complaining – some about volatility and the massive drop in value, others about the fact that they were pure importers. For example, virtually every surgical instrument, every surgical implant that's used in South Africa, is imported.' A substantial portion of South Africa's medicines is also imported, albeit it at a somewhat reduced rate as domestic production of medicines has been increasing.

All the while, Wakeford was thinking of everyone he represented, but he somehow seemed sensitised, perhaps negatively, to the elites. After Wakeford had been chosen as the new CEO of SACOB, Raymond Parsons, the long-standing director general of SACOB, who was about to commence his compulsory retirement, commented that Wakeford should realise that piloting a Cessna was vastly different to piloting a jumbo jet. Wakeford did not believe that he was the preferred candidate – certainly not on the shortlist in Parsons's head.

Wakeford suspected that Parsons believed he should be allowed to continue after his retirement as, in the opinion of Parsons, there was nobody good enough to fill his boots. If the truth is to be known, Wakeford had heard from staffers and board members that Parsons had reached his sell-by date. And his style, which was moulded by lobbying in the apartheid era, was not conducive to maintaining SACOB's relevance in a progressive environment. What kind of an 'environment' was a crashed rand? The overall impact of the heavily damaged rand was double-sided, according to Wakeford:

It was a crisis of confidence in the system for the consumer and for the investor. Now, if you consider Argentina at that very time, people were literally storming the banks. The Argentine currency was collapsing as well. In South Africa a group of right-wingers were arrested during that time, but post facto, I'm talking post-December, they were amassing weapons. What gave them the confidence to amass weapons? Were their plans linked to the inevitable socio-economic fallout?

So clearly there was a crisis and I was literally battered by the concern of ordinary members during that time – in fact it spoilt my whole holiday. Late December I was actually phoned by the press, who asked: 'What do you have to say about this?' My response was: 'Perhaps we should consider a commission of inquiry.' They went on to print my comments.

Wakeford found himself on a television show on SABC with Iraj Abedian, an economist, and others. Nobody had a clear view on what was going on with the currency. Abedian referred to all kinds of possibilities, including derivatives-markets and single-stock futures. At that stage, says Wakeford, he realised that he was still fairly naive in terms of market culture:

I was perhaps at times a little bit raw, but I still believe I was a clear thinker when I applied my mind to policy and events. When I lobbied matters, I was very successful – whether it was on issues related to public holidays, whether it was on government regulation, on the small-business statutory framework, all of that stuff – I think my record speaks for itself. But I was a bit naive. I thought that this was going to be quick and clinical.

Wakeford had received information that pointed to a pattern and required a comprehensive commission of inquiry to uncover what had really taken place in the currency markets.

However, even at that early stage, Wakeford was pretty damn close to putting his finger on who were the real culprits:

A lot of what was wrong was because of bad governance – bad governance in terms of the regulators and bad governance in terms of those who were scripting and pulling together the deals. And the deals that I put forward were because people were sitting on the inside and were part of the scrutiny of the deals. When I met with the Presidency in early 2002, it was stated unequivocally that they had already had information from other sources that was confirmed by what I told them. Bheki Khumalo, the president's spokesperson, had stated publicly that multiple complaints and information had been received pertaining to delinquency in the currency markets. My source had also told me that these matters had been raised with all possible regulators.

Little did Wakeford know that the Reserve Bank authorities had long been alerted – for good or for ill – about specific transactions that were going through the rand market during 2001: deals that were questionable in terms of compliance with exchange controls. As mentioned, South Africa's foreign-exchange regulations are administered by the South African Reserve Bank, backed by some of the most draconian legislation in the country, aimed at preserving the country's foreign reserves to the maximum possible extent.

Many months before Wakeford blew the whistle on the possibly dodgy transactions, there had been other whistle-blowers, who took the details to ... the Reserve Bank. This is how it took place. Towards the end of August 2001, James Cross, deputy governor at the South African Reserve Bank, had been approached by the head of a Johannesburg-based branch of a foreign bank. This person, along with a colleague, requested an appointment with Cross. The local branch of the foreign bank wished to 'test' a financing mechanism for offshore acquisitions by South African companies, Cross was told.

South African companies and banks are not allowed to finance foreign acquisitions by simply exporting rands. Companies – and there were only a handful – that had sufficient clout in foreign markets could, of course, borrow money in foreign jurisdictions, or raise equity if listed on a foreign market. The Reserve Bank had no say in that. These possibilities applied to the likes of AngloGold, later to become AngloGold Ashanti, with its listings in Johannesburg and on the New York Stock Exchange. Companies that had moved primary domicile offshore, such as Anglo American, were likewise restricted in moving capital outside South Africa for the purpose of making acquisitions outside South Africa. This was one of the reasons – largely misunderstood – that Anglo American had switched its head office to London. A presence in the City meant that Anglo American was close to its biggest investors, in the event that the corporation needed to tap the markets for capital.

Cross invited to the meeting at the Reserve Bank his colleague Lambertus van Zyl, the then general manager of the International Banking Department, and Tom Coetzee, assistant general manager of the Exchange-Control Department. At the meeting, a complicated deal was described. Cross would later recall: 'We were asked whether or not the Reserve Bank would object to such a structure being put in place.' The gist of the proposed deal was that the South African company, let's call it XYZ, would be loaned hard currency by the London branch of the bank. The cash would be used to finance the foreign acquisition.

To repay the loan, Johannesburg-based XYZ would institute an upfront issue of shares to the London-based branch of the foreign bank. These shares would then be sold by the London bank to foreign investors, for hard currency, over a 12-month period. This cash would be used to redeem the South African company's debt owed to the London bank. In some ways, at least, the structure seemed to make some sense: there would be no negative impact on the rand market. The overall transaction was, indeed, designed to be currency-neutral for South Africa – or so it was said. Also discussed were some further technical aspects of the proposed deal.

Cross and his colleagues asked the party about the benefit from the profit or loss on such a transaction. In the view of Cross and his colleagues, this issue seemed to be extraneous to the proposed structure. Says Cross: 'We were not given a definite answer to this question.' It was clear to Cross and his colleagues that the proposed transaction would generate substantial fees for the foreign bank.[4]

The so-called catch in the structure of the transaction was that the London-based branch of the foreign bank would be protected against changes in the value of the rand by means of a forward sale of rands. It was accepted and common practice for the Reserve Bank to provide companies with forward cover – in essence, a form of insurance. This way, an importer planning to buy $10 million worth of goods in three months' time could secure a forward-cover contract from its bank, which was, in turn, covered by the Reserve Bank. The benefit for the importer was that if the rand weakened, the importer would still only have to pay the rand equivalent of $10 million, and no more. This mechanism provided importers with a significant degree of confidence in the conduct of business.

Similarly, exporters who believed the rand might strengthen could secure forward-cover contracts from commercial banks, again covered by the Reserve Bank. The Reserve Bank's generosity in offering cover had led to the creation of the so-called net open forward position (NOFP), long perceived as a liability in the hands of the Reserve Bank.

Although the Reserve Bank conducts NOFP transactions and manages the overall book, the NOFP is in fact a liability held by South Africa's private sector. Chris Stals, a former Reserve Bank governor, explained why:

> There is a misconception that a reduction in the NOFP of the Reserve Bank absorbs an equivalent amount of foreign exchange in the market and therefore reduces the supply of foreign currency. Most of the Reserve Bank's forward book was a duplication of the South African private sector – mainly importers – which means the underlying foreign currency commitments of the NOFP were already covered by liabilities in the private sector, and did not represent a liability to the Reserve Bank.[5]

When the Reserve Bank acts to reduce the NOFP, it buys foreign currency (typically dollars) in the rand spot market, and then sells the dollars for rands to holders of forward contracts. The overall impact on the foreign-exchange market is neutral.

The liability arose mainly because of the long-term depreciation of the rand, and because the individuals who took a view on the forward value of the rand were repetitively wrong. However, during and after 1995, a policy decision was made to eliminate the NOFP as soon as was practical. This was an admission that the account was unmanageable. The NOFP had created a serious monster: during 1995 the liability on the account had exceeded $25 billion, a gigantic figure.

In 2001 the Reserve Bank bought $4.4 billion, financed by the South African government's foreign bond issues, and two large corporate deals. Added to other dollar purchases by the Reserve Bank in previous years, the balance on the NOFP declined to $4.8 billion by the end of 2001. This continued and on 12 March 2002, the NOFP stood at $2.9 billion. During 2003 the balance on the NOFP was finally eliminated.

Immediately after 14 October 2001, when the Reserve Bank announced a stringent tightening in the administration of foreign-exchange controls, the Reserve Bank made it clear that it was continuing to reduce the NOFP. It also said that it would no longer buy dollars on the spot market, but would use proceeds from privatisation and foreign loans. The bank had not intervened to support the rand because it did not want the level of the NOFP to rise again. In other words, the Reserve Bank's objective of reducing the NOFP was myopic: not even something in the nature of an emergency would make the Reserve Bank put on hold its buying of dollars, never mind temporarily reverse the policy and sell dollars.

Back to James Cross. Let's assume the hypothetical scenario that XYZ wanted to make an acquisition in France for the equivalent of $100 million. First, the London-based branch of the foreign bank would lend XYZ $100 million in cash, enabling it to pay for its foreign acquisition. XYZ then has a liability to the London bank. At the same time, to secure the debt, XYZ would issue the London-based branch of the foreign bank the rand equivalent of $100 million worth of fresh XYZ shares. Over the next 12 months, all else being equal, the shares would be sold in London and elsewhere in foreign markets, raising $100 million, which would be used to repay XYZ's loan.

It was all but impossible in practice to predict that the sale of XYZ's shares would raise exactly $100 million over such a long period of time, given all the variables at play. This is why the London-based branch of the foreign bank proposed that the South African Reserve Bank provide it with forward cover, protecting it against changes in the variables. Essentially, the Reserve Bank was being asked to insure the commercial risks of a foreign bank. It was a very cheeky proposal. For Cross, the bottom line was that 'after discussing the matter for some time and asking further questions, the meeting concluded that we could, inter alia, not agree to the forward sale of rand as requested'.

And that was that. Only it wasn't. Sometime later in September or early October, as Cross recalls it, he received a phone call

> from another person working for the same institution. This person stated that according to information received by their bank, certain offshore acquisitions by South African companies had been financed by using the domestic balance sheets of the company in question to fund the offshore acquisition, which would normally have been in contravention of the exchange-control regulations.[6]

This was very serious indeed. In other words, the transactions were not rand-neutral. This meant that certain unnamed South African corporates were benefiting from the naked sale of rands in the currency markets, and the purchase of hard foreign currency. Normally, this would have been in blatant violation of South Africa's exchange-control laws. It seemed, however, that some corporates had somehow obtained permission to literally break the law. Seen another way, permission may not have been obtained at all, and exchange controls had simply been contravened.

So there it was: incontrovertible proof that certain investment bankers and certain top officials at the Reserve Bank knew that some seriously dodgy transactions had been taking place, and no doubt still were, in the rand market during 2001. The game was on, months before Kevin Wakeford blew the whistle.

There were potent clues that certain elites were working hand in glove to circumvent South Africa's exchange-control laws. As mentioned, these laws are incredibly strict, and punishment for contravention can be severe, to say the least. At the same time, these laws are smothered in a great swathe of secrecy which has remained unchanged since apartheid days. Various descriptions can be accorded to this fear mentality; suffice it to say that it has reflected insecurities that have changed substantially in nature over the years and the decades, but somehow continue to tap down to similar roots.

Exchange controls have been in place in South Africa forever, but were heavily reinforced in 1961 following the Sharpeville massacre. The current legislation is set out in the Exchange Control Regulations promulgated in 1961 in terms of the Currency and Exchanges Act, which dates from 1933. Exchange controls in South Africa were applied ever more stringently during the apartheid era, especially after 1985 when international sanctions, trade boycotts, disinvestment campaigns and the withdrawal of loan funding to South Africa exerted severe pressure on the balance of payments (of which the trade account is the main component) and the domestic economy as a whole.

South Africa then introduced a dual currency system in an attempt to address some of the problems. The 'financial rand' system was used for capital-account transactions. Any outward transfers of funds other than normal trade-related transactions were subject to prior approval by the exchange-control authorities. Following the first democratic elections in 1994, the new government initiated the process of liberalising exchange controls. The first major step in this direction was the abolition of the financial rand in March 1995.

Stals, who was Reserve Bank governor until 1999, preceding Tito Mboweni, has argued that exchange controls make it impossible for companies to hedge and cover themselves against currency fluctuations, putting the onus onto the state instead. Hence the NOFP, which ballooned to unbelievable levels.

One corollary of the NOFP was that in times of crisis when nobody else wanted rands, in order to ensure that the forex market didn't seize up, the Reserve Bank was forced to swap precious hard currency for unwanted rands.

The way Stals tells it, if there were no exchange controls, companies would be able to protect themselves through structured vehicles available in the international currency markets. Foreigners considering long-term investments in new factories and plants South Africa desperately needs are discouraged from making affirmative decisions, given the negative influence of exchange controls. Abolishing exchange control would take the Reserve Bank, and hence taxpayers, out of the loop. It would also remove one of the biggest concerns of any potential long-term investor.

Seen on a longer-term basis, the rand has been a one-way downwards gamble. Foreign investors 'bet' with odds on that by holding off converting dollars, euros or pounds into rands today, more of the currency can be bought tomorrow. This raises questions of the amount – not that it could ever be established – of foreign investment that has been put on permanent hold.

Stals, for one, had long believed that the last remnants of exchange control should be completely eliminated. Exchange controls carry a massive administrative cost, adding to the opportunity cost of indefinitely postponed foreign investment. The system has also spawned any number of illegal schemes, aimed at circumventing the controls. At the same time, exchange control requires compliance not only with the law, but with the *spirit* of the law. Competition among financial institutions is normally fierce, given the eternal promise of big bonuses. This encourages some of the best legal brains to seek out loopholes in the system, so generating perfectly lawful but hugely damaging big-money schemes used by foreign-exchange dealers (under the roof of one bank or another) and multinational corporations.

So it was that on 8 January 2002, Kevin Wakeford wrote a letter to

President Mbeki. Wakeford's allegations were fierce and could not be ignored. As a result, the Rand Commission was appointed:

EMBARGO — FOR IMMEDIATE RELEASE

PRESS STATEMENT: COMMENCEMENT OF PUBLIC HEARINGS OF THE COMMISSION OF INQUIRY INTO THE RAPID DEPRECIATION OF THE EXCHANGE RATE OF THE RAND AND RELATED MATTERS

This statement serves as notification of the commencement of public hearings in terms of Section 4 of the Commissions Act, 1947 (Act No. 8 of 1947), of the Commission of Inquiry into the Rapid Depreciation of the Exchange Rate of the Rand and Related Matters (hereafter 'the Commission').

The public hearings will commence on 4 March 2002 at 10:00 in Committee Room 4, Level 4 of the Sandton Convention Centre, cnr Maude and Fifth Street, Sandown, Sandton. Parking with direct access to the Sandton Convention Centre is available in Alice Lane at a cost.

The members of the media and the public who wish to attend the hearings are requested to be seated by no later than 09:45.

The first two weeks, 4 to 15 March 2002, will be devoted to hearing the evidence of:

- a number of experts in different disciplines;
- the South African Reserve Bank;
- the National Treasury;
- the Banking Council of South Africa.

ISSUED BY THE CHIEF DIRECTORATE: PUBLIC EDUCATION AND COMMUNICATION SERVICES OF THE DEPARTMENT OF JUSTICE AND CONSTITUTIONAL DEVELOPMENT ON BEHALF OF THE COMMISSION OF INQUIRY INTO THE RAPID DEPRECIATION OF THE EXCHANGE RATE OF THE RAND AND RELATED MATTERS

25 FEBRUARY 2002

PRETORIA

A few days after this announcement, Reserve Bank governor Tito Mboweni launched a 'scathing attack', as one newspaper put it, on Wakeford.

Mboweni dismissed Wakeford's claims about the cause of the rand's depreciation as 'populist'. In an address to students at the University of the Witwatersrand, Mboweni said he felt sorry for the Rand Commission. He boomed it out that the commission would be 'worthy of a Nobel Peace Prize' if it managed to trace all the transactions concerned – which in itself was a fascinating comment.[7]

And so Wakeford was given another taste of the elite group of South Africans who treated the country's foreign-exchange markets as their own.

Few, if any, understood exactly what was behind Mboweni's petulant reaction. What became clear, however, as time went by, was that Mboweni's attitude towards the commission only hardened. Mboweni would go to any lengths in his attempt to focus attention anywhere but on the Reserve Bank.

Whether Wakeford liked it or not, whether he knew it or not, he had taken on the entire system. It was going to be a rough ride.

4
The red horse

Boom and bust of markets: the aftermath of bursting bubbles ... Along comes Enron to set a whole new standard of depravity ... The wider press ignores Enron ... The stench of Eland Platinum ... The hucksterism of the daily press ... Lessons from Watergate ... Lessons from the Hell's Angels story ... *Omertà* – the conspiracy of silence and its role in 'legitimate' business ... More on HSBC and Mexican drug traffickers ... Stinky tax havens ... The savage and vicious 1998 campaign against the Hong Kong dollar ... Weird rand trades in Johannesburg ... The South African press as agents for banks, big business and more.

'Then another horse came out, a fiery red one. Its rider was given power to take peace from the earth and to make men slay each other. To him was given a large sword.' – Revelation 6:4

Market volatility has long been a key characteristic of the human appetite for trading: if markets went sideways forever, it would be inhuman – nobody would make money.

A common description of market realities is 'boom and bust': when the good times roll, everyone makes money, but when the bottom falls out of the market, the consequences can be extremely painful and may resonate for years. Market volatility is also commonly characterised by 'overshooting' on the upside, and also overshooting on the downside. This is almost akin to love and hate, except that money is the fortune made on the way up, and money is the fortune lost on the way down.

Bubbles develop when the prices of securities increase to way above their intrinsic, underlying value, and then sink below their intrinsic value after the bottom falls out of the market. Hence the aphoristic expressions 'buy at the bottom' and 'sell at the top'. The problem is that no one knows for sure when the top has been reached or when the bottom has been touched. When a bubble bursts, downside action can be violent. One of the biggest incidents ever experienced was in Tokyo early in the 1990s, when the Nikkei 225 index traded close to 40 000 points on the back of an explosion in asset prices led by the property market. In due course, the index collapsed; it traded below 10 000 points during 2008 and has spent the past few years gyrating around that level. Almost a generation later, the Japanese are wondering how the index could have traded so high decades ago.

At the Rand Commission, Iraj Abedian argued that financial markets, including the capital (bond and stock markets) and foreign-exchange markets, display two key characteristics: both are imperfect and incomplete. Abedian further argued that financial markets are 'neither efficient nor socially optimal'. He said that markets are structurally prone to short-lived as well as prolonged bubbles, in which prices and quantities can deviate from private and socially optimal levels. Information is considered to play a vital role in these markets. 'Such financial markets are vulnerable to information manipulation, rumours and speculation,' he said.

Abedian argued that foreign-exchange markets are commonly subject to overshooting and undershooting, which 'in small open economies entail a high degree of volatility with resultant financial and social costs'.[1] The bulk of these 'costs' refers to structural damages to the economy and shorter macroeconomic imbalances in the form of higher interest and inflation rates, and welfare losses. This seemed to be another way of saying that foreign-exchange markets are a necessary evil. Currencies of various brands are essential, and indeed unavoidable, in international trade. Currency also plays an indispensable role within the borders of every country.

This raises the question of what lessons, if any, have been learnt from well-documented cases of boom and bust. One of the most dramatic market examples of this – and shattering in terms of its absolute-value destruction – was seen in March 2000, when the US NASDAQ Composite Index imploded.

The NASDAQ, an electronic market, ranks as one of the US's most traded indexes. From its inception in the 1970s, it has attracted an unusually high proportion of listings by technology companies, some of which prefer it to the New York Stock Exchange. The NYSE and NASDAQ are known, along with other major exchanges, as the generic 'Wall Street', the world's biggest capital market, where stocks are traded in the thousands, and where companies raise capital, either by issuing fresh equity or by selling corporate bonds. The intermediaries are stockbrokers, many of whom reside in the hallowed halls of investment banks.

The evidence shows that an unsustainable bubble started forming on or around 9 August 1995, when Netscape Communications, which had launched the original browser for the World Wide Web, went public. Netscape had planned to offer 3.5 million shares (about 10 per cent of its issued shares) in its initial public offering (IPO) at $14 a share. That would raise $49 million in cash and put the company's value at close to $500 million, given that about 36 million shares would be in issue. In the six months before listing, Netscape had recorded sales – not profits – of just $17 million. So the idea that the company could suddenly be worth half a billion dollars was impressive.

For an established and successful company with a track record, a typical market value (or market capitalisation, based on issued shares multiplied by the share price) would be about 10 times a company's annual earnings. If Netscape had earned, say, $1 million in its latest financial year, the stock could expect to achieve a market capitalisation of $10 million. Netscape, however, was in loss. But if investors were convinced that its browser was literally going to take over the world, its market capitalisation would be pushed into the stratosphere as the scramble for shares set in. The herd mentality took hold. In consultation with Morgan Stanley, Netscape's investment bank and advisor, the decision was made ahead of listing to offer five million shares at $28 apiece. That would raise $140 million in cash. On the day Netscape listed on the NASDAQ, it opened at $71 a share and traded as high as $75 before finally closing at $58.25.

Therefore, investors had valued Netscape at $2.1 billion, whereas, on the basis of traditional investment valuation, it would have been worth just a few million dollars. Over the next few months, the Netscape stock price would rise as high as $171 a share, which meant the company was valued at just over $6 billion. Netscape's revenue soared – from $85 million in 1995 to $346 million in 1996 and then to $534 million in 1997. But during 1998, Microsoft's browser, Explorer, began to take over, stalling growth at Netscape and pushing the company into loss. From its December 1995 high of $171 a share, Netscape plummeted to $16 a share in January 1998. Later in the year, America Online announced that it would buy Netscape for $4 billion in an all-paper deal. The apparently sad story of Netscape aside, the demand for internet stocks, or anything remotely connected to the internet, had exploded. The so-called boom age of TMT – technology, media and telecommunications – saw 850 companies selling shares for the first time in 1996 alone, notching up an all-time record on Wall Street and raising a total of $52 billion in cash.

In April 1996, Yahoo! listed at $13 a share and immediately moved up to $33. For investors, and especially speculators, these were times of plenty. But 'professionalism' fell into disuse. In his book *The Number*, Alex Berenson summed up the situation as follows:

> After 1990, only two factors prevented analysts from totally prostituting themselves in the service of investment banking. The first was professional pride, always a thin reed. The second was that an analyst who recommended too many losing stocks could lose the respect of institutional investors. They might punish his firm by sending trades to other banks, by refusing to buy its stock and bond offerings. Securities firms made more money from investment banking than commission, but they still needed big investors to buy stock to make the system work. With the IPO boom, the easiest way for institutional investors to make money was by getting shares in hot offerings. What happened to the offerings in the long run made little difference; big investors often sold most of their IPO shares in the first few days after a company opened for trading. The old quid pro quo of good research for commissions had turned into a new currency: hot IPOs for commissions. Institutional investors no longer even pretended to care about research.[2]

These were times when the excesses of greed – and fear – would assume biblical proportions. It was all about avarice, covetousness and rapacity. The retail investor – the little person, the man in the street – was seen as easy meat. In honouring competition, investment professionals were almost as savage with each other. In his book *F.I.A.S.C.O.: Blood in the Water on Wall Street*, Frank Partnoy, who sold derivatives at so-called bulge-bracket firms on Wall Street between 1993 and 1995, recalls:

> Following [John] Mack's lead, my ingenious bosses became feral multimillionaires: half geek, half wolf. When they weren't performing

complex computer calculations, they were screaming about how they were going to 'rip someone's face off' or 'blow someone up'. Outside of work they honed their killer instincts at private skeet-shooting clubs, on safaris and dove hunts in Africa and South America ... After April 1994, when these [derivatives] losses began to increase, John Mack's instructions were clear: 'There's blood in the water. Let's go kill someone.' We were prepared to kill someone, and we did. The battlefields of the derivatives world are littered with our victims. As you may have read in the newspapers, at Orange County and Barings Bank and Daiwa Bank and Sumitomo Corporation and perhaps others no one knows about yet, a single person lost more than a billion dollars.[3]

On 5 December 1996, Alan Greenspan, chairman of the Federal Reserve, gave a speech at the annual dinner and Francis Boyer Lecture of the American Enterprise Institute for Public Policy Research in Washington, DC.[4] Apparently concerned about the rate at which stock prices were rising, Greenspan asked: 'But how do we know when irrational exuberance has unduly escalated asset values?'

The phrase 'irrational exuberance' would become one of the best-known in the investment world. Later, Greenspan observed:

We as central bankers need not be concerned if a collapsing financial asset bubble does not threaten to impair the real economy, its production, jobs and price stability. Indeed, the sharp stock market break of 1987 had few negative consequences for the economy. But we should not underestimate or become complacent about the complexity of the interactions of asset markets and the economy.[5]

The 'real economy' is where the vast majority of humankind finds itself – trying to scratch out a living. On the way up, the financial markets occasionally resemble some kind of reality, but for most of the time the illusion is thin.

In March 2000, the NASDAQ Composite peaked at just above 5 000 points. Towards the end of 2002, it was looking to test 1 000 points – a loss of around 80 per cent. The index would rise above 2 000 points in

2004, and would again go through the 3 000-points level in 2012 – a level it first traded at way back in 1999.

Such bull and bear markets – the boom and the bust – now seem to be institutionalised as a dark, perhaps inevitable, corner of human experience. It is a dark corner indeed, one that bewitches, beguiles and seduces, and then spits out the bounty. On 4 December 1928, blessed by booming stock markets, US president Calvin Coolidge sent his last message on the State of the Union to the reconvening Congress: 'No Congress of the United States has met with a more pleasing prospect than that which appears at the present time. In the domestic field there is tranquillity and content-ment … and the highest record of years of prosperity. In the foreign field there is peace, the goodwill which comes from mutual understanding …'

As it turned out, 1929 marked one of the biggest stock-market crashes in history, an accident that would resonate across the US for years, across the real economy and across the world forever. The Great Depression is a key component of sociopolitical history. Politicians are also human, and humans can err – usually in the economic and marital fields.

Yet markets have endured, and are all but embedded in our DNA, and there are no signs, yet, that any respect is to be given to the cliché that history repeats itself. Improved communications have changed nothing: mankind's lust for greed remains entrenched. What we have learnt, but not necessarily applied with much success, is that great evil can be bred and fostered during the boom times.

The technology bubble that imploded on the NASDAQ and other markets in 2000 left many casualties; there were also hybrid firms that tried to jump on the bubble's bandwagon as it rose incessantly upwards. When Kevin Wakeford was camping at Keurbooms, one of the world's more dramatic corporate stories continued to blow up on the other side of the Atlantic. The eruptions would reverberate for years and change the way the world regarded corporate entities. This was all about Enron Corpora-tion, a name that would become synonymous with corporate rottenness of the most degenerate kind.

Enron was an American energy, commodities and services company based in Houston, Texas. It was listed on the New York Stock Exchange, where it was heavily traded. Before it filed for bankruptcy on 2 December 2001, Enron boasted a payroll of some 20 000 staffers and was by its own account one of the world's major electricity, natural gas, communications, and pulp and paper companies. Its attempt to cash in on the technology boom was seen when it established supposedly sophisticated markets for trading in highly specialised futures contracts, such as for weather.

Enron claimed revenues of nearly $101 billion during 2000. Towards the end of 2001, the truth started to emerge: Enron's supposed financial situation had been substantially sustained by institutionalised, systematic and creatively planned accounting fraud. A number of other significant corporate frauds exploded across the US at this time, including Tyco International, Adelphia, Peregrine Systems and WorldCom.

It was Enron, however, that proved to be the low-water standard setter of wilful corporate fraud and corruption. The Enron debacle and others brought into question the accounting practices and activities of many entities in the US, and led to the passing of the Sarbanes-Oxley Act of 2002, aimed, in essence, at preventing another Enron. After Enron went down, so did the once iconic Arthur Andersen accounting company.

Much of what occurs during bull and bear markets is driven by two key sets of players – the professional investment analysts employed by stockbrokers, and those employed by institutional investors, operating amid all other market players, not least speculators and traders. Those employed at stockbrokers are known as 'sell side', in that their role is to market investment ideas to clients. The investment analysts employed at institutional and other funds are known as 'buy side': their role is to find the best possible 'buys' from among all kinds of tradable securities. If an investment fund gains a good reputation, it will draw increasing fund flows, especially during rising markets. Hence the 'buy' status of the fund's analysts.

In following a well-established human tradition, a number of investment analysts employed on Wall Street by the various bulge-bracket stockbrokers were either threatened or fired for taking up the case against Enron before it went bust. And then there was the press, specifically the financial press. It is of note that the well-known magazine *Fortune*, which prides itself on its status in the financial and business arena, named Enron 'America's most innovative company'. This happened not once, but for six consecutive years.[6] For at least six years, Enron had fooled the entire world … or had it? In practice, it was left to a small number of journalists to expose the Enron scandal before it blew up, literally overnight, in the world's face.

As the Nieman Reports put it:

> With Enron ... it is not just that the scandal was not missed by the news media. Rather, the scandal was actually uncovered by the relentless, careful, intelligent work of two *Wall Street Journal* reporters, Rebecca Smith and John Emshwiller.
>
> Without their reporting, the Enron scandal almost certainly would not have come to light when it did and conceivably might never have surfaced. Yet their reporting was largely ignored, not by investors, among whom it has had major impact, but by many of the nation's news media pundits.
>
> Indeed, many in the press leapt with a vengeance onto the Enron story only when it seemed to have the makings of a political scandal rather than being a 'business story'. Members of the press, not unlike members of Congress, seem to have an easier time recounting tales of political contributions and influence peddling than matters of accounting, regulation and financial disclosure.[7]

Truer words have possibly not been strung together: the press has a seemingly incurable attraction to political – and also celebrity – dirt and filth. The mere idea that corporate entities are rotten or, indeed, outright corrupt ... well, who's really bothered about that? The most direct link that one should always bear in mind is the well-established practice of corporates and banks providing advertising revenue for the mainstream press. *private money runs the press*

There may have been seismic shifts in the structure of the press over the past decade or so, mainly in the ongoing transition from print to electronic format, but there is no question that there still exists what may be broadly described as the 'mainstream press'. There are times, however, when even the mainstream press will rise to the task at hand, as in the case of the *Wall Street Journal*'s Smith and Emshwiller. The US has the world's largest economy, and there is little surprise that the depth of coverage is to be found in the US's press. But how was it that such a large chunk of the press ignored the work of Smith and Emshwiller?

Paul E. Steiger of the Nieman Reports continued his analysis:

The real Enron scandal resides in the failure of institutions – account-ants, lawyers and outside corporate directors – that have been relied upon for more than half a century to keep America's capital markets the most honest, transparent and, therefore, the most successful in the world. Far more than the corrupting influence of corporate money on politics, the story of Enron speaks to the corrupting temptations for corporate managements to maintain at all costs the appearance of consistently rising profits – of 'beating the Street'.

In more ways than one, it was dogged investigative reporting that pushed Enron into a lake of sewage:

Smith and Emshwiller ... decisively cracked the Enron mystery ... pub-lication of their reporting triggered the collapse of the energy giant. Their reporting showed that Enron's profits were heavily based on aggressive accounting, the liberal use of off-balance-sheet partnerships and misleading statements to regulators and the public. In 10 days, beginning with the publication of the *Journal*'s first explosive story on 17 October 2001, Enron's stock plunged 60%. By December, a com-pany that a year before was valued by the stock market at $70 billion sought bankruptcy protection and became the subject of a Securities and Exchange Commission investigation and Congressional probes.

Steiger argued that the collapse of Enron was 'the first great American scandal of the 21st century'. On 8 November 2001, Enron restated its earn-ings for the previous five years, admitting that almost half of its profits were bogus. 'Coverage of a story like this,' Steiger further argued, 'makes few people happy. Thousands of Enron employees lost their jobs, while tens of thousands of investors lost major money in the stock market after mischief in the company was exposed ...'[8] All over again, it seemed that nothing succeeded like success: failure was not a favoured subject.

Exposing dodgy corporate behaviour is not as difficult as it sounds, but events can sometimes be easily lost in the sands of time. There has always been, and always will be, a big divide between reality and percep-tion, even between who supposedly said what and who really said it. Take the example of Tarzan, who never said 'Me Tarzan, you Jane'; or Bogart, who never said 'Play it again, Sam'; or Sergeant Friday, who never said 'Just the facts, ma'am'; or Shakespeare, who did not write 'Hell hath no fury like a woman scorned' (those words are from *The Mourning Bride* [1697] by William Congreve).

A fine South African example can be found in Eland Platinum, once listed in Johannesburg. The people who managed the stock – who were not limited to its directors and management – were wont to do whatever it took to prevent supposedly strange 'facts' getting to certain speculators. On 13 June 2007, when Eland was trading at around R119.00 a share, I wrote that London-listed 'Xstrata was prepared to offer around R70.00 a share for Eland, including premiums'. The reaction was quick, with the stock price falling by as much as 26 per cent in just a few hours.[9]

In round figures, the company's stock value declined by more than R2 billion in a few hours. A number of 'investors' and other geniuses in suits were after me: there were attempts to interdict me in court, and some or other loser, or losers, reported me to the authorities. I told Gerhard van Deventer of the Financial Services Board that he could lock me up and throw away the key before I would tell him where my information had come from. I never heard from him again. It was another sad case of the authorities going after the wrong person. Someone, or some people, had been 'confidentially' letting it be known that Xstrata was going to bid R120.00 a share for Eland. At the time, it was hardly a secret as to which pack of jackals in the Johannesburg securities industry had been front-running the Eland stock price.

This was a particularly egregious case of market misconduct, and I relished taking on the entire system – and taking a billion or two rands out of some greedy pockets. Eland's valuations rose in due course and, finally, on 6 August 2007, Xstrata offered R105.00 per Eland share, equal to $1.1 billion. It still ranks today as the most overvalued acquisition in the history of the global platinum industry. By the time of Xstrata's takeover, Eland had been given various new prospecting rights, and had cleared up some of the issues around land title on its existing properties.

Amid the stench around Eland, after just two years, nine individual founding shareholders in Eland innocently scored R2.3 billion as a result of the firm cash bid for the company by Xstrata. Just four directors, J.A. Clark, J.M. Jansen van Vuuren, David Salter and Loucas Pouroulis, scored with a collective gain of R1.3 billion. The biggest individual gain was notched up by Pouroulis – R819 million pre-tax. A handful of people who made more than two billion rands have never been heard of again. To be fair, Pouroulis tried, like a man inspired, to become involved in platinum mining in Zimbabwe. I have for years requested interviews with Pouroulis, to no avail. As for Xstrata, it was clear to me during the latter part of 2012 that the London-listed corporation was as keen as razor blades to discuss anything about the progress, or otherwise, of Eland Platinum. Had Eland Platinum remained listed, it would have been up there for public scrutiny. But when it disappeared into the maw of Xstrata in 2008, the Swiss-based transnational mining company buried its newly acquired assets as deeply as it could in its South African chrome division.

Back to Enron. To be fair to *Fortune*, one of its reporters, Bethany McLean, wrote an exposé that the magazine published in its March 2001 edition: 'Is Enron overpriced?' McLean was to co-author *The Smartest Guys in the Room*; and in 2010 she co-authored *All the Devils are Here: The Hidden History of the Financial Crisis*,[10] which covered three decades of corporate and related scandals. Asked in an interview if 'everyone was equally to blame', McLean replied:

> I think it's really hard to apportion blame. But if I had to, I would say: politicians and regulators because it was their job to protect people and protect the system and they failed. I guess the other group is the rating agencies and that's because they too had an explicit job. It wasn't to make investment banks happy, it wasn't to grow their bottom lines, it was to rate bonds and they failed abysmally. And they did so through some level of self-delusion which we all fell victim to but also a fair degree of venality …
>
> Someone said the problem with the crisis is that it's really hard to find the line between self-delusion, venality and corruption. It's what makes the crisis this complicated story of human nature. And that's what makes the narrative somewhat unsatisfying because we all want to have someone that we can parade in front of TV cameras and say here's why it all went sour. But it's more complicated than that and it's an explanation for why there haven't been many criminal prosecutions in the wake of the crisis.[11]

The Enron scandal marked the early age of whistle-blowing. On 30 December 2002, *Time* magazine awarded its 'Person of the Year' to three people: Cynthia Cooper of WorldCom, Coleen Rowley of the FBI and Sherron Watkins of Enron. All three were whistle-blowers. Watkins, in particular, was one of a number of people at Enron who quietly helped certain journalists expose the mind-boggling scandal. It could have been argued that the US had learnt something from Enron – something that could have healed and restored its national roots to something more akin to what the founding fathers had intended, or at least hoped for.

No such luck. The next scandal was bigger than any previous one and, to boot, it shattered the world economy: the global credit-markets crisis, which exploded in the world's face around October 2007. This crisis was not about a single entity, such as Enron. It was seemingly about the entire establishment. It raises the very real issue of whether 'communications' – and in particular the press – can be more of an enemy to society than a friend.

***

So much so often lies beyond the hucksterism of the daily press, and increasingly over the past decade as 'readers' increasingly resort to online news sources. In the electronic press, there is no print deadline: news rolls out on a 24/7 basis, and spreads via social media, blogs and micro-blogs. Even so, one old principle has remained very much in place: broadly, this can be characterised as 'mood', or the general approach that the press, professional and otherwise, adopts in regard to a particular story. An American who is murdered on home ground by a killer with a shady profile is one thing; an innocent child who is killed by a US drone in Pakistan is another thing completely. This may oversimplify the situation, but the underlying point is that the innocent child who has been killed is seen as collateral damage in the US's broad 'war' against terrorism. A more subtle example is where only certain parts of the press pay any attention to a particular story, as in the two journalists at the *Wall Street Journal* who found themselves working in relative isolation in their unravelling of one of the most deceitful schemes of all time.

One of the most extraordinary narratives in the history of the press – and of a nation – kicked into its ugly life on 17 June 1972, when five burglars were caught by plain-clothes police with drawn guns in the act of breaking into the headquarters of the Democratic Party at the Watergate office complex in Washington, DC. The break-in took place when a US presidential campaign was fully on the boil, and, as such, the incident was regarded as a 'local' Washington story. There was also nothing visual in the story; the break-in was instantly history. Much of what would follow was leaked by faceless people.

Earlier, in January 1972, G. Gordon Liddy, general counsel to the Committee for the Re-election of the President (CRP, known to some as 'CREEP'), had presented a campaign intelligence plan to the CRP's acting chairman Jeb Stuart Magruder, the Attorney General John Mitchell and presidential counsel John Dean. The plan proposed extensive illegal activities against the Democrats. Two months later, a reduced version of the plan was approved. Liddy was to head the operation, assisted by former CIA agent E. Howard Hunt, and committee security coordinator James McCord. John Mitchell resigned as Attorney General to become chairman of the committee.

Sadly for the CRP, within hours of the burglars' arrest, the FBI discovered the name of E. Howard Hunt, sitting like a chunk of caviar in a notebook belonging to one of the burglars. Two days after the Watergate break-in, information was made available in the public domain that one of the burglars was a Republican Party security aide. President Richard Nixon's lead spin doctor, Ron Ziegler, described the break-in as 'a third-rate burglary attempt'. The way things turned out, there is no knowing just what Ziegler would have described as a 'first-rate burglary attempt'.[12]

On 29 August, Nixon said Dean had completed a 'thorough investigation of the matter ... I can say categorically that ... no one in the White House staff, no one in this Administration, presently employed, was involved in this very bizarre incident.' It was not the first time that a politician was telling bald-faced lies. On 15 September, Nixon said of Dean: 'The way you've handled it, it seems to me, has been very skillful ... putting your fingers in the dykes every time that leaks have sprung here and sprung there.'[13] On the same day, a grand jury indicted a number of individuals involved in the Watergate scandal, including Liddy and Hunt, on charges that included conspiracy, burglary and violation of federal wiretapping laws.

Even so, the press remained heavily concentrated around the US presidential campaign. The five burglars who broke into the Democratic Party office were tried by Judge John Sirica and convicted on 30 January 1973. Then, on 23 March, one of the convicted burglars, James McCord, wrote to Judge Sirica, mentioning a high-level cover-up. The Nixon administration and its supporters accused the press of levelling 'wild accusations' and of exhibiting a heavy liberal bias.

Stepping beyond the politicking, what shone through like a massive bolt of lightning in the Watergate scandal was the unfettered determination of the US law-enforcement system, and its ability to discharge its duties without fear, favour or prejudice. In the final count, 69 government officials were charged and 48 were found guilty, including:

- John Mitchell, Attorney General – convicted of perjury;
- Richard Kleindienst, Attorney General – 'refusing to answer questions';
- Jeb Stuart Magruder, head of the committee to re-elect the president – conspiracy;
- Frederick LaRue, advisor to John Mitchell – obstruction of justice;
- H.R. Haldeman, chief of staff for Nixon – conspiracy, obstruction of justice and perjury;
- John Ehrlichman, counsel to Nixon – conspiracy, obstruction of justice and perjury;
- G. Gordon Liddy, special-investigations group – burglary;
- E. Howard Hunt, security consultant – burglary; and
- James W. McCord, Jr – burglary, conspiracy and wiretapping.

Most of the senior White House staff ended up as a loosely connected pack of convicts. President Nixon blamed the press for just about everything. He went so far as to say that if he had followed liberal policies espoused by the press, Watergate would have been nothing more than a 'blip'. The conflagration continued month after month. Finally, Nixon resigned on 9 August 1974. No doubt in line with a prearranged deal, Nixon was immediately granted a pardon by the default new president, Gerald Ford.

The Watergate scandal was a low-water mark of a very special kind. It was one thing that Nixon's re-election ranked as the biggest landslide in US presidential history, and that he was subsequently shown up to be nothing more than a cheap-shot hustler who had run a criminal enterprise from the office of the world's most powerful person. What lingered far longer, however, is that what had started out as one of the greatest bungles in the history of the press finally emerged as one of the most comprehensively and professionally covered stories in US, and world, journalism.

Watergate was also a crucial reintroduction to the world of (attempted) executive abuse of law enforcement. On 5 August 1974, a few days before Nixon resigned, the White House released a previously unknown audio tape from 23 June 1972, just days after the infamous event at the Watergate complex. Nixon and Haldeman were together in the Oval Office plotting how to block investigations by somehow having the CIA inform the FBI that 'the issue' was about national security. It was Nixon taking another cheap shot, and missing, all over again.

***

> 'The daily press is the evil principle of the modern world,
> and time will only serve to disclose this fact with greater and
> greater clearness. The capacity of the newspaper for degeneration
> is sophistically without limit, since it can always sink lower and
> lower in its choice of readers. At last it will stir up all those dregs
> of humanity which no state or government can control.'
> – *Søren Kierkegaard*, The Last Years: Journals 1853–1855

One of the more painful issues is that sometimes the press simply makes things up. There are many descriptors that can be unfurled on this mast; a lawyer may use phrases such as 'fraudulent misrepresentation'. There are any number of benchmarks that can be referred to, but one of the most comprehensive comes courtesy of American journalist and author Hunter S. Thompson, who used the quote above from Kierkegaard at the beginning of his book *Hell's Angels,* published in 1966.[14] The book includes a harrowing and fascinating – and highly important – benchmark exposé of a certain pattern of conduct in the mainstream press. In my world, it has always been important for me to understand Thompson's analysis, and very useful when I extended its interpretation to an examination of the role the press played in and around the Rand Commission.

Money was at the root of the Rand Commission, as in the case of Enron and other scandals of that era, as well as the systemic 2008 global credit-markets crisis. In Thompson's book, the events had little to do with money, in the sense of financial markets, but lots to do with how the press 'educated' the public. At any point in time, the press is desperate for some big breaking story. This is, in turn, a function of money: the press needs customers – readers – in order to generate circulation, which, in turn, determines how much advertisers are prepared to spend with a particular media organisation. It also determines to a large extent how much readers are prepared to pay for a news product, if anything at all. The way the press handled the Hell's Angels story was also to do with money – no matter how indirectly.

In Thompson's book, a sustained piece of underground reportage, the opening parts deal with events involving various outlaw motorcycle gangs on the Labour Day weekend in 1964, in California. Such was the uproar following the 'Monterey events' that unfolded, that California's Attorney General, Thomas C. Lynch, commissioned an investigation culminating in a report that included results from a questionnaire sent to various law-enforcement officials across the state.

There was little new or startling in the report, which was published six months after the Monterey events. There was some local newspaper coverage of the Lynch Report, and that was it ... until a *New York Times* correspondent in Los Angeles picked up on the story, and ran a lurid commentary. Then the race was on: *Time* ran a piece under the headline 'The wilder ones', and *Newsweek* ripped in with an article under the headline 'The wild ones'. The story had gone national. As a matter of record, the first 'invasion' by bikers of a small California town had been recorded in 1947, which inspired *The Wild One*, a film released in 1953 starring Marlon Brando. Ten years after that, bikers 'invaded' another town. But it seemed that for the heavyweight press to get into the story, the Lynch Report was compulsory as a cover: why bother digging out the facts when you can lean on the Lynch Report?

The beefy mainstream editors were suddenly alarmed. As Thompson put it, 'The Huns were real! They've been holed up somewhere for eighteen years, polishing their motorcycles and greasing their chain whips until California's Attorney General decided to introduce them to the Press.' As *Time* absorbed the fumes, it rattled out that Lynch had 'amassed a mountain of evidence about Hell's Angels ... the thrust of which shows that the group has more than lived up to its sinister moniker ... It was a rape case that ignited Lynch's investigation. Last fall, two teenage girls were taken forcibly from their dates and raped by several members of the gang.' The heavyweight reporting in general created the impression that the Hell's Angels were a gang that numbered in the thousands. The truth was that in March 1965, the gang hardly existed, with a count, at the most, of about 85 members, all in California.

There were others who had effectively retired from the gang or moved on; some would don their colours and appear once a year, at a big event. The Lynch Report carried no such qualifiers: it stated that there were 463 identified members of the gang, and that of those, 51 had felony convictions. Yet elsewhere, the report referred to just 16 specific arrests and a paltry two convictions. It seemed that neither Lynch nor the mainstream press feared any backlash for printing libellous falsehoods. It helped that the Hell's Angels had no real means of contesting the lies. The Angels reacted to their newfound national notoriety by trying to charge for photographs.

***

'A good reporter, if he chooses a cat or an Arab, can understand a cat or an Arab. The choice is the problem, and if he chooses wrong he will come away scratched or baffled.' – A.J. Liebling

Seemingly determined to fully resist the facts getting in the way of a story, real or otherwise, the *New York Times*, *Newsweek* and *Time* virtually created the Hell's Angels. One *New York Times* article was nothing more than a condensed version of the Lynch Report, but the lead was, says Thompson, 'pure fiction'. It ran, as Thompson recalls in his book, as follows:

A hinterland tavern is invaded by a group of motorcycle hoodlums. They seize a female patron and rape her. Departing, they brandish weapons and threaten bystanders with dire reprisals if they tell what they saw. Authorities have trouble finding a communicative witness, let alone arresting and prosecuting the offenders.

Thompson, who spent many months with the Hell's Angels, drinking, socialising and motorcycling with members, and was present at the Monterey events, complained that this incident never occurred. It was created, as a sort of journalistic montage, by the correspondent who distilled the report, but the *Times* is neither written by fools nor edited by fools, and anyone who has worked on a newspaper for more than two months knows how technical safeguards can be built into even the wildest story, without fear of losing reader impact. What they amount to, basically, is the art of printing a story without taking legal responsibility for it. The word 'alleged' is a key to this art. Other keys are 'so-and-so said' (or 'claimed'), 'it was reported', and 'according to'…

The *New York Times* article in question included no fewer than nine qualifiers in just 14 paragraphs. Perhaps the most crucial was the 'alleged gang rape last Labour Day of two girls, 14 and 15 years old, by five to ten members of the Hell's Angels'. This was flagrant libel, argued Thompson, as was *Time*'s assertion that two teenage girls had been forcibly taken from their dates and raped by members of the gang. The heavyweight newspapers were seemingly blind to page one of the Lynch Report. This stated in black and white that 'by letter dated September 25, 1964, the District Attorney of Monterey County requested dismissal of charges in the Monterey-Carmel Municipal Court, which request was with the concurrence of the Grand Jury'. There were also material facts omitted from the Lynch Report, such as the following comments of a deputy district attorney for the county: 'A doctor examined the girls and found no evidence to support the charges of forcible rape … And besides, one girl refused to testify and the other was given a lie-detector test and found to be wholly unreliable.'[15]

But the heavyweight news organs continued, regardless. *Time* faked a platoon of statistics on the Hell's Angels:

> Founded in 1950 at Fontana, a steel town 50 miles east of Los Angeles, the club now numbers more than 450 in California. Their logbook of kicks run from sexual perversion and drug addiction to simple assault and thievery. Among them they boast 874 felony arrests, 300 felony convictions, 1 682 misdemeanour arrests and 1 023 misdemeanour convictions; only 85 have ever served time in prisons or reform schools.
>
> No act is too degrading for the pack. Their initiation rite, for

example, demands that any new member bring a woman or a girl (called a 'sheep') who is willing to submit to sexual intercourse with each member of the club. But their favourite activity seems to be terrorizing whole towns ...[16]

Fast-forward more than four decades and to somewhere on the other side of the world: South Africa. This time it was not about finding the motorcycle outlaws; it was about finding the dark forces that sometimes rise to the surface in the financial-services sector.

***

The drama of the rand during 2001 was irresistible – certainly for me. I started checking out what facts were available with various contacts in and around the markets. After a while, there was no doubt in my mind that delinquent capital was at work. One of my contacts in London said it was a 'done deal' that the rand had been 'raided'. The problem was that there was no clear way of having facts confirmed. In more ways than one, Johannesburg is a relatively small place. The legal fraternity is closely knit, as are the chartered accountants, architects, and so on. There are also only a relatively small number of stockbrokers, bond traders and currency traders. These cliques are hardened, and show no hesitation in choosing silence when something goes badly wrong.

At this point, it seems worth taking a slight diversion to consider the Mafia's oath of silence, *omertà*. There are signs that the modern Mafia has become a little shabby, but many of its habits and practices remain intact. On 20 January 2011, federal agents in the US announced the 'biggest mob roundup in FBI history', involving 127 individuals and covering seven organised crime families of La Cosa Nostra – the American Mafia. Attorney General Eric H. Holder, Jr, spoke of investigations that involved 'unprecedented scope and cooperation'. Around 800 federal agents were involved in the sweep when the accused were arrested, or sought for arrest. These included 34 members of the five historical mob families based in New York State and New Jersey, viz., Bonanno, Colombo, Gambino, Genovese and Lucchese.[17]

Seen as a whole, the mob sector in the US had been in decline for two decades. Even so, Holder said that organised crime remained a top priority for federal agents. Among the indictments served in the mass arrests was a double homicide prompted by a spilt drink at the Shamrock Bar in the Woodhaven neighbourhood of Queens. The indictment served on Bartolomeo Vernace included charges dating to 1981, when Richard Godkin took a single gunshot to the face and John D'Agnese took a point-blank bullet to the chest.[18]

Holder added that mobsters in general remained a continuing major threat to the 'economic well-being of this country'.[19] As dangerous as the mobsters can be, caricatures have become all but passé. Among the many arrested were Joseph 'Junior Lollipops' Carna, Vincenzo 'Vinny Carwash' Frogiero, Luigi 'Baby Shacks' Manocchio, Giuseppe 'Pooch' Destefano, Andrew 'Mush' Russo, Vincent 'Jimmy Gooch' Febbraro, Benjamin 'The Fang' Castellazzo and Anthony 'Firehawk' Licata. It seemed that the mobsters, who took themselves very seriously, were keen on hilarious nicknames to lighten up their daily endeavours.

Among the ranking mobsters arrested were Colombo street boss Andrew Russo, acting underboss Benjamin Castellazzo, *consigliore* Richard Fusco and two high-ranking members of the Gambino family hierarchy, *consigliore* Joseph Corozzo and ruling panel member Bartolomeo Vernace.

When considering Mario Puzo's book *The Godfather*, which spawned one of the most successful motion-picture series in history, one should never lose sight of the reality that it was a fictional work. Extensive analysis of non-fictional US crime families has established a chain of command starting with the Commission (dominated by the five New York mob families), followed by the boss (Don), underboss, *consigliore* (advisor), *caporegime* (captain) and soldiers. Associates fall into a completely separate category.

A crucial and common characteristic of all these individuals – excluding associates – is that they rank as 'made men', also known as men of honour, or mafiosi. The accolade is earned after official induction, which must be sponsored, into the American Mafia (La Cosa Nostra) or the Sicilian Mafia (Cosa Nostra). Only in rare cases are men without Italian blood accepted for induction as a mafioso. Made men initially rank as 'soldiers' within the organisation. At the very top end, the term for the 'boss of bosses', *capo di tutti capi* or *capo dei capi*, is not known to have been bestowed on any individual in the US since 1997 (Puzo's book was published in 1969). The term has never been used by the Sicilian Mafia. In the 'Ndrangheta, an insidious crime organisation centred in Calabria, Italy, the *capo crimine* (crime boss) is elected annually, but enjoys relatively little power.

Members of these crime organisations are bound by loyalty, akin to a blood bond, if not indeed a blood bond, and that loyalty characterises them more than anything else. According to Holder, 'members and associates of La Cosa Nostra are among the most dangerous criminals in our country. The very oath of allegiance sworn by these mafia members during their initiation ceremony binds them to a life of crime.'[20] Murder and conspiracy to murder are always possibilities for mobsters, but they engage in a never-ending smorgasbord of crime: fraud schemes of all kinds; the illegal imposition of mob 'taxes' at ports, in construction industries and on small businesses; mail and wire corruption; perjury; obstruction of justice; receipt of stolen property; possession of contraband cigarettes; corruption of virtually any kind; and so the list goes on. Among the crimes where violence is always a possibility, mobsters are involved in extortion ('protection', one of the original favourites, also known as 'shaking down'), narcotics trafficking, prostitution, illegal gambling, arson, loan sharking, labour racketeering, blackmail, robbery, and so on.

A killer may be caught red-handed with a 'smoking gun', but in the case of mob enterprises layers and layers of activity have long frustrated law-enforcement agents, who *know* who is involved but where is the proof – especially proof pertaining to the involvement of the higher echelons? In response, most countries have legislated special statutory measures to combat organised crime. The US was among the first, with the enactment in 1970 of the Racketeer Influenced and Corrupt Organizations Act, known as RICO. In 1998, South Africa enacted the Prevention of Organised Crime Act (POCA), aimed at combating organised crime, money laundering, criminal gang activities and racketeering. The legislation is fairly wideranging: convicted individuals can be fined up to R1 billion or sentenced to life imprisonment. Statutory laws targeting organised crime are generally characterised by gentle relaxations in the onus of proof.

The Mafia's business model has some considerable history. La Cosa Nostra has been active in the US for well over a century, and in Sicily for many centuries. In the US, each and every made man contributes to the

YWAM and the Mafia seem like twins.

organisation. If members have any rules, the first is loyalty to the organisation. Each made man is expected, on pain of having his head taken off, to be rational, to be honourable, to be a stand-up man, no matter the circumstances, and to have class. *Omertà*, the oath of silence, is hard-wired into the DNA of a mafioso.

The term 'Mafia' and its variations must be used with circumspection. It was a prosecuting magistrate in Italy, Giovanni Falcone, who objected to the misuse of the term 'Mafia', when he said that he was 'no longer willing to accept the habit of speaking of the Mafia in descriptive and all-inclusive terms that make it possible to stack up phenomena that are indeed related to the field of organized crime but that have little or nothing in common with the Mafia'.[21] Falcone was murdered by the Mafia in 1992.

There is an increasingly compelling case to be made that the modern financial-services sector has been developing various kinds of evil profit-making products and services. In a number of instances, the amounts of money involved make the Mafia look like a bunch of squint-headed amateurs. In December 2012, as mentioned earlier, HSBC, the global bank, paid $1.9 billion to US authorities to settle allegations that it had laundered billions of dollars for drug barons, potential terrorists and certain rogue states for nearly a decade until 2010. The US Department of Justice said HSBC had moved $881 million for two drug cartels in Mexico and Colombia, and had accepted $15 billion in unexplained 'bulk cash' across its counters in Mexico, Russia and other countries. In some branches, the boxes of cash were so big that the tellers' windows had to be enlarged.

The specific case against HSBC had never looked pretty. Do bankers need reminding that these activities are seriously illegal? HSBC's US unit – of all places, it may be said – accepted $7 billion in cash from Mexican drug cartels, conducted 25 000 Iranian transactions amounting to $19 billion in just one week, and assisted certain Saudi Arabian banks to finance groups such as al-Qaeda. These activities all seemed to be truly unbelievable, and yet they attracted very little in the way of headlines. As foul as this conduct may have been, it has been said in some quarters that these activities assisted HSBC through a particularly tough time in the global financial-services sector: jobs were saved. If this is to be believed, then financial institutions – or at least some among their ranks – have seemingly created

e financial sector holds governments in ransom
ause governments want the economy to grow
fail.

a whole new level of deviant conduct. Have politicians and bureaucrats unwittingly reached the point where miscreant conduct in the financial markets is to be seen as a set-off for job retention during depressed economic times?

Another level to consider here is that crooked conduct in financial markets can often be very difficult to detect, never mind prove. But there are exceptions, as in the HSBC case. In February 2008, Mexican authorities told the CEO of HSBC's Mexico unit that a local drug lord said that HSBC was 'the place to launder money'. According to prosecutors and federal court documents, incompetence, in essence, had allowed two cartels, in Mexico and Colombia, to launder nearly a billion dollars in drug-trafficking proceeds through HSBC. Prosecutors said a multi-agency probe into such transactions over several years showed how HSBC had degenerated into the 'preferred financial institution' for drug traffickers and money launderers.[22]

At a news conference in Brooklyn, New York, top US law-enforcement officials gave details of how HSBC was used. In one species of money-laundering transaction, millions of dollars of drug cash flowed through HSBC as Colombian traffickers used the so-called Black Market Peso Exchange to convert dollars to Colombian pesos. In this multi-step process, middlemen – referred to as peso brokers – used dollars from drug traffickers to buy consumer goods such as washing machines, no doubt to baptise the money laundering that was very much under way. The goods were then exported to Colombia and sold. Part of the laundered proceeds, in Colombian pesos, went back to the drug cartels. During the investigations, a significant sum was eventually traced to the city of Culiacán in the outback Mexican state of Sinaloa, home to one of Mexico's most powerful drug gangs and controlled by Mexico's most wanted man, Joaquin 'Shorty' Guzmán. In 2001 Guzmán escaped from a maximum-security prison in a laundry cart.

According to documents made public by law-enforcement authorities, between 2006 and 2008 HSBC's Mexican unit moved $1.1 billion from Sinaloa to the bank's US branches. The United Nations Office on Drugs and Crime estimates that drug cartels earn an estimated $60 billion a year from trafficking in the US. Around half this sum is rerouted to Mexico to pay off politicians, fund private arsenals and fuel violence that has seen more than 60 000 people killed over the last six years.

Among key HSBC figures, Sir John Bond left HSBC in 2006 after 45 years with the bank. He had been both chairman and CEO of HSBC. After leaving the bank, he went on to become chairman of Vodafone (until 2011) and mining company Xstrata. Stephen Green quit HSBC in 2010 to take up a seat in the UK's House of Lords and a seat as trade minister for the coalition government. He had been CEO at HSBC and then chairman before joining the government. He is a lay preacher. Michael Geoghegan left HSBC after Green decided to join the government. He was also CEO of HSBC and was earmarked for the chairman's position, but lost out in an internal battle. Sandy Flockhart was at HSBC for four decades before retiring in July 2012, days before the US Senate levelled its first accusations about the bank's operations in Mexico. He had been head of the Mexican business from 2002 to 2006. David Bagley, head of compliance at HSBC, quit just before the July 2012 Senate committee hearing in the US.

The US authorities said HSBC did not face criminal charges because the bank was 'too big' to prosecute. No individuals were implicated.

Some may say that severe misconduct in the financial-services arena has reached epidemic proportions. In July 2012, MasterCard and Visa agreed to a $7.3 billion settlement to resolve lawsuits initiated by retailers alleging collusion over credit-card fees. MasterCard and Visa denied the allegations but settled in the belief that such an outcome was 'in the best interests of all parties'. On 6 August 2012, Standard Chartered Bank hit the headlines when Benjamin Lawsky, superintendent of the New York State Department of Financial Services, stated that the bank had 'schemed with the government of Iran and hid from regulators roughly 60 000 secret transactions involving at least $250 billion and reaping SCB hundreds of millions of dollars in fees'. Standard Chartered Bank rigorously denied the accusations. A spokesman for Deloitte, one of the Big Four global accountancy firms, also dismissed the allegations.[23]

On 14 August 2012, Lawsky announced that Standard Chartered Bank had reached a settlement that allowed the bank to keep its licence in New York. According to the terms, the bank agreed to pay a $340 million fine.

Size counts: if the Mafia had been involved in money laundering of the kind indulged in by HSBC for a decade, there is no doubt that the likes of Benjamin 'The Fang' Castellazzo would have been arrested and would have faced many serious charges of organised crime, including money laundering and racketeering. But global banks, in particular, are treated with kid gloves. Their bosses, past or present, are regarded as above the law. Where banks once operated in what may be described as grey areas, it seems that during the past decade or so, they have become accustomed to venturing with impunity into areas where no individual can go.

There are other, overlapping areas where entire global systems have become polluted. Tax havens have long been an ongoing frontier, deepening the gigantic sewer. In January 2011, Bob Diamond, the then boss at Barclays Bank, was embarrassed when he could not answer a British lawmaker's question on how many subsidiaries the bank operated in the Isle of Man, Jersey and the Cayman Islands. The answer, as it turned out, was 249. Action Aid, a charity, published research in October 2011 showing that the top 100 companies listed in London operate 8 492 entities registered in tax havens. This leads to a massive skew in investment flows: Mauritius, a small island, ranks as the biggest investor in India, while the tiny UK territory of the British Virgin Islands, sitting quietly in the Caribbean, ranks as one of the biggest investors in China. Tax havens have a well-developed habit of cropping up in financial scandals. A notorious example can be found in the form of the Cayman Islands, the favoured domicile for hedge funds. It seems that every time a hedge fund blows up, the Caymans are in the news.

Tax havens are used for more than tax reasons. In 2001, when Enron went bust, it emerged that the group had concealed the majority of its debt in locations dotted around the Caribbean. Tax havens are also notorious for companies profiting from transfer pricing. In a given country of origin, manufacturers often aim to break even; output is then marked up in a tax haven, where the resulting profits are taxed at minimal rates compared to those that apply in the country of origin. The goods are then sold into consumer markets, where, once again, the markup is minimal – for the manufacturer, that is. Viewed as a whole, the vast majority of 'profits' earned by the manufacturer are earned in tax havens so overall tax payments are minimised.

In recent years, Switzerland, which manages a third of the world's cross-border wealth, has yielded to pressure to be more transparent, but its concessions have not amounted to much more than advanced window dressing. The country's policy-makers see tax as a morally neutral issue, as a battleground where the wits of taxpayers are played off against the depredations of fiscal authorities. As such, the Swiss see tax avoidance, and possibly also tax evasion, as something completely different from money laundering or fraud.

Society is growing more wary of tax havens, which are increasingly targeted by activists. Global Financial Integrity, a campaign group, estimates that around $1 trillion a year flows from poor countries to tax havens. It estimates that two-thirds of that figure can be classified as tax avoidance (which is 'legal') and tax evasion (which is illegal) but, more tellingly, that the balance of one-third includes transfers by criminals and the corrupt.

Pressures to reform tax havens have met with little success. Singapore has taken advantage of this situation, aggressively marketing itself as an emerging tax haven, and grabbing business from long-favoured destinations. Companies resist change, arguing that every taxpayer has the right to minimise tax (tax avoidance). At the same time, companies argue that tax havens are an essential part of their business models, crucial to at least maintaining their competitive positions. The societal value of transfer pricing is vague, if not unknown.

In yet another related area, insider trading, there are signs that law enforcement has had enough – certainly in the US. While US law enforcement remains wary of chasing after investment banks, or other banks, it had become increasingly willing to focus on insider traders, who tend to operate as individuals rather than in bloodthirsty packs. Among insider traders, the most advanced cases of psychopathy tend to occur in hedge-fund managers. On 13 October 2011, Raj Rajaratnam, a hedge-fund manager, was sentenced to 11 years in prison by Judge Richard J. Holwell in the federal district court in Manhattan. Justice Department officials were quick to point out that the sentence ranked as the longest so far imposed for an insider-trading case. Judge Holwell said in his judgment that 'insider trading is an assault on the free markets ... His crimes reflect a virus in our business culture that needs to be eradicated.'[24]

Rajaratnam was convicted in May 2011 on 14 counts of insider trading and conspiracy, and was slapped with a $10 million fine and ordered to forfeit $53.8 million in 'ill-gotten profits'. At the time, Rajaratnam ranked as the 54th individual who had been prosecuted for insider trading over the past two years; no fewer than 50 of them had pleaded guilty or were convicted. The other cases were pending, although one individual had fled the US. When Rajaratnam was sentenced, federal prosecutor Reed Brodsky was quoted as saying that the crimes were 'brazen, pervasive and egregious'. The case, like so many others, produced a fresh set of superlatives. According to Brodsky, there was nobody to equal Rajaratnam 'in terms of the breadth and scope of his insider trading crimes'.[25] Various studies have shown that some of the most successful insider traders are far less interested in making millions than in impressing others, a very select band of 'others'.

***

Sometimes the underlying story simply doesn't make it into the press. 'The story' – such as news that the president of a country has fallen ill – may take up countless headlines, but sometimes the process of getting the story is more important than the story itself. This, in turn, becomes a story. In an address to the Credit Suisse First Boston Asia Investment Conference on 28 March 1999, Joseph Yam, chief executive of the Hong Kong Monetary Authority, recalled monumental events in currency markets. It was all about a sustained attack on the Hong Kong dollar:

> At the height of these attacks, during the summer of 1998, there was clear evidence that the free market in Hong Kong was in danger of failing to fulfil its functions. Specifically, the currency, securities and futures markets were being distorted to the point where efficient resource allocation had given way to speculative manipulation ...
>
> Strong evidence suggests that a very small group of players were responsible for a preponderant proportion of the short futures contracts open at the time. We also estimate that currency borrowings to the tune of HK$30 billion, arranged in advance to avoid the expected interest rate volatility they were hoping to generate in Hong Kong, had been made by a similarly small group of players to be quickly dumped at a time when the markets were most vulnerable. In short, we were far from the model of 'atomistic competition' among small individual actors envisaged by thinkers such as Adam Smith. The invisible hand of the market had been replaced by a very visible club being wielded by a concentrated group of speculators.

In many other jurisdictions, this cornering of the markets would have been subject to investigation under anti-trust legislation: the Salomon Brothers scandal in the US in the early 1990s springs to mind.

In Hong Kong we have no such law: it is probably time that we thought out the cases for and against having them. We should also look at safeguards against market concentration.

As a referee, with limited powers, but with responsibility for preserving the basic integrity of the game, we intervened using the quickest, most efficient, and fairest methods that we had at our disposal.[26]

In other words, Yam and his colleagues at the Hong Kong Monetary Authority mounted a counterattack. The message was clear: in certain markets, especially emerging markets with an open economy, there was no question that securities, including the currency, could come under attack from a small and concentrated club bent on generating profits in any manner, no matter how disgraceful. Whether any of South Africa's monetary authorities or policy-makers ever took anything in from what Yam said will perhaps never be known. There was, however, certainly no evidence that South Africa moved to implement any safeguards that could have detected, or even prevented, the 2001 attack on the rand.

It is of note that when the Hong Kong dollar was so viciously attacked in 1998, the press reflected, accurately, the panic in the markets. Yam's approach was to get behind the story: his was the process of *getting* the story. He does not disclose the details of how he learnt about the small number of big players that ganged up on the Hong Kong dollar. This is understandable: market intelligence is to be used, not abused.

At the best of times, traders are crafty. Currencies can be traded directly – or indirectly, by anticipating the effect of a move in a currency on a country's stock and bond markets. While the rand market was shown to be relatively illiquid, particularly after 14 October 2001, when the Reserve Bank issued a circular that demanded immediate compliance with its exchange-control regulations and rules, the demonstrable fact is that the rand suffered a cataclysmic loss in value over the next two months. There had been traders who took a 'long dollar, short rand' position for most of 2001. A smaller number of traders, after 14 October, really and truly went short on the rand. The impact on the stock market was completely predictable: firms involved heavily in the export markets, so-called rand hedges, stood to benefit heavily. It was axiomatic that the stock prices for such rand hedges, not least the mining companies, and the likes of Sasol, would boom.

According to a Johannesburg-based derivatives trader, during the closing months of 2001,

> depreciation of the rand always occurred in early-morning trading just before or just after our local stock market opened. It is clear that the rand was used as a mechanism to boost the local equity market where the 'real money' was made by certain institutions.
>
> If US players were actively speculating against the rand, we would have seen the exchange rate move 'overnight' to correspond with US trading hours. Instead, most volumes and movements occurred during Johannesburg stock exchange trading hours, which start an hour or two, depending on the season, before London opens.
>
> It is clear to me that there has been an abnormal decline in our currency to such an extent that it cannot be justified using any economic, social or financial arguments of any kind. I am of the belief that there are local financial institutions or counterparties that have not only benefited from a decline in the currency per se by taking a long dollar–short rand position, but have also profited from these adverse moves in the currency by taking positions on the ALSI40 Index.[27]

The index referred to was based on the 40 most valuable stocks listed on the JSE Securities Exchange. If this trader's observations are analysed, it means that speculators were shorting the rand to weaken it, and at the same time going long on the stock market as a whole. Most of the value in the ALSI40 Index can be sourced to the resources sector, which rose strongly on a weakening rand. Seen another way, the trashing of the rand during 2001 was only a sideshow in the bigger game of making a fortune on the one-way bet that equity prices would rise.

Another factor at play was the two-way trade in dual-listed shares – those listed in both Johannesburg and London, such as Anglo American. One trader put it so:

A rand-exchange speculator – any foreign institutional stockbroker, and not necessarily a bank – can implement extremely large rand-dollar exposures by buying dual-listed shares in South Africa. The purchase of these shares can be financed by rand borrowed in South Africa. The shares are then sold in London. The manipulator or arbitrageur – the difference is only in the size of the transaction – promises to sell the shares offshore for a fixed dollar amount. As a share trader, the speculator has effectively created an exposure to currency without assuming real ownership of any underlying shares.

The speculator can settle his exposure and realise his gains (and, in some case, losses) when he transfers the South African-held shares to the London register, or he can unwind the trades in each market without touching the authorised currency dealers.

Whether or not this trader or traders exist, I do not know. But we deserve to know.[28]

***

'It is well enough that people of the nation do not understand our banking and monetary system, for if they did, I believe there would be a revolution before morning.' – Henry Ford

Early in 2002, when it became apparent that Kevin Wakeford was going to take on the system to establish what had happened to the rand during the previous year, I found it impossible to resist the opportunity of taking on not so much the system, but, rather, the press.

I asked myself, who in the press has the stomach to wrestle with this one? So it was that I went to see the country's top spy: Brett Kebble. Within 24 hours, he gave me the details of the parties that Wakeford would be naming. Kebble also gave me the details of the 'schemes' that were involved. In essence, these amounted to, first, misrepresentations to the Reserve Bank regarding so-called asset swaps, and, second, trade delinquency in the rand currency markets. In other words, there were certain traders in certain entities who had worked ruthlessly to profit from the rand as a 'one-way bet'. There was no question that there was parallel trade in the equity markets: traders taking a short position on the rand simultaneously took a long position on resources stocks listed in Johannesburg.

In the case of the asset swaps, the schemes were cloaked behind com-plex mechanisms. While the Reserve Bank may have approved a few components of the scheme, I was told, it would never have approved the full scheme.

For my part, the initial move was a walk in the park. At the time, I was freelancing for *Finance Week*. I told the editor, Rikus Delport, and the deputy editor, Amanda Vermeulen, that I was preparing a hard-core series of articles on what had happened to the rand during 2001. It was agreed that the initial articles would be published. The first one hit the news-stands on 8 March 2002. A few days after my article was published in *Finance Week*, Byron Kennedy, of Johannesburg-based Moneyweb, wrote that I had 'opened a can of worms by fingering Deutsche Bank' in what I had dubbed 'Randgate'.

At this point, Wakeford had not mentioned any 'names': he was yet to testify at the Rand Commission.

Kennedy continued along the lines that corporates were next on my 'hit list':

If this week's *Finance Week* cover story is to be believed, the Rand Commission is wasting not only precious taxpayers' money but also a substantial quantity of time. In an article titled 'What led to the meltdown', referring to the shock destruction of the South African currency in December last year, author Barry Sergeant states that local investment banks are squarely to blame, singling out Deutsche Bank as one of the major culprits. Sergeant also outlines a seemingly complex methodology in which investment bankers made obscene amounts of cash in a scandal he brands as 'Randgate'....

But Deutsche Bank, the largest banking group in Europe, has dismissed Sergeant's work as one of a loose cannon and said in an official statement that 'Deutsche Bank at no time executed a transac-tion that bears any resemblance to the "Randgate product" presented by *Finance Week*'. The South African arm of Deutsche Bank adds: 'The allegations regarding Deutsche Bank are entirely incorrect and without foundation.' ...

But David Shapiro, the MD of brokerage SG Securities, is not convinced that the elaborate round-tripping process, described at length during Sergeant's interview, is entirely unique. According to Shapiro, corporates and individuals used similar processes in the nineties 'or even further back' to take more than their required limit of rand out of South Africa. Shapiro admits that this is 'a little more sophisticated' as the 'numbers are huge'....

While logic suggests that a global banking group like Deutsche Bank would hardly risk its well-established reputation on what amounts to currency trading in a free market, Sergeant is standing by his story and reckons that South African corporates involved in this elaborate scheme will probably be named in the next week.[29]

Moneyweb founder Alec Hogg argued that

although it was never part of the original brief, logic suggests the key conclusion from the Rand Commission must be that most of the SA currency's problems start and end with Exchange Control – so remove what's left of it, and quickly. Such action may well give the rand another sharp hit. But with companies and forex market players then able to use derivatives and futures contracts to hedge themselves, welcome stability is certain to be injected into the rand market. And at the very least, taxpayers will no longer be burdened with the cost of 'providing liquidity' when sentiment turns for whatever reason. That alone would turn the commission into one of the best investments the nation has made.[30]

At least Moneyweb, a relatively small corner of the press, and always internet-based, was attempting to take the story into the broader public domain. On 9 March 2002, Moneyweb's Belinda Anderson penned an article that collated various viewpoints:

Moneyweb spoke to a few economists about whether the 'Randgate' saga set out in this week's *Finance Week* was plausible. The answer was a resounding 'yes'.

Economists canvassed for a view on the plausibility of the argument set out in this week's *Finance Week* for 'Randgate' – the series of transactions allegedly used to weaken the rand in order to profit from its fall – say the saga is certainly feasible.

The article fingers Deutsche Bank SA for its involvement in the rand's fall, a claim that Deutsche firmly denies.

One economist, who preferred not to be named, said Deutsche was known in the market for speculating and its name had been mentioned on more than one occasion by international institutions for allegedly having been involved in the rand's fall.

Standard Bank chief economist Iraj Abedian said that his submission to the commission had presented a similar possibility: 'I hypothesised that a case of this nature is certainly feasible.'

Nedcor economist Dennis Dykes says he has no knowledge of the specific case referred to as 'Randgate', but: 'something like this could feasibly have happened'. Dykes said similar things had happened in international markets, for example one specific scandal in the Hong Kong market. But whether it had happened in SA remained to be seen, he said, also saying it would only have been possible in a thin market. Abedian says: 'I would be absolutely amazed if this were the only case.'

The Rand Commission had started to hear evidence on 4 March 2002. Testimony of a generic nature was given by various economists. No banks or individuals were named. Instead the evidence focused on the workings of currency markets and the possible impact of political and economic events, both domestic and global.

Then there was evidence from Tito Mboweni, governor of the South African Reserve Bank; Maria Ramos, director general of the Treasury; and Trevor Manuel, the minister of finance. Once again, the scope of the material was of a general and generic nature.

On 10 March, Hogg wrote, as published on the Moneyweb website:

South Africa's old Apartheid Government loved Commissions of Inquiry. They were the perfect tools when tricky issues needed burying, ensuring the problem was tied up in committees for years. And when the recommendations finally came, they were nothing more than that – mere suggestions which could easily be ignored. No surprise, then, that sceptics abounded when the National Party's successor recently launched its Rand Commission, tasked with investigating reasons for the currency's plunge in December. For the wrong reasons, though, this Commission looks like being worth every cent of the R25m it is costing taxpayers.

The return on our collective investment will not be derived from finding some 'perpetrator' who can be punished. Rather, the Commission has unintentionally brought a fierce public focus onto Exchange Control – those outdated and very leaky laws supposed to stop capital outflows, but which seem to be having precisely the opposite effect. One expert after another has explained to the Commissioner John Myburgh and his team that Exchange Controls are actually costing the country billions. By extension that means it's a financial burden eventually borne by taxpayers, a crucial constituency for any Government.

From 4 March until 13 March, the Rand Commission heard evidence of an 'educational' nature. There is no question that this was of value to the three commissioners, John Myburgh (a lawyer), Mandla Gantsho (a chartered accountant) and Christine Qunta (a lawyer). Myburgh had taken silk – i.e. became a senior counsel – in 1986. He had been a judge of the High Court and also judge president of the Labour Appeal Court.

After two weeks of hearing this material, the commission adjourned until 2 April, when Kevin Wakeford would give evidence. One of the many obstacles faced by the commission was its very terms of reference. The inquiry, which had judicial powers, was targeted at unpacking specific transactions that Wakeford had named – and which he had not yet put in the public domain.

The Rand Commission's terms of reference, inter alia, were to inquire into and report on whether between 1 January and 31 December 2001:

- any person or any other juristic entity entered into, concluded or caused any transactions that contributed or gave rise to the rapid depreciation of the rand;
- any of the transactions in question involved collusion and resulted in any improper gain or avoided loss;
- in respect of any of the transactions in question, any authorised dealer in foreign exchange deviated from the terms and conditions of its appointment;

- in respect of any of the transactions in question, existing regulations and/or restrictions on the export of capital from South
  Africa were contravened;
- in respect of any of the transactions in question, regulations and/or
  restrictions on the maximum period within which exports proceeds must be repatriated to South Africa were contravened; and
- in respect of any of the transactions in question, transactions were
  entered into that were in contravention of the letter or spirit of the
  exchange-control regulations.[31]

The commission was also required to advise the president on any relevant recommendations, such as 'the effectiveness of the current administrative system of ensuring adherence to exchange controls and other regulatory measures in guarding against the occurrence of such transactions'.

It is crucial to note that, as such, the Rand Commission was not asked to investigate which non-transactional factors had an impact on the exchange rate during the course of 2001. It was asked to deal with certain foreign-exchange transactions, and to determine whether or not those transactions, and not anything else, had an impact on the value of the rand. The terms of reference were criticised, of course. But at the same time it was clear that the authorities were distancing their position from 'the transactions'. As Wakeford recalls, 'Maria Ramos herself was beating the drum of innocence before the commission had even started. She made public announcements saying that Treasury never approved the deals.'

While Moneyweb had taken in the various angles on 'Randgate', the influence of the press in this case could not be underestimated. As soon as I published the first Randgate story in *Finance Week*, I knew that my days there were numbered. The 'average' reception among the press to Wakeford's whistle-blowing was negative. It is arguable that the biggest press hit on Wakeford came from Caroline Southey, the then editor of the *Financial Mail*. At the time, the *Financial Mail* could be described as among the most influential voices in South African financial journal-ism. The weekly magazine's stature peaked in the 1980s – not because I worked there for seven years in that decade – but because of the mer-curial Steve Mulholland, the editor who had an eye for what readers wanted to read. The reputation of the *Financial Mail* has been on the decline since Mulholland departed; its circulation has been falling incessantly, not for years, but for decades.

The *Financial Mail* decided that it would break its 'own' Randgate story by publishing Wakeford's letter late on 27 March – just days before he was due to testify at the commission.

Wakeford's letter read as follows:

Introduction

The weakness of the rand is no surprise but the extent and pace of the currency's depreciation [have] been more severe than analysts' wildest expectations. The rand's recent woes have been ascribed to a number of implausible reasons given by commentators. The popular causes given by commentators are: the Argentinian debt crisis; the Zimbabwean situation; the slow pace of privatisation in SA; the AIDS pandemic in SA.

These issues were priced into the market on a gradual basis over a considerable period of time and are now muddying the waters when analysing the demise of the rand. At the core of the problem lies the usage of dubious financial methods that have undermined the value of our currency. This is not to say that there is not scope for economic policy considerations that would contribute to strengthening and stabilising our currency. There are obviously numerous structural financial instruments that are potentially undermining the value of our currency. These instruments serve the narrow interests of institutions, companies and their clients at the expense of our national economic interest. This report will highlight one of these instruments and the parties to one of the deals that utilised such a method.

Deutsche Bank/Sasol deal

The original deal was for Sasol to purchase a German chemical company, Condea. This was an offshore deal for which Sasol obtained Reserve Bank permission a considerable time ago. This deal was fully compliant with exchange-control regulations as it was 100% funded offshore.

Sources began raising concerns two to three months ago when Sasol announced that it managed to shift in a structured financial product deal, which domestically funds 40% of the original value of the Condea acquisition. This move seemingly is not compliant with the original Reserve Bank authorisation.

When examining this we came across a dubious and peculiar share transaction. Deutsche Bank structured this transaction. The transaction unfolded in the following manner: Sasol bought back a portion of their shares from the market; Sasol then obtained Reserve Bank approval to issue new shares and sell them offshore to Deutsche Bank UK.

This deal was ±R6 bn (it has been difficult to verify the actual figure); this foreign capital obtained from the sale of these new shares issued assisted Sasol in funding the Condea acquisition potentially under false pretences.

This left Deutsche Bank overexposed to the rand via rand-denominated shares (Sasol shares). This induced the sale of rand by Deutsche Bank into our domestic market. These actions obviously contributed to the rand's depreciation. There is therefore a strong likelihood that Sasol and Deutsche Bank were colluding to cause a drop in the value of the rand in order to strengthen their economic position in relation to falling oil prices, i.e. a weaker rand boosts resources stocks and commodity prices for companies in the market.

Deutsche Bank could also speculate against the falling rand during this process and hence enrich itself. This could have induced market manipulation and insider trading.

On 4 December 2001 Deutsche Bank issued a market commentary via their bulletin titled 'Capitulation of our rand view finally!' Interestingly during the same period the *Sunday Times* carried a headline article concerning 'the big bang' approach to exchange control and the consequent free fall of the rand.

It is possible that these two articles were mutually reinforcing. This was taken very seriously by the markets because Deutsche Bank's credibility is reinforced by its core management members who have very strong links and relationships with the Department of Finance and the Reserve Bank. Market jitters at that stage set in and the rapid downward spiral of the rand began reaching an all-time low of R13.84 to the US dollar during December 2001.

Simultaneously this was further confounded as mentioned earlier by Deutsche Bank's dumping of rand in the local market due to their over-exposure to rand-dominated Sasol shares. In addition, the SA currency market was technically vulnerable with fairly thin trade due to the Reserve Bank governor's public warning in October that more vigilance would be applied when inspecting transactions.

Strangely this statement effectively locked out speculators who would have bought an undervalued rand and thereby could have strengthened our rapidly ailing currency. Deutsche Bank was potentially left with a monopoly situation to manipulate the currency due to the absence of a significant challenge from the usual speculation.

Further to this, Deutsche Bank UK could now start selling their strengthening Sasol shares (being a natural hedge in the domestic market), which they have purchased and paid for, offshore. This will cause further capital outflows if these shares are sold in the domestic market. In market jargon this is known as a 'double whammy', referring to outflows of capital.

It is of great concern that Deutsche Bank's core management have a historically privileged position and relationship with the Department of Finance and the Reserve Bank and have therefore created the impression in the market that they specifically could offer these financial products to other companies.

It is rumoured that Nampak, M-Cell and Billiton are in the process of following similar strategies. We note with interest that Deutsche Bank currently owns 7% of Billiton.

Conclusion

It is obvious that there could be many more permutations of such dubious financial methods and a repeat of the method highlighted above. Should we ignore the weaknesses in our foreign exchange regime actions of this nature are bound to continue to the peril of our country. Failure to substantively intervene will perpetuate the dramatic downward spiral of our currency's value.[32]

Wakeford would later explain that he had met President Thabo Mbeki's advisor, Wiseman Nkuhlu, at the Sandton Towers, Johannesburg, in January and had been asked to 'immediately write something down ... I need it today.' This explained the nature of Wakeford's note-form missive.

Southey attacked Wakeford head-on (ad hominem, as it is known) in an article in the *Financial Mail* on 29 March 2002:

The incredible lightness of Kevin Wakeford's letter

In January, when President Thabo Mbeki was prompted to launch a commission of inquiry into the dramatic depreciation of the rand late last year, he did so primarily on the basis of a letter from Kevin Wakeford, CEO of the SA Chamber of Business. The commission will cost an estimated R25 m, not to mention the extensive resources banks have had to dedicate towards the commission's requests for information.

The letter clearly was not written to stand up to the type of scrutiny it now will receive. It was a letter written by one man to another. But that does not obscure the fact that it has, whatever Wakeford's intentions, become a key document in our attempt to understand the Myburgh Commission. The *FM* has now had an opportunity to read the document – though it was not made available to us by Wakeford. It is published on this page. We should point out that the letter was not signed by Wakeford, and did not appear on a letterhead; but extensive investigations by the *FM* have convinced us it is genuine.

In our view, the document raises serious doubts over the need to call a commission of inquiry into the collapse of the rand. The allegations are neither substantiated nor even, in some cases, coherent. Organisations and individuals are maligned, their integrity impugned, their motives and actions condemned.

There appears little chance that the most damning charges in the letter will ever be proven: they are conjectural and lack evidence. It is precisely the kind of document that needs formal scrutiny by the Myburgh Commission – if only to verify its source and be the platform for detailed and testable evidence ...

The article carried on and on, never once so much as even contemplating that there was a remote possibility that there had been delinquency in the markets. Southey, indeed, made so many judgements and reached so many absolute conclusions that it seems pointless to count all of them. She was playing the man and not the ball. Her attack was a nakedly degenerate piece of editorial comment: it could have been written by Deutsche Bank and/or Sasol. The apparent objective was to deflect attention from the underlying issues and focus on discrediting the messenger. Most heinous, however, was Southey's reference, almost religious in its nature, to 'the integrity and efficacy of SA's financial institutions'. Southey was simply inventing things, things that she had no proof of either way.

In the fullness of time, what would emerge was incontrovertible evidence that South Africa's financial institutions were wanting in integrity, and wanting in efficacy. A fuller picture shows that private-sector financial institutions – the five biggest, in particular – work hand in glove to perpetuate a system that, if stripped naked, would be shown up to be little short of disgraceful. This is a system that aims, and succeeds, to extract banking profit margins that rank among the highest in the world. At the same time, when something goes awry, or even off the rails, the financial institutions, along with the Reserve Bank, will work like peas in a pod to cover the mess up. Welcome to the Rand Commission.

The Rand Commission was to show that the private-sector financial institutions would in fact increasingly differ from the Reserve Bank. This served the South African citizen immensely: for the first time, at least some of the inner workings of a banking cartel, benignly and unofficially authorised by the Reserve Bank, were unveiled in the public domain. The problem was that nobody seemed to have the vaguest idea of what they were looking at.

One persistent factor was that Wakeford was identified as a colossal enemy of the banking cartel. Somebody had leaked the Wakeford letter to Southey with the intention of discrediting him. Southey had gleefully accepted the task at hand, like a simpering lapdog. Beyond her flagrant attempts to crush Wakeford like a bug, the latent innuendo in her approach was to defend unnamed individuals and unnamed entities on the predetermined basis that all were paragons of virtue – simply perfect. In her tiny, microscopic world, Wakeford was the enemy. The person who had, on his personal neck, spoken out on what he believed to be an issue of national importance was going to be hunted down like a rat.

Just what this meant for Southey would be seen in the years ahead. What it meant for the *Financial Mail*, certainly in the short term, was not clear.

Two *Financial Mail* readers reacted, on the *Financial Mail*'s website, to Southey's article as follows:

An extraordinary crisis led to the rand declining [during 2001] by 45% of which a 20% decline took place during two weeks in December 2001. This is dramatic, the consequences of which filter through in higher prices every day. Yet we're told it's business as usual and that the transactions that led to the decline of the rand can't be traced. To have been so dramatic there must have been some huge transactions that depleted the nation's reserves. Yet, we're told they can't be traced. We are a gullible public. (Bill Mitchell)

It takes courage to stand up to big corporate shenanigans – and I fear that there is far too much protestation to Wakeford's stand. Perhaps the manner in which the so-called letter was presented was not cricket, but if we look at a number of global companies involved in off-the-wall creative accounting – some big names at that – let's give the man a chance – I don't like the idea of having to pay more on my bond and R4/litre for fuel because of some greedy individuals. (Richard Crosby)

Southey, it should be noted, was obsessed with the idea of digging out Wakeford's source. It seemed that some weird piece of logic progressing through her mind held that if the source was indeed identified, then the currency collapse of 2001 would suddenly be fully explained and could be laughed off as some accident of history, and then ignored as if it had never happened. She had absolutely no interest in trying to interrogate the events of 2001 that lay behind, and would hopefully explain, the trashing of the rand. She also seemed completely ignorant of the fact that whether or not the 'source' was employed at a competitor to Deutsche Bank, the information that had been given to Wakeford had national implications.

Southey also complained about the cost of the Rand Commission, without even referring to the cost of the crashed rand to the country, and how much further that cost could have risen had the rand's plummeting towards its would-be demise not been at least halted.

Wakeford recalls:

I was attacked viciously by the banks and their acolytes for causing them so much pain and cost. They now had to gather all this information for submission. It's taking their eye off the ball, I was told. But the truth be known, they were let off lightly. I mean, for a commission in the midst of a crisis like this to only cost R15 million – it was joke. It should have cost R1.5 billion, and then it would have made a difference: just during the rand's collapse, our economy's balance sheet lost R300 billion – that's beside damages to the consumer's buying power, the pending explosion of the inflation rate, and everything else.

In more ways than one, Wakeford had been forced onto the back foot. The financial-services sector was gunning for him; certain disgruntled corporates wanted him to vanish; the government was forced to sit on the fence; and the negative press, led by Southey, painted him as some kind of monster, an evil menace to society.

The war was on.

***

'I am a most unhappy man. I have unwittingly ruined my country.
A great industrial nation is controlled by its system of credit.
Our system of credit is concentrated. The growth of the nation,
therefore, and all our activities are in the hands of a few men. No longer
a government by free opinion, no longer a government by conviction
and vote of majority, but a government by the opinion and duress of
a small group of dominant men.' – President Woodrow Wilson
(regretting signing into law the Federal Reserve Act)

I spent a lot of time in 2002 with Carolyn Pritchard, a student and budding journalist visiting from the US. She would later write in an academic paper, in part fulfilment of her university course requirements:

Journalism in South Africa suffers from a crippling inferiority complex. Even the reporters and the editors themselves refer to it as a trade, and not a profession. By any name, it is not an industry that anyone in the country will admit to being proud of.

Journalism is never put to the test more than in times of crisis. If nothing else, the spectacular fall in the country's currency, the rand, re-lived more than just the problems of outdated capital controls, but a conspicuous absence of hard investigative journalism by the country's financial print media. An investigation into the media itself finds many reasons why.[33]

Pritchard then goes on to discuss apartheid's 'long tentacles'. She observes that 'in addition to the pressures exerted on South Africa's print media by politics, the industry is also squeezed by economics. It is inordinately dependent on advertising revenue, with as much as 88–90% of revenue derived from advertising, versus just 10–12% from cover price and circulation.'

Under the subheading 'A dearth of knowledge', Pritchard said:

It could be argued that too many of the country's business journalists are simply not qualified ... Dr Michael Samson, an economist with the Economic Policy Research Institute, agrees that he is 'misquoted more often' than he is quoted. 'They don't take good notes and they don't record conversations,' says Samson. 'They don't even get the simple facts straight.' Samson added that 'I don't think journalism is unbiased anywhere, so I'm not surprised to see it be biased here'. In the US, he says, the bias is 'more subtle'.

Looking at the rand meltdown, Pritchard stated: 'The print media went to the pundits: economists, analysts, and even the Reserve Bank ... the press talked to the people who study money and make policy on money, but, curiously, failed to talk to the people who move money in order to make more of it.'

Pritchard quoted Moneyweb's Alec Hogg: 'No matter how antagonistic the whispering campaign, in the court of public opinion, Wakeford is the clear winner. Emails, phone calls and comments from the Moneyweb community are overwhelmingly supportive of what he did.'

Pritchard continued:

No one in the press thought to take Wakeford's letter any further and investigate it for themselves.

'How the fuck would you investigate the fall of the rand?' exclaims *Business Day*'s editor, Peter Bruce. 'It's like investigating grass growing – it's a natural thing.'

Barry Sergeant didn't think so ... it was only after Sergeant had pitched and written the piece for *Finance Week* that he spoke to Wakeford, 'and he refused to tell me anything until he had testified before the Rand Commission'.

5
The black horse

Deutsche Bank Johannesburg, Martin Kingston and realpolitik ... Mzi
Khumalo and his 'friends' ... The obsessive witch-hunt for Wakeford's
source ... Wakeford called by the likes of Maria Ramos, Gill Marcus and
Jayendra Naidoo ... The strange world of Christoph Köpke.

'The black horse's rider was holding a pair of scales in his hand:
"A quart of wheat for a day's wages, and three quarts of barley for a
day's wages, and do not damage the oil and the wine!"' – Revelation 6:5–6

In times of famine, the elite will continue to do all right. More to the
point, perhaps, is that investment banks will do all right whatever the
economic environment. Deutsche Bank was the common denominator
during the Rand Commission's hearings; the corporates were, of course,
Sasol; to a far lesser extent, M-Cell and Nampak; and, further out, Billiton.

Deutsche Bank Johannesburg chairman Martin Kingston had had a
long-standing relationship with the financial leadership of the ANC –
those who had been part of the economics desk in the build-up to liberation and were part of that process post facto as well. They were in key
government positions. The line-up included Tito Mboweni, Maria Ramos
and Trevor Manuel. Kingston means different things to different people.
Broadly speaking, he is someone who commands an ambivalent audience.
Just what his fan base thinks of him wouldn't surprise anyone. What's
more revealing, however, is what his detractors made of the man.

Kingston had often been mercilessly lampooned by the late Brett Kebble;
he was accused of being 'married to the ANC'. He had married Thembi
Tambo, whose father, Oliver Tambo, was one of the most important figures
in the ruling party's history. Kingston later divorced Thembi and married
Pulane, daughter of Manto Tshabalala-Msimang, Thabo Mbeki's health
minister and one of South Africa's most controversial politicians.

Kebble complained loudly about how Kingston would 'strut around like a peacock, advertising his unparalleled contacts' in the ANC and other spheres of influence. It took little prompting for Kebble to launch into Kingston with lusty inflection: 'I know the president. I know Mbeki. I know Mandela. I know Bill Clinton, and I know blah, blah, blah. Pleased to meet you, how can I help you, do you know my name?' Then Kebble would sing to the tune of the Rolling Stones song 'Sympathy for the Devil': 'Do you know my name, oh yeah …'[1]

Despite a growing population, boosted by large numbers of self-exiled Zimbabweans, post-apartheid South Africa developed into a smaller pool with fewer big fish. The elites rose further and further above the proletariat. These elites are the most public and also the most secret club in the country. None have ever broken ranks and spoken about the inner workings of this club, and there is no question any living member ever would. Perhaps an analysis of the elites provided by the late Brett Kebble would be in order. Kebble mixed with the best of them and used letters of the alphabet to describe how South Africa's power-mongers functioned – and malfunctioned:

- A says to everyone that 'Brett is a big white fish who must be fried'.
- His friends at the all-night drinking on Fridays at a certain 10-star hotel say, 'Fine, let's get B to heat up the frying pan'.
- My so-called ally C, who has finally accepted that he won't become president until he is a hundred years old, even so needs to build power bases. He says, 'Ah, I have a good relationship with Mbeki, we're both two bricks and a tickey[2] high, let's bring him in.'
- D approaches me and says, 'I worry about your friendship with E; he's using your support to finance his presidential ambitions. He's a person who will misuse power.' I ask: 'Who would use it better?' He replies: 'Me.'
- I write to the president to let him know what F is doing in the dark. I do not even get a thank you; these people think they're earls and dukes – royalty.
- G uses his official role to deter people from lending to me, at the request of his friend H.
- I's actions are motivated by inferiority and insecurity, aggravated by his wife rising to greater prominence than he.
- J pisses his pants before the Friday sessions end. Everyone knows it – they avoid him from about midnight.

- K is one of the 20 richest people in the country, despite having created no wealth at all. Very late at nights he says he's not earning enough. He announces that it is he who should be president.[3]

Funny? Indeed – but about as accurate as it gets. Kebble worked in the world of realpolitik. The merit of his alphabet soup is in the detail of recognising the functioning of South Africa's new elites. Kebble was as cynical of white business as he was of black business: he saw the two as variations on the same dull tune:

- One day M said to Julian Baring in London, 'If I were you, old boy, I should be careful of my new partners. You might wake up one morning and find an assegai up your arse.'
- N had built himself from the kind of background where there was a lot of building to do. Now he wanted the sun to shine on his gold ambitions. He asked me to help him swing a deal with O, who he called 'the thickest hairy back [a derogatory term for Afrikaner] in business'.
- P managed to tear himself away from his main task of shafting Lonmin long enough to shaft me too.
- Q spent the meeting telling me how he had taught Ernie Els to play golf, taught Michael Schumacher to drive and taught the world to do everything. To him, everyone in Anglo American had the same first name, 'Fucking'. Then he joined forces with Anglo American because they had one community of interest, which was to stop our rise.
- R is possibly the most loathsome person you could ever meet.

If Kebble seemed to be talking in riddles, he was referring in broader terms to his bid to merge all the companies under his control into a large single entity. That was during 1999. The overall transactions were thwarted forever when Kebble and some of his sidekicks were caught in what Kebble described as 'technical infringements' in late 1999. Eventually he would be indicted, along with his father, Roger Kebble, plus Hennie Buitendag and Western Areas, in December 2002 on charges of incitement, conspiracy, insider trading and fraud. The investigation had been conducted by KPMG Services and financed by Business Against Crime, which was financed by a number of entities in the private sector.

Kebble's take on the situation cut right down to the bone: 'What it boils down to is, if my deal had gone ahead, the mining industry today would be ten times better off. But my deal died because egos were threatened. There it is. That is the essence.'[4] Kebble, of course, has been separately exposed as one of the most talented fraudsters in South African history. His account of his high life in high business, which extended from early 1997 until his murder on 27 September 2005, referred in numerous instances to how he was forced into corners by elite individuals.

On this score, Kebble's main complaint was over what he called 'selective prosecution' – members of the elites were, in effect, immune. Enemies or threats to the elites were hunted down, in one way or another. Within the context of exchange controls, were certain people immune to action from the Reserve Bank? Despite the draconian nature of the system, political connectivity counts – perhaps not always, but certainly sometimes. Possibly the most infamous individual case of illicit export of South African cash can be traced to April 2001, when a three-way deal between the state-owned Industrial Development Corporation (IDC), formed in South Africa in the 1950s, Harmony Gold, a listed stock, and Komanani Mining set the scene for catapulting Mzilikazi Godfrey 'Mzi' Khumalo, a flamboyant businessman, into the big league.

The twist in the freakish story was that Komanani inexplicably bailed out of the deal on 17 August 2001. Within weeks, on 31 August 2001, an entity known as Simane, 67 per cent owned by Mzi Khumalo, secretly acquired Komanani's previous rights, free of charge. As it turned out, the magic of a weakening rand, combined with a strengthening dollar gold-bullion price, had explosive effects on Harmony's stock price, which increased from R37.30 a share on 3 April 2001, when the original Komanani deal was structured, to R96.50 a share on 4 February 2002. At these sorts of prices, the Komanani deal was very seriously 'in the money'.

Harmony had issued shares to Komanani and an equivalent amount of stock options on Harmony shares to the IDC. The idea was that if Harmony's stock price rose to sufficient levels, the IDC could convert its options to stock in Harmony, sell the stock and pay off the debt that Simane owed the IDC. With the Harmony Gold stock price slowly going into orbit, so it was that on 4 February 2002, the IDC converted its options into shares and sold them, leaving the black economic empowerment

(BEE) partner the debt-free owner of 11 million shares in Harmony. On 24 May 2002, when Harmony's stock hit an astonishing R186.80 a share, the 11 million unencumbered Harmony shares were worth a stupendous debt-free R2 billion.

Khumalo bought out Simane's remaining minorities, his fellow black brethren, for R82 million, a pathetic sum in the context and one that hardly made a dent on the R2 billion worth of Harmony shares that he owned. Prima facie evidence that certain individuals at the IDC had worked hand in glove with Khumalo, effectively handing him 11 million Harmony shares, was submitted to the Scorpions, then a division of the National Prosecuting Authority (NPA). Given Khumalo's self-confessed connections, naturally the case was assigned to the bottom drawer and was in due course designated to the oblivion file.

On 31 August 2001, when Simane had issued 200 new shares to Khumalo, 170 shares went to Efferton and 30 went to Nest Life. Both were foreign-registered entities; in effect, 57 per cent of Simane's owner-ship had been externalised from South Africa. When I asked about Efferton and related matters, Reserve Bank executive Alick Bruce-Brand offered a terse response: 'We are not in a position to comment.' Equally significant was Khumalo's investment in Cluff plc, a company listed in London but with certain operating assets in South Africa: how had Khumalo obtained permission to export rands to buy shares in a foreign stock? It was simply not permissible.

Khumalo made no attempt to hide the existence of his offshore invest-ments. As well as high living – hiring billionaires' yachts for parties in the Mediterranean and flaunting his wealth around the French Riviera – he made substantial (and public) investments abroad in foreign currency. Khumalo was in with the 'in' crowd. He was a personal friend of Bulelani Ngcuka, who headed the NPA, and a regular visitor to Ngcuka's wife, Phumzile Mlambo-Ngcuka, the minister of mines from 1999 to 2005. Khumalo would boast that he and the minister 'shared a birthday'. The minister stridently promoted 'broad-based black economic empowerment' in the mining sector, and was instrumental in formulating all kinds of rules and regulations aimed at forcing mining companies into submission. If anyone knew that the Simane deal was anything but broad-based, besides Khumalo, it was Ngcuka and his wife. She would be appointed deputy president of South Africa on 22 June 2005 by President Thabo Mbeki. The week before, Mbeki had infamously relieved Jacob Zuma of the position, following Ngcuka's announcement that there was a prima facie criminal case against Zuma.

Just prior to the ANC's December 2007 elective conference in Polokwane, the NPA controversially announced that the charges against Zuma had been dropped due to political interference in the process. At Polokwane, Mlambo-Ngcuka lost all her positions; she was even dropped from the ANC's National Executive Committee. The Zuma 'slate' had won a landslide victory. This was not good for Mzi Khumalo. Years back, in Durban, Zuma had clashed with Khumalo over certain treasury matters at the local branch of the ANC. After Zuma swept to power at the national level, Khumalo suddenly found himself out in the cold. Five years after I had published extensive details on how Simane had exported hundreds of millions of rands offshore, Khumalo suddenly became the subject of a heavy-duty investigation by the Reserve Bank. The administrators of South Africa's draconian exchange controls appointed a highly skilled, very expensive team of professionals to investigate the Khumalo saga. Overseas travel was part of what turned out to be a lark.

Unofficially, very little was found of at least R760 million that Khumalo had shipped offshore. Deutsche Bank had assisted in transferring the R760 million, involving Deutsche Bank Johannesburg and Deutsche Bank London. There was never any rationale for the transfer, and no evidence that Khumalo had been given any kind of exemption from South Africa's strict prohibition on residents from transferring more than fairly nominal amounts offshore. Khumalo fought the case tooth and nail, raising complaints that his constitutional rights had been violated. One of the investigators told me that the action taken against Khumalo looked unlikely to deliver any real results, given that precious little of his 'offshore' loot could be traced. It was weird, all right. Khumalo had effectively been given years to implement various schemes to ensure that his exported gains were going to be almost impossible to trace. It's possible, of course, that he blew most of his fortune on wine, women and song. When he hired the *Christina O* in the Mediterranean, Khumalo would delight in telling woman seated on the yacht's bar stools that they were sitting on a whale's foreskin.

So within months of the Rand Commission closing in July 2002,

Deutsche Bank was involved in Mzi Khumalo's transaction, which, years later, would be heavily investigated by the South African Reserve Bank. Whatever Deutsche Bank had stood accused of at the Rand Commission, it certainly experienced no nerves in helping Khumalo make transactions that no ordinary person could ever have been permitted to do. In his heyday, Khumalo was hooked into the ruling elite and he gave every appearance of being untouchable. The extent of Khumalo's connectivity – again, in his heyday – was deep-rooted. It was Kebble who shoved the network into the public domain.

In October 2003, Kebble had publicly lashed out at the NPA and the Scorpions. Kebble claimed that Bulelani Ngcuka, head of the NPA since 1999, had made

> a shocking series of slanderous and racist statements about me during an off-the-record briefing to selected journalists on 24 July 2003 …
> it was an extraordinary gathering in which Ngcuka set himself up as prosecutor and judge, delivered his verdicts and then sought the editors' help to spread those verdicts through the pages of their newspapers.[5]

At the time, an NPA spokesman said Kebble's claims had been noted: 'As we have pointed out to Kebble in writing some time ago, we categorically deny any wrongdoing or irregularity by the NPA or any of its members insofar as it relates to criminal proceedings against Kebble or any of his family members.'

So far as Kebble was concerned, the NPA was being used for private agendas, and he pointed specifically to Khumalo, who, Kebble stated,

> is a close friend of Ngcuka … [Khumalo] has declared himself my enemy in part because I am taking legal action against him seeking repayment of moneys owed by him to me in excess of R50 million. Khumalo has sworn he will bring about my downfall and to my face has told me that he will use his friendship with Ngcuka to achieve that.

One of the crucial points from the series of events is that Khumalo's flaunting of exchange control happened many months after the Rand

Commission. This raises key questions over whether or not certain parties involved in the 2001 trashing of the rand were let off the hook – either due to political connectivity or pure political expediency.

That aside, the use of public institutions in South Africa for private purposes is now a fairly regular feature in an increasingly bleak law-enforcement landscape. And South Africa is not alone: the use of public entities and agencies as, in effect, extensions of the private sector is becoming an increasing feature across the West.

On 22 December 2012, the US's Partnership for Civil Justice Fund (PCJF) announced that it had obtained documents, pursuant to the Freedom of Information Act, showing that from its inception, the FBI had treated the Occupy Wall Street (OWS) movement as 'a potential criminal and terrorist threat', even though the FBI itself acknowledges in documents that organisers explicitly called for peaceful protest and did 'not condone the use of violence' at protests. Heavily redacted documents show that FBI offices and agents around the US 'were in high gear conducting surveillance against the movement even as early as August 2011', a month prior to the establishment of the OWS encampment in Zuccotti Park, New York City, and other OWS actions across the US. The PCJF said it believed the documents it obtained were 'just the tip of the iceberg', and a 'window into the nationwide scope of the FBI's surveillance, monitoring, and reporting on peaceful protestors organizing with the OWS movement'.[6]

PCJF executive director Mara Verheyden-Hilliard said that 'these documents show that the FBI and the Department of Homeland Security are treating protests against the corporate and banking structure of America as potential criminal and terrorist activity. These documents also show these federal agencies functioning as a *de facto* intelligence arm of Wall Street and Corporate America.' From as early as 19 August 2011, the FBI in New York was meeting with the New York Stock Exchange to discuss the OWS's plans. Among documents showing coordination between the FBI, the Department of Homeland Security and corporate America is a report by the Domestic Security Alliance Council, described by the federal government as a 'strategic partnership between the FBI, the Department of Homeland Security and the private sector'. The report discusses the OWS protests at the west coast ports to 'raise awareness concerning this type of criminal activity'. The Domestic Security Alliance Council issued several tips to its corporate clients on 'civil unrest', which it defines as ranging from 'small, organized rallies to large-scale demonstrations and rioting'.

Among the heavily redacted 112 pages released to the PCJF, it was apparent that the FBI had encountered a plan to identify and execute members of the OWS:

> An identified [redacted] of October planned to engage in sniper attacks against protesters in Houston, Texas, if deemed necessary. An identified [redacted] had received intelligence that indicated the protesters in New York and Seattle planned similar protests in Houston, Dallas, San Antonio and Austin, Texas. [Redacted] planned to gather intelligence against the leaders of the protest groups and obtain photographs then formulate a plan to kill the leadership via suppressed sniper rifles.[7]

There was no evidence that the FBI had taken any steps to warn the targeted individuals that their lives could be in danger. Equally, there is no evidence that the FBI took any action against those planning the executions.

Welcome to the World of Big Money.

***

'I believe banking institutions pose a greater threat to our liberties than standing armies.' – Thomas Jefferson

There were hints here and there, but there has never been any hard evidence of any plots to assassinate Kevin Wakeford – assassinate in the physical sense, that is. Instead, there were other plots. Before, during and after Wakeford blew the whistle on the rand in January 2002, he may have had little, if any, idea of the kind of elites he was up against. As a political analyst, he was aware of the elites, to be sure, but he was not aware of all the detail. Wakeford had conceded a degree of naivety in his decision to blow the whistle. He has always argued that he was motivated by wanting to act in the best interests of the country.

After Wakeford blew the whistle, it was another CEO who offered his services – this time for Wakeford. Dave Brink, non-executive chairman of construction company Murray & Roberts and non-executive director of ABSA, called and offered Wakeford bodyguards. Says Wakeford:

But the point is – why did Dave Brink offer me bodyguards? Everyone knows that if you're a leader of a country the people you've got to be the most circumspect about are your bodyguards. Your bodyguards are the guys who assassinate presidents and they are guys who are wonderful listening posts for the opposition. I turned it down and my response was, which at the time was a white lie, but I did it to protect myself: 'Look, the National Intelligence Agency has a permanent team monitoring me and protecting my best interests.' Of course, that wasn't the case – I had no form of protection whatsoever. I had met with the National Intelligence Agency prior to the establishment of the commission and thereafter but I had never requested assistance of any sort. They were, however, very interested in my interpretation of events and often implied that my information was deadly accurate.

Wakeford was fearful, but at the same time he felt that his own best instincts were to be trusted above all else. His approach in trying to expose what had happened to the rand rattled any number of cages. He was called by other high-profile people, including Geoff Rothschild of Sasfin Frankel Pollak Securities. Rothschild's words went along the lines of:

> Kevin, this is a bunch of nonsense, what's going on here? This is bad for business, it's bad for the business mood, and it's not good in the context of a corrupt government – that's where the focus should be. We should be focusing on public-sector corruption because that's where the real corruption is, that's where the market failures are actually induced and unacceptable. Why are you pursuing this? This is not good.[8]

As far as Wakeford was concerned, Rothschild was 'speaking in innuendo'. Says Wakeford: 'He wasn't as forthright as he should have been with me.'

Wakeford had overwhelming support from the man and woman in the street, and from small and medium-sized businesses. By contrast, people at the top of the pecking order, that shallow, thin band of economic and political elites, wanted the Rand Commission to be stillborn. Wakeford didn't trust anyone among the elite structures, even though the two sets of elites lived in a state of healthy competition – against each other. And like so many big private-sector voices in South Africa, the likes of Rothschild reverted to type: pretend that the private sector is nothing less than perfect, and shift 100 per cent of the focus to the public sector. Wakeford remained steadfast in his belief that although there may have been short-falls in certain parts of the public sector, the rot in the rand during 2001 had been rooted in the private sector.

Wakeford's information had come from

a trusted person and, no, I'm not revealing my source – I can't do that – I gave my word. But my source gave very specific financial transactions, foreign transactions, which I put in the public domain. I'll tell you why I know that for a fact. There were a number of people at the banks, at specific banks at that time, for example Deutsche Bank, who knew about these transactions because they were the architects.

This could have been an understatement: Kebble, who most certainly did not speak to Wakeford, was able to establish the details of the transactions within 24 hours, and had named Deutsche Bank as the common denominator. Separately, I had been able to obtain wider information about the trading patterns that had characterised 2001. And, of course, the Reserve Bank itself had been informed in August 2001 of potentially dodgy deals in the rand market.

Even so, Wakeford was the target: the witch-hunt was on. He was called by the Reserve Bank in March 2002, along the lines of: 'Mr Wakeford, could we teleconference with you because we have an enquiry into one of our staff members.' James Cross had retired as deputy governor of the Reserve Bank in December 2001. It had been asserted that it was he who had leaked the information, and because it was a labour inquiry, Wakeford agreed to the teleconference. Cross's lawyer asked Wakeford questions in the presence of everyone in the Reserve Bank committee room, or, as Wakeford puts it, 'wherever it was, where Reserve Bank offi-cials from both employer and employee were represented. I was asked, "Was James Cross your informant?"'

Wakeford continued:

I've never met James Cross in all my life. Okay? ... And by the way, straight after that question, because that's all they needed to hear from me as part of the leading of evidence – Cross was possibly trying to protect his pension and his reputation because he was now retired: the guy could have lost everything. And then I was asked, 'Surely, Mr Wakeford it was from …' – no, I must be very careful in terms of what I say: 'Mr Wakeford, was it then somebody else perhaps?' In other words, implying it was one of his colleagues at the Reserve Bank. I said, 'I've had no contact with the Reserve Bank other than a Mr Van Staden, who phoned me after I called for the commission. He wanted to meet with me.'

Echoing strongly the approach taken by the *Financial Mail*'s Caroline Southey, the Reserve Bank elite appeared to believe that if the identity of the 'source' could be dug out, then the Rand Commission would some-how disappear. This was truly twisted logic, as if finding the source would mean that nothing had happened to the rand during 2001 – it had spent the whole year doing nothing, going sideways.

Wakeford received a request from Deanne Gordon, who in March had moved from the South African branch of investment bank J.P. Morgan, one of Wall Street's oldest names, to Rand Merchant Bank, a home-grown outfit. Wakeford recalls that

there were vicious rumours flying around that she was in fact the 'source'. And she was facing, I think, the wrath of her employer, and perhaps the wrath of business in general. I was requested by an inter-mediary to sign an affidavit to the effect that I had never met her, nor seen her, not even seen a photograph of her in my life. Which I did. Apparently she was under a lot of pressure … I just received this affi-davit, I read it through, I was happy to sign it. I went down to the Rosebank Police Station, which was down the road from SACOB, I had it authenticated, ratified – whatever you call it – authorised by a com-missioner of oaths and then I had it couriered back to her attorney.

Jayendra Naidoo, a prominent political figure, had also called, early in January. Wakeford was by the Sundays River with an old colleague, his aca-demic mentor, Gavin Bradshaw, from the Nelson Mandela Metropolitan University, a professor of political science and conflict resolution. Bradshaw had made a significant contribution in this field during the early 1990s, the era of the National Peace Initiative. He was one of the key role players in the initiative, primarily in the Eastern Cape but also nationally, and he was in a sense mentored by John Burton, one of the pioneers of the human needs theory in politics and resolving conflict. Bradshaw, a sharp thinker and progressive academic, was a friend who had mentored Wakeford academically.

Naidoo said words along the lines of: 'Look, we really need to meet with you.'

Wakeford asked, 'Who's "we"?'

Naidoo replied: 'A few political heavyweights. They're currently in Cape Town and we would like to meet and get together with you.'

This was after Wakeford had gone public: 'It was now in the public domain, in a sense; it was in the press. To protect myself, I was advised by the likes of Bradshaw and others go public because it's very difficult to silence someone once the cat's out of the bag.' Phillip Dexter, treasurer general of the South African Communist Party, also called. Gill Marcus, deputy governor of the Reserve Bank, also called, indirectly, through SACOB, as did Maria Ramos, director general of the Treasury. Wakeford did not reply to Dexter, Marcus or Ramos. 'Smuts Ngonyama, head of the Presidency at Luthuli House and key confidant of Mbeki, said that I should refrain from speaking to anybody, as the commission was there to establish the facts; he spoke with an attitude that suggested that they knew my information was spot on and that their comrades who were potentially involved should not have a "heads-up or inside track".'

Wakeford was saying little, if anything. There were three people who could be seen as key in terms of linkages to the Mbeki Presidency. The first was head of the Presidency in Luthuli House, Smuts Ngonyama, whom Wakeford knew from the Eastern Cape. 'I didn't know him very well,' Wakeford recalls, 'but I knew him well enough – in fact when I was head of the Port Elizabeth Chamber he was MEC [Member of the Executive Council] of Economic Affairs in the Eastern Cape, so there were times when we engaged around the Coega project, et cetera, and he was very helpful.' Ngonyama said it was important for Wakeford to keep his head under the radar: 'You have now handed the information over to the Presidency,' he told Wakeford. 'The Presidency has commissioned an inquiry, a judicial inquiry. The information you have in a sense is *sub judice* because this commission has judicial powers and it's now up to the commission to establish the facts, it's not up to you to play a role any further than you have.'

The second was Professor Wiseman Nkuhlu, South Africa's first-ever black chartered accountant, and economic advisor to Mbeki. And third, Bheki Khumalo, government spokesperson for the president. All three had a common refrain: whenever Wakeford called them for advice, the response was along the lines of: 'Quite frankly, this whole thing is now in the hands of the commission, it's not in your hands any more. You don't have to respond to anything. They can't get information from you because the commission is now custodian of that information.'

Mervyn King, former SACOB president, had offered Wakeford the services of the legal team at Brait, a financial-services niche player, to assist him, as he had been given a paltry budget of R30 000 by SACOB to defend himself. The budget was provided by former head of BMW in South Africa, Rainer Hagemann, treasurer of SACOB, who told Wakeford that he was 'only getting R30 000. Anything over and above that is your problem.' The budget dried up very quickly. This would seem to mean that the defence of the rand was only worth R30 000. Wakeford recalls that his lawyer, Andrew Cadman, 'was a lovely youngster but it was almost like going to a first-team rugby game with the under-13A team. It was going to be like going to a gunfight with a knife.'

After Mervyn King's 'counselling' of Wakeford, King said something like: 'Kevin, I've heard that this has some validity, what you're saying.' King referred to the 'attorneys across the road', meaning Fricker Road in Illovo, Johannesburg, home to a number of prestigious financial houses, law firms and the like. King said that the attorneys had been formally commissioned by the Reserve Bank 'to defend the institutions'.

King told Wakeford: 'You stood on a rat's tail, my boy.' He asked: 'Kevin, are Investec involved?' It was no secret that King had friends at Investec. Wakeford replied: 'I don't know if they are involved.' Wakeford believed that King was 'feeding back information'. He also believed that King, under heavy pressure, was 'using the trust relationship we had to almost try and mediate some kind of outcome'. Wakeford felt that SACOB's leadership, particularly King and Christoph Köpke, president of SACOB, possibly had a caucus to keep Wakeford reined in, in order to be able to lever some kind of control over Wakeford's actions during these critical times. It can be noted that Köpke, along with his second wife, Rosie, had become a house friend of Wakeford's. 'In the same vein, I was a house friend of Mervyn King and his wife. Mervyn spoke at my 40th birthday event with Theo Qabaka.' Even so, Wakeford still gave both King and Köpke the benefit of the doubt, as they seemed to be concerned and supportive. 'I regarded both of them as friends. If they were in trouble, even today, I would assist them. They were both probably under huge pressure from the corporate membership because of my stand on the rand.'

If nothing else, Köpke seemed to have a pragmatic and expedient approach to doing business in South Africa. He once explained 'transfer pricing' to Wakeford. Transfer pricing is, in essence, the transfer of profits from one jurisdiction to a second one, with a low tax rate, or where there is a large assessed tax loss. In the case of DaimlerChrysler, which manufactured in South Africa, this could have involved the marking up of imported components by artificially setting currency prices at a central treasury at the corporate HQ in Germany or elsewhere. There are a number of auto manufacturers in South Africa, but each unit produced locally includes a good number of imported components. These tend to be higher-value parts, such as fuel injectors and electronics, which today represent a fairly high percentage of the overall finished unit's cost. In the case of a DaimlerChrysler vehicle, it could be that high-value components, many of which are manufactured in Germany, are routed through a tax haven, and marked up at that point. These items are then relatively highly priced in South Africa. It could mean that the domestic DaimlerChrysler unit made very little in overall profit, thereby incurring minimal tax within the South African jurisdiction.

According to industry analysis, about 65 per cent of a vehicle's cost in South Africa comprises imported parts. The domestic component of about 35 per cent is 'much lower than elsewhere, except when component manufacturers also export'. The real problem, however, is that South African component manufacturers are 'not yet globally cost competitive'. The South African auto sector has for many years been able to claim 'duty credits', which, the analysis found, only 'encouraged more imports'.[9]

In line with international harmonisation, moreover, not least that of the World Trade Organization, the duty imposed by South Africa on auto imports of ready-to-use units had fallen from 115 per cent in 1994 to 25 per cent in 2012. In line with the reduction in import duties, fully imported auto sales increased at a sharp rate, rising from just over 40 per cent of the South African auto market in 2005 to 70 per cent in 2010. Things changed for South Africa's auto sector when the Department of Trade and Industry finally announced the Automotive Production and Development Programme to replace the long-standing Motor Industry Development Plan from 2013, to be in place until 2020.

Many European OEMs (original equipment manufacturers) and suppliers already buy components from South Africa – amounting to trade of more than €2 billion a year. The South African auto sector is expanding its capabilities and, according to analysis, 'gearing up for the higher production and localisation levels of the Automotive Production and Development Programme'.[10] Given the incentives on offer, it was hardly a surprise that 10 new large multinational suppliers started production in South Africa between 2010 and 2012.

For many years, the South African taxpayer has stood behind the domestic auto sector. In a cruel irony, this industry has become South Africa's biggest manufacturing sector. What South Africa desperately needs is direct foreign investment, especially in manufacturing, and elimination of subsidies for the domestic auto manufacturing sector.

Whether or not DaimlerChrysler was involved in transfer pricing regarding its South African operation, it seemed, separately, that Daimler-Chrysler had an interesting approach to foreign direct investment. Köpke once told Wakeford that DaimlerChrysler had borrowed a substantial sum from the IDC. If this took place, it meant that DaimlerChrysler South Africa was financing at least one expansion with rands borrowed from the IDC. This placed zero risk on the DaimlerChrysler parent company's balance sheet, and would have eliminated any currency risk on the expansion, at least at the capital-investment level.

Add that to the possibility that DaimlerChrysler was practising transfer pricing, and there is no question that the South African manufacturing unit was a fantastic investment with practically no downside.

If nothing else, Köpke was at best a pragmatist, and at worst a cynical corporate operator. As would be shown, he had an unusually strong interest in the goings-on at the Rand Commission. He had self-serving interests in ensuring that the least possible fallout was suffered by Deutsche Bank and Sasol. This is something Wakeford had established in the latter part of the commission. He has never confronted Köpke on this matter.

Köpke chose to remain absolutely in control as president of SACOB. Rather than recognising the impossible potential conflicts of interest that he faced and stepping down from SACOB, or at least standing aside until the Rand Commission had completed its work, Köpke, on the contrary, was going to stage-manage as much as was possible.

In February Köpke warned Wakeford: 'Mr [Pat] Davies at Sasol is not happy with you.' The contents of Wakeford's letter to President Thabo Mbeki had, of course, been leaked. At that stage, Davies was an executive director of Sasol and answered to CEO Pieter Cox and the inscrutable chairman, Paul Kruger.

6
The white horse

Myburgh threatens Wakeford ... Wakeford, badgered and badgered ...
Papadakis unleashes devastating evidence, also suffers heavy badgering
... Deutsche Bank takes more heat ... Rand Commission squirms with
conflicts of interest ... Deutsche Bank capitulates ... More from James
Cross.

'The white horse's rider held a bow, and he was given a crown,
and he rode out as a conqueror bent on conquest.' – Revelation 6:2

When the Rand Commission opened for business early in March 2002, the
rand was trading at six-week highs against the dollar. Literally from the day
that Kevin Wakeford blew the whistle, the rand had been appreciating.
The currency would continue gaining, but this seemed of only peripheral
interest to those anticipating the kind of dirty linen that some expected
to be unveiled at the hearings.

On 1 April 2002, the day before Wakeford was due to testify before the
Rand Commission, the chairman, John Myburgh, read Wakeford the riot
act, so to speak. Wakeford recalls:

> I was told the night before by Myburgh – I'm not sure whether I phoned
> him or he phoned me. I remember him saying to me, 'Tomorrow's your
> day, have you taken your Calmettes? Take sleeping pills, it'll be hard
> for you to sleep tonight.' And then he said to me, 'Also bear in mind
> I have powers to arrest you if you don't reveal your source.'

Wakeford paused and then replied to Myburgh: 'John, my bags are packed,
I've signed over power of attorney to my ex-wife, and I'm ready for anything you can throw at me. Be my guest, you're going to make me the most
popular guy in town. Why don't you do that?'

That was the end of the conversation. It seemed as clear as clear can get that the establishment was unanimous that Wakeford's source should be hunted down. The next part of that strategy, no doubt, would find purchase by wheezing propaganda that the source – no matter who it was – had motives that were impure. That way, the next part of the strategy would kick into place: there would be thunderous demands to halt the commission in its tracks. It seemed that everybody, including Myburgh, wanted the entire rand catastrophe to be covered up, or at least not exposed.

No such luck, but certainly the intrigue continued. Mbeki's office had started going quiet, says Wakeford, 'and it didn't really worry me'. Just before the commission started its hearings, Wiseman Nkuhlu stopped returning Wakeford's calls. Wakeford remembers:

> Then I knew – I'm going in to be battered, like a lamb to the slaughter, sacrificial lamb type of thing. I hate claiming victimhood but the day I walked in there, besides a few friends who were sitting in the gallery, I was alone – one man. Little Andrew Cadman, who was my lawyer – he still couldn't put his tie on properly – insisted on sitting next to me but he couldn't advise me on anything during my testimony. He is probably a damn smart operator today – at the time he was just very young and inexperienced. I had to literally think on my feet there because when I walked in to bat, I saw the big hired legal guns that were representing the commission and the other parties. One of the commission's lawyers from the law firm Tabacks came to me and said, 'We want you to read out these documents, your first one and your second one.' Then I realised this was a set-up to try to discredit me.

The various parties giving evidence at the commission had appointed very serious, and very expensive, legal brains. Even so, the members of the legal fraternity that did appear during the commission's hearing were hardly impressive on this controversial and crucial occasion. Everyone knew that the rand had been horribly screwed during 2001, yet only Wakeford and a few others were determined to find out why. Everyone else, almost by definition, was involved in some cover-up or other. This is not meant to suggest that all the parties that appeared at the commission were implicated; on the contrary, a good number of the guilty parties simply never appeared.

Alec Brooks, an attorney who had the appearance and demeanour of an overworked sheriff from the old Wild West, on behalf of the Rand Commission, started quietly by asking Wakeford about the role of SACOB. Wakeford responded:

The chamber movement goes back to close to 400 years; it started in France. There are over 10 000 chambers worldwide today, most of whom are affiliated to the International Chamber of Commerce. South Africa has four different chamber movements, one of which is the South African Chamber of Business. Its core focus essentially stands on two legs, one to represent and advocate [the] economic interests of the broad membership through the chambers of commerce at local level, together with the sector representation and of course the corporate membership for direct members of SACOB at a national level. Ultimately to sum up the representative side, it is to protect certain economic interests of the general membership of the chamber movement. The second leg is obviously to facilitate trade and investment through local chambers and through the national chamber.

Wakeford then confirmed that his filings about the rand meltdown had been made in his personal capacity, not as CEO of SACOB, but as a 'concerned citizen of this country'. As he was reading his report into the record, Brooks repeatedly asked about 'the source', with questions such as: 'And whilst you are referring to the source, are you prepared to disclose the source to the commission?' Wakeford made it clear that he was 'not prepared to disclose' his source. A cynical listener may have started to gain the impression that Brooks was badgering Wakeford. Brooks asked, for instance, 'Did you have any proof of that or is this once again your source talking?'

Wakeford replied: 'It is my source talking.' It was as if Brooks failed to understand that Wakeford was a messenger. Brooks continued: 'So you relied solely on what your source told you?' Wakeford replied: 'I relied on that and my source had also indicated, as reflected further in the documentation, that in fact this matter had been reported to the Reserve Bank.'

This was a crucial point. While the likes of Caroline Southey of the *Financial Mail* led the pack of heavies trying to hunt down the identity of the source, it was absolutely clear that the same source, or someone with essentially the same information as Wakeford's source, had started to report the dodgy deals to the Reserve Bank as early as August 2001. All told, it was a wonderful version of smoke-and-mirror tactics. Whether or not the name of the source, or sources, was disclosed, nothing could change what had happened to the rand during 2001. The real questions were whether or not there had been manipulation of the currency during 2001; whether or not unjust profits had been garnered from such manipulation; and which parties had benefited from such profits. It would then be a matter of examining whether such profits could be regarded as licit. If insiders had taken positions in related markets, that had to come out as well. If there were pervasively suspicious trades of short rand and long South African equities, the market makers in those transactions would have to be subpoenaed to give evidence to the commission.

That was never going to happen, and it didn't.

The bloodthirsty bounty hunters chasing down the identity of the 'source' were beyond disingenuous. It seemed that their logic would have been along these lines: if the name of the source is made public, then anything illicit that may have happened involving the rand during 2001 will *ipso facto* become legitimate and legal. It seemed unimaginable that the hunt to find out who had been behind South Africa's biggest financial disaster had long degenerated into a witch-hunt. If the proponents of this propaganda had a more sophisticated plan, or a Plan B, which seemed unlikely, it would probably be that such a witch-hunt would conveniently divert attention from the real issues in play. And as mentioned, there may well have been a case to argue that the commission should have simply shut down before it even started.

Given Brooks's status as an experienced attorney, it is worth further examining his relentless – and hapless – attempts to root out the name of the source:

'Did your source tell you who at the Reserve Bank it was reported to?'
'No.'
'Did your source tell you when it was reported?'
'During the course of last year.'

These were cynical questions. But Wakeford was far too alert to fall into the traps.

'So for the purpose of this sentence you rely solely on what your source said?'
'That is correct.'
'No first-hand knowledge yourself?'
'No first-hand knowledge.'

Brooks seemed almost to be asking if Wakeford had possibly worked at one of the banks, or companies, involved in the deals.

'So could you stop there? Is that what the source told you again?'
'That is correct.'
'Did you check up on that information?'
'No, I did not ...'
'Could you stop there? That information, source information?'
'Source information.'
'Did you check up whether Sasol issued new shares?'
'No, I did not.'

Wakeford had always made it clear that all the information he put forward was based on source information. Eventually, even John Myburgh seemed to feel that Brooks was going too far.

'Mr Brooks, can we not keep this short? Mr Wakeford, this is all based on what somebody told you?'
'That is correct.'
'You do not need to do it sentence by sentence. None of this is from your personal knowledge, am I right?'
'That is correct.'

Wakeford was clear in his criticisms:

Deutsche Bank could also speculate against the falling rand ... and hence enrich itself ... It is of great concern that Deutsche Bank's core management have historically privileged positions and relationships with the Department of Finance and the Reserve Bank, and had therefore created the impression in the market that they specifically could offer these financial products to other companies.

Brooks asked Wakeford what he meant by 'historically privileged positions and relationships'. Wakeford replied: 'I was told that they have great standing; they are revered in those circles. That they also have historically strong connections and the market is fully aware of those, and hence the ability to execute certain transactions.'

Possibly because he was determined to show that a lawyer will do anything for money, Brooks repeatedly tried to catch Wakeford out. He apparently wanted Wakeford to trip up, falter, stutter and stumble. If Brooks had any idea of Wakeford's development as a human being, he may well have chosen a different path of interrogation – something that would have left Brooks looking at least marginally fair and nonpartisan.

Later on, the redoubtable advocate Jeremy Gauntlett, representing the National Treasury, cross-examined Wakeford. There is little doubt that Gauntlett carries wherever he goes one of South Africa's more talented legal minds. It was always going to be interesting to see what kind of interrogation he would put Wakeford through. Gauntlett started by referring to the fact that Wakeford was obliged by circumstances to act in a great rush when he prepared his original letter addressed to President Thabo Mbeki:

'One of the things I wanted to ask you arising from that is that, as you know, in the original report there was a suggestion by your source of some collusion, some kind of unhealthy close relationship between Deutsche Bank and the National Treasury. That of course is not in the second one – is that one of the aspects you thought that actually responsibly you could not include?'

'Yes, that is correct.'

'You in fact, Mr Wakeford, no doubt through your position of CEO of SACOB have a working relationship with the minister of finance and the DG, do you not?'

'We have contacts at various levels in the Department of Finance.'

'Yes, you know the minister and the director general, Mr Wakeford, do you not?'

'I know the minister and the DG, yes, I do.'

'And I take it you would not intend for a moment to reflect either on their integrity and capacity to investigate this matter themselves?'

'No, the investigating body, as I understand it, Sir, is not the Treasury, the investigating or the statutory authority that investigates anything relating to the currency or any, let us call it illegal or unethical behaviour, should be the Reserve Bank.'

'The point is this, that you were raising macroeconomic issues and, I am correct, aren't I, in saying that you did not approach either the minister or the director general before these allegations were made public, did you?'

'I did not.'

Macroeconomic issues included the likes of monetary policy, of which interest-rate adjustment is one of the main tools. Wakeford's main focus had always been on unearthing details of misconduct in the markets. But for reasons unknown, Gauntlett was running Wakeford around with a red herring. On this point, it is worth bearing in mind that South Africa's Constitution provides that 'the primary object of the South African Reserve Bank is to protect the value of the currency ...'

'They [the minister and the director general] in fact tried to reach you, did they not?

'That is after I had already established contact with the Presidency.'

'But you avoided contact with them, did you not?'

'I did, yes.'

'In fact, your PA cancelled one particular meeting which had been set up by the DG with you to try and understand what you had so that at the highest level these aspects could be examined, is that right?'

'That is correct.'

'Is there a reason for this?'

'Well, my understanding at the time, Mr Gauntlett, was that, firstly, according to my source, this had been reported to the Reserve Bank. There was no action on this and as far as I understand, the Ministry of Finance is responsible for policy frameworking and not for the execution of anything in relation to the currency and I saw it fit to make contact with the Presidency and to hand over the information to the president.'

'But did you ask your source when precisely and who was contacted in the Reserve Bank or Treasury in relation to these very serious matters?'

'No, I did not ask my source.'

Gauntlett's intentions were suddenly clear: like every man and his dog, among the elites, that is, the advocate had joined the obsessive hunt for Wakeford's source. Once again, there was no way that Wakeford was going to be led astray by a lawyer's curve balls:

'Did you not think it was obviously important?'

'I think it is important to understand that when you are dealing with a source where a person is frightened and scared and under normal conditions who would not have come forward and provided this information, that the moment you mention a name in the Reserve Bank your source is exposed as well.'

'So you did not verify the source, but then did you then attempt to verify through the sources open to you, given your position in SACOB, which is to ask the Reserve Bank or Treasury has this matter been raised with you during the last year?'

'No, I did not verify it with the Reserve Bank or Treasury.'

'I see. And your report then was compiled during one hour, I think you have indicated, is that right?'

'That is an expression of speech; it was a very short period of time.'

'All right, let us say about an hour, less, more, it does not matter. When you had done this, did you read it back to the source? Did you verify that the source's source was right?'

'I did not read it back to the source, no.'

'Did you try and verify it against any benchmark, the information report?'

'Well, obviously I had made notes and I referred to those notes.'

Wakeford was frustrating Gauntlett at every twist and turn. Gauntlett seemed to think that this was good enough reason to let off some steam:

'But that is senseless, Mr Wakeford. The notes you made came from the source; I am asking about a benchmark outside, you do understand the question? Have you done that?'

'I have not verified it with an outside benchmark, no.'

'Did you, because of the seriousness of the allegations, raise it with the president of SACOB – whether or not you should go public at this stage with what you had?'

'No, I did not raise it with the president or any other executive member of SACOB.'

How much did Gauntlett *really* know about Christoph Köpke, president of SACOB? Who was Köpke connected to, and what were the implications?

'This morning you suggested ... that you speak, I think, in your personal capacity. Is that right?'

'Well, I was approached certainly as the head of SACOB – I cannot imagine why they would approach me for any other reason – but my source approached me as the chief executive officer of SACOB. But one has to say that I did not go to my executive council, to my governing body. I deemed the information to be too sensitive and I believe that it was appropriate to hand over to the president.'

'The information too sensitive for Mr Köpke, the president of SACOB – are you saying that under oath, Mr Wakeford?'

'Too sensitive to hand over to anybody at SACOB.'

'But without being verified by any extraneous source, it could go to the president and the horse [would be] let out of the stable, as you have indicated earlier. Is that right?'

'That is correct.'

'Now, lastly, in relation to the capacity in which you speak because I am a little bit confused. Your later statement indicates in two places that you received the information clearly by virtue of your position in SACOB?'

'That is correct.'

'I see. However, you say in one place that you went to the president as CEO of SACOB and as a concerned citizen, is that right?'

'That is correct.'

'But as I understood your evidence earlier when you were indicating that you spoke in a private capacity, the information that you have passed on, do you say that you passed that on behalf of SACOB or do you not? Which hat, Mr Wakeford, or both?'

'I would say that one could actually try and figure that with two hats. In terms of my general mandate to serve and protect the general interests of my members, I handed it over as CEO of SACOB, but to assume and to say that I had a broad-based knowledgeable mandate amongst my members I think would be false and incorrect.'

'Now, you have said in your statement that Mr Dykes of Nedcor was a believer in something sinister having happened in the marketplace but when you put this view to Mr Mervyn King, the past president of SACOB, and to Köpke, the present president of SACOB, both individuals with enormous standing in the business community in South Africa, they were agnostic on this point, not so?'

'Well, they did not provide further explanations; they were very concerned, I might tell you, but they did not have additional information.'

'And before you made [your claims], what you say in paragraph 1.10 at page 8 was your ultimate judgment call, did you make a separate telephone call to them or anybody else?'

'No, I did not.'

In South Africa's little world of foreign-exchange-control rules, there were no clear-cut channels of approach or communication. That much had been shown in Jeremy Gauntlett's cross-questioning of Wakeford, when he asked why Wakeford had not approached the director general of finance or the finance minister. Likewise, while a number of approaches had been made to the Reserve Bank's James Cross, there was separate information about how Deutsche Bank had approached the National Treasury.

Treasury director general Maria Ramos had found it 'unacceptable and annoying' that she had been approached by Deutsche Bank's Neil Morrison. As managing director of Deutsche Bank Johannesburg, Morrison had sent Ramos a letter asking for her 'in principle view' regarding the proposed structuring of Sasol's acquisition of Condea. She forwarded the letter, marked urgent, to Chris Malan, the Treasury's chief director of financial regulation, for handing over to the Reserve Bank.

The bank's exchange-control department, in turn, was supposedly 'very unhappy' that Deutsche Bank had made a direct appeal to Ramos, as shown in an email that Malan sent to Ramos. Ramos in reply stated: 'Given the circumstances, we should only deal with [Sasol] through the [Reserve Bank]. I am not interested in ensuring that banks get business. I am also quite annoyed by [Deutsche Bank's] behaviour.'[1]

Before he testified, Wakeford and I had met, and I gave him the names that he would be naming in his testimony. He said that he could not comment before he appeared before the commission, but it can be assumed that he had a certain peace of mind that I had independently established what his source had told him. For Wakeford, however, his trump card was that Gobodo Forensics, which had been contracted by the commission as investigators, had independently established that Wakeford's testimony on the transactions was correct: the deals in question involved Deutsche Bank as the common denominator, plus Sasol, Nampak and M-Cell.

The other major accounting houses that had been appointed prior to Gobodo failed to come up with anything relevant – that's when the Presidency intervened and insisted that Gobodo Forensics be appointed, apparently in the belief that Gobodo was not conflicted. The other audit firms were potentially conflicted in relation to their lucrative audit and consulting contracts with the banks. This turned out to be a good decision and the unravelling of vital evidence began to manifest under the un-biased and very smart efforts of Gobodo Forensics, led by one of South Africa's leading lights in the art of forensic accounting: the inimitable George Papadakis.

There were increasing signs that Deutsche Bank was feeling the heat. While Wakeford was testifying before the commission, news leaked out that the head of foreign-exchange dealing at Deutsche Bank Johannesburg, Danny Pienaar, had suddenly quit. He said, of course, that his resignation had nothing to do with the commission. He said that he would be travel-ling abroad for the next four to six months. 'I was just working too much from September [2001] onwards, 16- to 18-hour days,' he told Vernon

Wessels of *Business Report*.[2] Which seemed a little strange: the rand market had been relatively quiet – albeit extremely volatile – after the Reserve Bank had released a new circular on 14 October 2001. It would have been purely speculative to say that had Pienaar been subpoenaed to appear before the commission, the excuse would have been that he had gone fishing. He was going on holiday to Argentina, or so the whispers went: perhaps the rand's implosion was not enough for him. Argentina was very busy with a gigantic economic crisis.

In some senses, Wakeford had split the country. During the lunch break on the day that he testified, I went downstairs from the Sandton Convention Centre to a coffee shop across the street, which had indoor and outdoor tables. It was a pleasant enough pre-autumn day. After a while, Peter Bruce, then editor of *Business Day*, strolled across the road with Hilary Joffe, who had progressed to writing editorials for the newspaper. She was also doing lots of work covering the Rand Commission. They sat down at a table next to me and after a short while, one of them suddenly seemed to realise what they had done. They both stood up and moved to a table as far as possible from me. No doubt if I had overheard their conversation, the world would have come to an abrupt end. The problem was that I had no interest in their conversation, which meant that the world would have been saved.

Apart from Caroline Southey of the *Financial Mail*, it was going to be Amanda Vermeulen at *Finance Week* and Hilary Joffe who would give Wakeford the rudest press treatment. The more that the evidence at the commission confirmed what Wakeford had complained about, the more these three ladies stiffened their backs. All three exhibited bias, possibly in an innocent belief that bankers were the closest manifestations to saints that South Africa had ever been blessed with.

Meanwhile, big-business pressure on Wakeford continued apace. On 8 April, Tony Phillips, the CEO of Barloworld, which in those days was still a relatively notable player in the private sector, sent a letter to SACOB:

Gentlemen,

We have been following with great interest the submissions to the Myburgh Commission on the value of the rand.

We note that the Chief Executive of your organisation took it upon himself to write to the State President, which letter we understand was the reason for the setting up of the commission of inquiry. What is not clear is whether Mr Wakeford is acting as a private citizen or as the CEO of SACOB.

Your comments on his role and what mandate he may have or have had from the members of SACOB would be of great interest to us.

Yours faithfully,

(signed)

A.J. Phillips[3]

The letter from Tony Phillips was like a cardboard cut-out of so much that had preceded it during 2002: an absolute obsession with Wakeford, but no real interest in why, what and how the rand had been trashed during 2001. This was surprising, given Barloworld's ranking as a major importer. It was very strange indeed.

Like so many others, Phillips appeared to be happy to go with the notion that Wakeford's complaint should never have been made at all. At the same time, Phillips was somewhat prejudging the outcome of the commission's work. He knew as well as anyone that the commission was still sitting, and was possibly a long way from handing in its final report. The best of the commission still lay ahead.

***

'In a time of universal deceit – telling the truth
is a revolutionary act.' – George Orwell

On 2 May 2002, George Papadakis of Gobodo Forensics gave evidence to the Rand Commission. When all the expert evidence that was heard by the commission is analysed, this was testimony that ranked among the highest quality.

The investigating team appointed by the commission comprised various experts, with Papadakis as forensic accountant. There were also structured finance specialists and legal resources. Papadakis was team leader. After being appointed, the team reviewed the contents of the Wakeford letter. It then proceeded to interact with the various parties mentioned in the letter, held discussions with the parties and collated documentation. The investigation was limited to Sasol, Nampak and M-Cell, but the team also consulted with Deutsche Bank Johannesburg and Deutsche Securities, also its Johannesburg branch, both representatives of the Deutsche Bank Group. The Papadakis team also consulted with the Department of Finance and the National Treasury as well as the South African Reserve Bank.

Papadakis read into the record that 'we as a team did not verify the validity or authenticity of the relevant records and documentation subjected to an analysis by ourselves. We accepted such documentation at face value unless stated to the contrary in the report.' However, 'should new documentation and/or information be provided to us for whatever reason, our opinions and interpretations may change and an amended report issued if considered necessary'.

Despite the apparent complexities, the Sasol transaction, as structured and implemented by Deutsche Bank, was straightforward. To conclude the purchase of Condea in Germany, Sasol had to pay €350 million to the sellers. To finance this, Sasol would have needed to somehow convert R2.5 billion into €350 million. Due to exchange controls, this was not allowed. Deutsche structured the deal such that Deutsche Bank London would sell R2.5 billion worth of Sasol shares to foreign investors – for hard currency – over a period of 12 months. Sasol bought back the requisite number of shares in itself on the JSE Securities Exchange, and loaned the required bundle to Deutsche Bank London, where it served as security for the €350 million loan that Deutsche Bank London had made to Sasol.

The proceeds from selling the Sasol shares abroad would be used to reduce and finally eliminate the €350 million loan made to Sasol. Any of the Sasol shares on-sold by Deutsche Bank London to non-residents that were later sold to a South African investor were known as flow-back shares. The overall idea was that the net transactions would be 'neutral' for the rand. The foreign shareholders who bought the Sasol shares may one day sell the shares back to a South African investor, but for at least a period of time there would be neutrality for the rand. Eventually, the shares would be sold and that would be negative for the rand. Seen that way, the overall transactions would not be neutral for the rand.

The Papadakis team dealt with the Sasol transaction by taking cognisance of all the legs of the deal, as implemented by Deutsche. This included analysing whether there had been any flow back to South Africa of the Sasol shares. The team conducted this exercise with reference to the definition of flow back as provided by Deutsche Bank. The team understood that the Reserve Bank was approving a share placement. However, after looking carefully at all the legs of the deal, the team was unable to decide whether the transaction was an asset swap or a share placement. If it was an asset swap, the implications would have been negative for the rand.

Then the shockers started. The team established and confirmed that there had in fact been an exchange of rands for foreign currency. An analysis of the implementation of the Sasol transaction indicates that rands were exchanged by Deutsche Bank London for foreign currency, predominantly in the South African foreign-exchange market. On 19 and 20 February 2001, Deutsche Bank London exchanged R2.5 billion for €350 million. The settlement date was 26 February 2001. It was no surprise that the rand had depreciated when this deal went through the market.

Also on 26 February 2001, Sasol paid R2.5 billion to Deutsche Securities Johannesburg. Deutsche Securities placed the R2.5 billion on deposit with Deutsche Bank Johannesburg. The rights to this deposit were ceded as collateral to Sasol International Holdings for the Sasol shares borrowed from Sasol Investment Holdings. On 26 February 2001, Deutsche Bank London paid euros, the equivalent of R2.5 billion, less Deutsche Bank London's fee, to Sasol Offshore; Deutsche Bank Johannesburg paid roughly R2.4 billion to Deutsche Bank London in terms of a South African government bond repurchase agreement concluded with Deutsche Bank London. At this point it may be noted that the Deutsche group had charged Sasol a 'fee' running into tens of millions of rands. It should also be noted that the Deutsche group is a significant player in the South African bond market. The bond 'repurchase' agreement referred to was subject to further investigation.

The next shocker was that the Papadakis team had found that Deutsche Bank did not, before the implementation of the transaction, disclose to the Reserve Bank, and particularly the exchange-control department of the Reserve Bank, the conversion of the rands for euros. Deutsche Bank only disclosed this fact to the Reserve Bank after a review of the Sasol transaction had been initiated – which no doubt had followed the complaints received by James Cross as early as August 2001.

There were more shockers – one on top of the other. The Papadakis team found that in the context of the asset-swap transaction implemented by Deutsche Bank, the following transactions had not been disclosed to the Reserve Bank:

- the scrip lending agreement concluded between Sasol Investment Holdings and Deutsche Securities;
- the conversion of approximately R2.5 billion for €350 million;
- the bond repurchase agreement concluded between Deutsche Bank London and Deutsche Bank Johannesburg;
- the transfer of South African government bonds by Deutsche Bank Johannesburg to Deutsche Bank London as security for the scrip lending agreement; and
- the scrip lending agreement between Deutsche Bank London and Deutsche Bank Johannesburg, whereby Deutsche Bank Johannesburg acted as agent for Deutsche Securities.

The forward sale of Sasol shares between Deutsche Bank London and Deutsche Securities was disclosed to the Reserve Bank, but was not disclosed in the context of the asset swap. The application for the forward sale was made on 9 February 2001, in terms of which permission to trade 50 million Sasol shares was sought. The maturity date of the contract was 31 December 2001.

In short, the Deutsche Group had represented one thing to the Reserve Bank, and had done something very different. The Papadakis team did not make any interpretations as to who had a duty or otherwise to disclose. Crucially, the team established that Deutsche had represented to the Reserve Bank that no currency conversion would take place. This was a specific representation, rather than an omission.

The investigation into the sale of Sasol shares by Deutsche Bank London was initiated, but according to Papadakis, it was not concluded; only certain of the representations made were tested. The Deutsche Bank Group indicated that as at 31 December 2001, possible flow back into South Africa of Sasol shares was about 6 per cent, that is, 2.5 million shares. This figure excluded the shares not on-sold by Deutsche Bank

London. In a letter dated 22 January 2002 – just weeks after Wakeford had blown the whistle – the Reserve Bank asked Deutsche Bank to request Sasol to refinance from abroad the amounts transferred from South Africa in respect of the flow-back sales in order to recoup the loss in foreign currency. This letter was forwarded to Sasol by Deutsche Bank on 4 February 2002. Before the commission even started its hearings, Deutsche and Sasol had been instructed to implement reversals to restore a neutral position to the rand. It was no wonder that nerves were fraying, and that such a gargantuan amount of negative energy had been hurled at Wakeford.

Deutsche Bank London, it must be noted, was not recorded as a shareholder in the Sasol share register. In terms of the Companies Act, the Papadakis team noted, the share register is the definitive source in determining ownership of shares in a company. Deutsche Bank's evidence was that it is difficult, if not impossible, to track flow back, which was a strange and feeble excuse.

The Deutsche Bank Group gave evidence that Sasol shares, to the equivalent of some R2.5 billion, were initially sold to Deutsche Bank London (which was represented to the Reserve Bank as a long-term investor). Deutsche Bank London was then to on-sell these shares to other long-term foreign investors.

Deutsche Bank London was a long-term foreign investor whose only benefit from the shares was the fee earned. According to Deutsche Bank, 39 735 600 Sasol shares were initially placed with Deutsche Bank London; according to the Deutsche Bank Group, as at 31 December 2001, 14 206 933 shares had been on-sold by Deutsche Bank London. The commission investigated a sample of the shares on-sold by Deutsche Bank London and based on the sample could find no evidence that the shares on-sold to long-term foreign investors were settled in foreign currency. All sales were settled in rands.

Deutsche had, of course, mischievously argued during the commission's hearings that its deals, once completed, would have resulted in an inflow of foreign currency. The incomplete analysis of flow backs indicated that Sasol shares had in fact been sold directly, in the first instance, to South African investors.

***

'The money power preys upon the nation in times of
peace and conspires against it in times of adversity. It is more
despotic than monarchy, more insolent than autocracy,
more selfish than bureaucracy.' – Abraham Lincoln

Also on the subject of who knew what, the Papadakis team found from documents and other evidence an indication that Sasol was unaware of all the detail surrounding the basis upon which the transaction was to be implemented by Deutsche Bank.

And the team's analysis of the implementation of the Nampak transaction indicated that rands were again exchanged by Deutsche Bank London for foreign currency in the South African foreign-exchange markets. The Nampak transaction was found to have had as many 'omissions' in terms of disclosure as the Sasol transaction. The Papadakis team again investigated a sample of Nampak shares to determine whether Deutsche Bank London had on-sold Nampak shares to other foreign investors. Based on the sample, and the information appearing in the Nampak share register, the team could not find the specific names of the shareholders that were represented in the Deutsche Bank documentation as being registered as the shareholders. Furthermore, the team could not identify Deutsche Bank London as a registered shareholder. An analysis of the Nampak shares on-sold by Deutsche Bank London to other foreign investors indicated on a sample basis that the shares were in fact on-sold by Deutsche Bank London and that, in fact, all the proceeds were received in rands. This did not look pretty. It seemed that Deutsche had scored a double whammy: it had nakedly sold rands and bought foreign currency, and then sold the Nampak shares to South African investors. As such, the Nampak transaction could not have been more detrimental for the rand.

As in Sasol's case, the documents and evidence indicated that Nampak was not aware of the detail surrounding the basis upon which the transaction was to be implemented by Deutsche.

The M-Cell transaction was similar to those implemented for both Sasol and Nampak, and again, the indication was that M-Cell was not aware of the details surrounding the basis upon which the transaction was to be implemented.

Papadakis was no doubt expecting an interesting time during testimony when he faced Advocate Johan Wasserman, who questioned Papadakis on whether he had 'expressed any views on the bonds purchased by Deutsche Bank London, of which you are well aware'. Papadakis replied that 'as contained in the evidence of the Reserve Bank', the bond transaction was 'effectively in legal terms a purchase and repurchase but in economic terms it was a loan'. This was a crucial distinction.

Then followed a long exchange in which Wasserman insisted that Deutsche Bank London had purchased South African government bonds, and that such a transaction meant that funds, to the tune of R1.2 billion, had flowed into South Africa. Wasserman was just trying to do his job, but he would have assisted himself and his clients greatly if he had instead mentioned a figure of R2.5 billion.

Papadakis was adamant that although he had been told that this was a purchase transaction, in fact it was a repurchase transaction. As such, it was a paper transaction. It was a loan to Deutsche Bank London; in other words, no cash had flowed into South Africa. The 'repurchase' agreement was a nifty piece of smoke and mirrors.

The loan of R2.5 billion had been made to Deutsche Bank London to buy the Sasol shares. As noted, the idea was that Deutsche Bank London would then sell the Sasol shares to investors in London and Europe, leaving the rand cash market out of the loop. Wasserman was heavy about the supposed *purchase* of South African government bonds:

'I just want to know, Mr Papadakis, do you admit or deny that you have been told about the purchase transactions?'

'I have been told about a purchase but it is in fact a repurchase transaction.'

Myburgh stepped in:

'Where is it recorded as a repurchase?'

'It is recorded in the document that I was given.'

'Yes, but is that in the agreement itself or in the records of Deutsche Bank?'

'In the records of Deutsche Bank.'

At which stage Wasserman stepped in again:

'I put it to you that it was in fact a purchase ...'

'The document does not reflect that.'

'But if it was a purchase you would have referred to that?'

'But with reference to the facts, those are not the facts. Now you are asking me to start assuming things that are not facts.'

'Because of the on-placement of shares, you do not think that would have triggered the inflow of currency into the country?'

'We considered that and we deal with it in the report, and we say in the report that we did consider the on-sale of shares by London to other foreign investors. The sample we analysed reflects that all those shares, share sales, were in fact settled in rand. If you now want to assume that those rand are generated by those foreign investors exchanging foreign currency for rand, that would be the correct interpretation. But there is no evidence that those foreign investors who then bought shares from Deutsche Bank London converted foreign currency to acquire rand. Those might have been rand balances that they held.'

Myburgh seemed to be as keen as Wasserman to find proof that foreign-currency cash had been used to buy rand:

'Does that not mean that there is an introduction of foreign currency into the country?'

'No, it means the opposite.'

Silence, and then Wasserman stepped back in:

'Mr Papadakis, the bonds had been acquired by the payment of foreign currency, any bond purchased from a resident involves the payment of foreign currency?'

'You assume the purchase from a resident?'

'From a resident, I put it to you that the purchases were from a resident, that would have the impact of the inflow of foreign currency?'

'I have seen no evidence that the purchase was from a resident.'

At this point, Wasserman, frustrated, decided to take the ad hominem route – play the man, not the ball:

'I see, there you express [yourself] as a chartered accountant?'

'As I said, that is the view we express as a team comprising not only me as a chartered accountant but structure-finance specialists as well that were involved in the analysis of the implementation of this transaction.'

It seemed strange that Wasserman wanted to wobble the hearings by questioning Papadakis's qualifications. The issue in focus was purely of an accounting nature: had there been a discrete flow of cash into South Africa, involving South African bonds?

'I see, the fact that the foreign currency that was generated was used to discharge a liability of a resident which the resident had to settle in foreign currency, would that have a negative or a positive impact on the currency reserves of the country?'

'Not in this instance.'

'Do you read as a chartered accountant or as a lawyer, or what [are] you reading as?'

'We read it as a team comprising forensic accountants and structure-finance specialists and the legal team as well, the legal resources.'

Wasserman wobbled further, and tried to put words into Papadakis's mouth:

'It is quite startling that in your final report, you had come to the conclusion that you do not have the in-house expertise to come to a positive conclusion as to the impact these transactions had on the depreciation of the rand. That is basically what you are saying. Correct?'

'We are saying we are not in a position to conclude whether these transactions caused, contributed or gave rise to the depreciation of the rand.'

Wasserman weakened to the point where he was beating around the proverbial bush:

'What I have said is we were surprised that he was called, being a chartered accountant, to come and to give recommendations to the commission in view of the fact that these are issues upon which only the commission can make the call.'

'We do not seek to make recommendations and I do not think our report makes any recommendations to the commission. Our objective is to place facts before the commission as we see them, as we investigate them and to allow the commissioners to make a decision. That is what we understand our role to be. Not to make recommendations.'

For anyone listening closely enough, the evidence presented by Papadakis, which aligned with the allegations that had been made by Wakeford, was devastating, particularly for Deutsche Bank. Deutsche's legal representatives were unable to counter, never mind deny, the long list of factors that the Deutsche Group had hidden from the Reserve Bank. These were rough times for many lawyers, who, nevertheless, were generating millions of rands in fees. Just as Gauntlett's line of questioning of Wakeford was strange and meandering, so Wasserman's futile attempts to badger Papadakis were embarrassing.

At this point, besides the poor showing of various legal representatives, it is worth considering some other constraints faced by the Rand Commission. For one thing, there was a degree of familiarity among some of the faces at the commission. Tito Mboweni, governor of the Reserve Bank, had come to know John Myburgh when the latter sat as a judge in the labour courts and Mboweni was minister of labour. This proved nothing, but it certainly raised the odd eyebrow. The issue of conflicts, or perhaps more politely, potential conflicts, applied to a great number of witnesses, and also to certain assistants to the commission. It is an understatement to say that the South African foreign-exchange market is small. As commissioner Christine Qunta would later put it in her minority report for the Rand Commission on 1 August 2002:

The assistants [to the commission] sometimes had rendered services or were still rendering services to particular institutions and had to recuse themselves. The commission tried its best to manage such conflicts of interest. For example, from among the local experts that gave evidence during the first week of hearings, only two economists, Jammine and Glynos, were not affiliated to a financial institution that fell within the terms of reference of the commission. It is important to point out though that the experts from various financial institutions indicated that they were making statements as independent witnesses.[4]

Among other constraints faced by the commission:

- There was insufficient time to complete the various investigations to the extent that would have been desirable, or even logical.
- The areas of investigations inevitably dealt with information that was of a very sensitive nature, and if such information fell into the hands of competitors or even the general public, it could harm the interest of certain corporates or institutions. A public hearing was probably not the most appropriate forum for conducting such investigations.
- The investigation undertaken by the commission involved a complex exercise, which, ideally, should have taken into account the experiences of other countries, given that financial markets are globalised. Only three international experts were called before the commission; none had specific expertise in the rand, and certainly not in the who, what and why of the rand currency market during 2001.

Then there was the question of how the authorised currency dealers were investigated. This covered the activities of ABSA, Standard Bank, Board of Executors, Citibank, J.P. Morgan, FirstRand, NIB Bank, Investec and Deutsche Bank. The information gathered by the commission's team relied entirely on the responses by the authorised dealers to a questionnaire drafted by the team and sent to them. There was no independent verification of the data. All information was aggregated.

As Qunta would explain:

The team could, for example, have selected a few transactions and investigated them in detail. The team gathered very valuable information about transactions and did observe some trends that should have prompted further investigation but did not. For example, the data collected showed that the average balances on the 10 largest client foreign-currency (CFC) accounts increased over the period October to

December 2001, which is an indication that clients of banks tended to hold more foreign currency and were reluctant to hold rand.

Yet nothing was done to investigate this phenomenon by way of sample investigations. No attempt was made to investigate the profits made by the authorised dealers and the fact that there was a correlation between such profits, the bid-offer spread and the depreciation of the rand. The team also found that an analysis of authorised dealers' client transactions showed that the clients of authorised dealers were reluctant to hold rand. The moving of clients' funds from rand into foreign currency resulted in a negative impact on the exchange rate of the rand. No further investigation was done.

There was overwhelming circumstantial evidence that the rand had been shorted during 2001, and viciously so during the final quarter. Despite the volume of transactions implemented in the markets, there is no question that data could have been accessed and analysed. From that, it would have been possible to identify the key traders who had shorted the rand. These individuals could then have been subpoenaed to give evidence at the commission.

I reiterate that there was never any chance of that.

What did emerge during evidence is that the Reserve Bank monitors just 1 per cent of foreign-exchange transactions. The balance of 99 per cent is administered by the authorised dealers. This raised the question of whether authorised dealers were complying with their obligations as co-administrators of exchange-control regulations. No proper investigation was undertaken on the management of CFC accounts, non-resident transactions on the JSE Securities Exchange and the Bond Exchange of South Africa, or the treasury departments of authorised dealers.

So yet another conflict of interest was exposed: authorised dealers were both exchange-control administrators and beneficiaries of business from corporates.

Separately, it was apparent from the figures provided by the Reserve Bank for outflows during the course of 2001 that institutional investors were responsible for a significant outflow of capital: this also warranted further, and very detailed, investigation. This was not done.

A number of interesting conclusions could be reached from certain statistics. Not only was participation by non-resident banks in the rand market reduced during the latter parts of 2001, but local authorised dealer activity also slid. According to data available from the South African Reserve Bank and cited by economist George Glynos, volumes traded by local banks reached a peak in October 2001 but then dropped off considerably in November and more so in December. According to Glynos, the extent of the decline of trading volumes by non-residents in the forward and spot market in December confirmed that there was speculation in those markets.

Qunta was of the view that in light of evidence placed before the commission, speculative activity, both legal and illegal, and both by non-residents and residents, contributed to the rapid depreciation of the rand, especially during the second half of 2001. On account of the lack of investigation of certain crucial areas of speculative activities, such as proprietary trading of authorised dealers and CFC accounts, Qunta concluded that the commission was unable to establish the exact percentage of such speculative activity.

***

'Give me control of a nation's money and I care not
who makes the laws.' – Amschel Rothschild

Towards the end of May 2002, as the Rand Commission was listening to the final batches of evidence that would be tendered, Deutsche Bank capitulated. It had attempted, cynically, to seal a confidential settlement with the Reserve Bank. But news leaked out and parts of the deal were made available in the public domain:

Confidential settlement agreement

This document sets out the basis on which Deutsche Bank AG, Johannesburg Branch ('DBJ') and the Exchange Control Department of the South African Reserve Bank ('Exchange Control') have agreed to settle their differences regarding the application for and implementation of the 'asset swaps'/share placements arranged by Deutsche Securities (Proprietary) Limited ('Deutsche Securities') for Sasol Limited ('Sasol'), Nampak Limited ('Nampak') and M-Cell Limited ('M-Cell') (the 'share placements') and the transactions entered into in relation thereto by members of the Deutsche Bank Group (the 'Asset Swaps/Share Placements and Related Transactions'). DBJ and Exchange Control have agreed that the Deutsche Bank Group will implement a set of transactions, described in Annexure 1. The intention is to address Exchange Control's concerns regarding reserves neutrality, while at the same time not requiring the unwinding of any of the Asset Swaps/Share Placements and Related Transactions. This settlement is made without admission of liability or wrongdoing on the part of the Deutsche Bank Group.[5]

Further details, however, leaked out and were recorded by journalist Vernon Wessels and published in *Business Report* on 29 May 2002. He put it so:

Deutsche Bank would replenish the R800 million foreign exchange it stripped out of the country through a complicated structured finance deal agreed by the Reserve Bank ... Deutsche, Europe's largest bank, has to put R10 million on deposit without interest with the central bank until it has reversed financing deals on behalf of Sasol and Nampak and replenished the perceived loss of foreign exchange from South Africa. Exchange control regulations state a number of ways in which an errant authorised dealer will be penalised for breaking the rules – one of which includes a deposit with the central bank which will not be returned should it again step over the line ...

Deutsche in London attracted fees of 2.5% of the total value of its deals on behalf of the local firms. This would amount to almost 9 million euros (R90 million) in the 350 million euros [Sasol] transaction.

The inconclusiveness of the deal brought into question whether exchange controls could be effectively policed as it showed the regulations were open to misinterpretation and manipulation, market players said.

The settlement[6] prevents the Reserve Bank from taking any further action against Deutsche. This has raised concerns that the commission may not be able to recommend that any fines be brought against Deutsche should it come to a different finding, as a penalty would have to be imposed on Deutsche by the Reserve Bank's exchange control department.

Business Day's 'Bottom Line' commentary took a somewhat philosophical line: 'The settlement hammered out between the Reserve Bank and Deutsche Bank after a seven-month review of asset-swap deals arranged by the bank, was sealed on the basis that they "agree to disagree" on their effect on reserves, and therefore on the depreciation of the currency.'[7]

With hindsight, offering to implement 'reserves-positive' transactions totalling R800 million as part of the settlement may not have been too wise on Deutsche's part: it created the perception that this was some form of punishment. The bank was adamant that the transactions were a gesture of goodwill and did not imply any admission of wrongdoing, but in politically charged circumstances, perceptions sometimes count more than reality.

It seemed a little eerie. Just months prior, on 27 March 2002, Deutsche Bank had denied allegations that it and Sasol had, according to one press report,

> colluded in a complex plan to thrash the rand thereby profiting from its collapse. Deutsche Bank Johannesburg MD Niall Carroll, commenting on a letter published this week in the *Financial Mail*, said there was no reason whatever for the bank to hammer the rand …
>
> Carroll insisted the allegations were completely inaccurate, and defamatory of Deutsche Bank. He said: 'We did a legitimate asset swap transaction with the permission of the Reserve Bank as it was currency neutral.'
>
> CEO of Sasol, Pieter Cox, also denied the allegations through a spokesman, and would not comment until the company had appeared before a commission.[8]

Perhaps the most significant aspect of Deutsche Bank's capitulation was simply that it became public knowledge. In a 'normal' situation, assuming the Reserve Bank had indeed decided to follow through and investigate the deals that James Cross was given information on, any settlement would have taken place in the background, completely sealed off from the public domain. First, this is in the nature of South Africa's exchange controls, administered under a monster cloud of secrecy. Second, it would have saved Deutsche Bank from any kind of embarrassment.

On this score, it is worth examining in more detail the evidence that Cross gave to the commission on 24 April 2002, to develop the issue of how in August 2001 the head of a local branch of a foreign bank had requested an interview with Cross together with a colleague. Cross was close to naming the bank and he directly mentioned the name of the major corporate. Cross wrote in an affidavit:

> On enquiring as to the reason for the interview, I was told that the bank wished to test a financing mechanism for offshore acquisitions by South African companies ... At the meeting a structure was described relating to bridging finance provided by the offshore parent bank pending the issue of shares offshore by the SA company, in order to acquire the offshore investment ... placing shares in a large parcel or a once-off transaction for a sizeable amount would, in all likelihood, damage the share price of the SA company in question.
>
> A method had been devised whereby the shares of the offshore company to be acquired would be purchased by means of an offshore loan. As and when the shares of the SA company were placed, piecemeal on the offshore markets, the loan would gradually be expunged until sufficient shares had been placed to make the acquisition in accordance with exchange-control regulations. In order to secure the offshore bridging finance the parent bank had to rely on security provided in SA by the corporate making the offshore acquisition.
>
> For credit purposes, the offshore bank was required to sell forward rand for dollars to the equivalent of the security provided by the domestic corporation. We were asked whether or not the Bank would object to such a structure being put in place. After discussing the matter for some time and asking further questions the meeting concluded that we could, inter alia, not agree to the forward sale of rand as requested.
>
> ... sometime later in September or early October I received a phone call from another person working for the same institution. This person stated that according to information received by their bank certain offshore acquisitions by SA companies had been financed by

using the domestic balance sheets of the company in question to fund the offshore acquisition, which would normally have been in contravention of the exchange-control regulations. From what I can recall, Sasol's name was mentioned. I said that I had no detailed knowledge of any specific approval given to this company and asked whether or not the methodology applied was the same or similar to the example given by a colleague in the interview mentioned above. It was intimated that the method used seemed to have been the same or similar and that the result would have been, in their view, negative for the domestic currency.[9]

This meant that from around early October 2001, the game was on: Deutsche Bank was under investigation along with various transactions it had implemented, not least the one involving Sasol. For his efforts, Cross was fingered as Wakeford's source – a claim that nobody could prove, and which was simply untrue: an invention of some degenerate mind.

Smaller fry than Deutsche Bank had a tougher time. Alick Bruce-Brand, a Reserve Bank official, told the commission that in 2001, 166 transactions, worth an aggregate R1.8 billion, had been referred to the Reserve Bank as suspicious. The bank had launched investigations into 71 of the cases, valued at R100 million; 39 cases, worth R203 million, had been referred to the South African Police Service.

Cross's evidence would never have vaguely seen the light of day were it not for the appointment of the Rand Commission. Likewise, it was because the Rand Commission was appointed that the details of the Deutsche Bank capitulation went public. And it was Kevin Wakeford's whistle-blowing that had led to the appointment of the Rand Commission in the first place. Whether or not the Reserve Bank would have investigated the deals in the absence of the Rand Commission remains a moot point.

7

Riding side-saddle

The commission delivers two reports … Southey continues her belly-aching campaign … Parker speaks of 'disuse' of exchange controls … Maduna opts for premature closing of commission … Sasol's Kruger launches vitriolic attack on Wakeford … Mboweni continues to lash out … Köpke fires Wakeford.

'Like wind currents and weather patterns, international capital flows carry with them a measure of benefits and risks. Let me try briefly to pin down what makes them so powerful and so protean in their effects on the international financial landscape. I find it helpful, as a mnemonic, to think of their main characteristics in terms of what I shall refer to as the six "V"s: Virtue, Volume, Variety, Velocity, Volatility, and Viciousness.'
– Joseph Yam, CEO of the Hong Kong Monetary Authority, at the Credit Suisse First Boston Asian Investment Conference, March 1999

The Rand Commission published two sets of findings. The majority report was signed on 30 June 2002 by John Myburgh and Mandla Gantsho, two of the three commissioners. The key conclusion was that the transactions put in place by Deutsche Bank for offshore financing deals it had implemented on behalf of Sasol and certain others had contributed to the long-term depreciation of the rand in 2001. A minority report was published by Christine Qunta, the other commissioner. She was far harsher in her findings.

At the heart of the Rand Commission was the distinction between the transactions that the commission investigated (of which the biggest, by far, involved Deutsche Bank and Sasol) and the trading – general and specific – of the rand during 2001. The commission had no mandate to investigate the trading of the rand during 2001, so when evidence at the heart of that process – such as the devastating testimony of Mark Parker, executive general manager, treasury, at Nedcor Bank – came to light, it was treated as interesting, but off limits.

At the same time, Deutsche Bank, in particular, had no motive to re-direct attention to the actual trading of the rand during 2001. There was every chance that Deutsche Bank would have done itself a severe injustice had it taken that route. This irony assisted those who had wished the commission away from day one – not least Mboweni and his apparent lapdogs, such as Caroline Southey. The trading of the rand during 2001 not only took place in a tainted regulatory environment, but it was also subject to the whims of traders who had little regard in general for rules and regulations. When those rules and regulations were being ignored, bypassed or blatantly messed with, the consequences of unethical behaviour were devastating.

Indeed, beyond rules and regulations, there were also ethics to be considered – or the lack of them. Mark Langley, the former head of foreign exchange at Crédit Agricole Indosuez, told the commission that although traders were expected to commit to a code of ethics, these were largely ignored. Asked if traders would pass an exam on ethics, Langley replied: 'They would all fail. The book is dumped in front of you. It is signed and never read.' Traders engaged in 'unethical' behaviour by colluding with dealers from other banks to drive a currency in one direction. There were also cases where trades were registered and then cancelled, creating the impression of a deal being done. Banks known to be very heavy transactors would sometimes attempt to disguise their activity by asking another bank to execute part of a trade on the big bank's behalf. Such unethical deals were limited, but did take place, said Langley, citing his 21 years of experience as a trader.[1]

***

During the commission's hearings, Deutsche Bank had it coming from all angles and tangents, and countered with weak responses such as claiming that Deutsche Bank London was not obliged to apply to the Reserve Bank for permission to implement certain legs of the deals. The situation was messy. Myburgh and Gantsho found that the deals were not unethical and recommended no further action be taken against Deutsche, as it had reached a settlement with the Reserve Bank. The commissioners found, however, that the Sasol and Nampak deals were 'contrary to the spirit of exchange controls' because of a lack of 'upfront and complete disclosure' by Deutsche on hedging transactions, which depleted South Africa's foreign reserves by more than R2 billion.

Somehow, it seemed that only the very finest of lines could be drawn between 'not unethical' and 'contrary to the spirit'. In her findings, Qunta said that the Reserve Bank in its evidence to the commission stated that Sasol and Deutsche Bank Johannesburg had contravened exchange-control regulations. The Reserve Bank, in response to a series of questions from the chairman of the commission, had on 6 June 2002 advised that Deutsche Bank Johannesburg had contravened exchange-control regulations. The evidence of the Reserve Bank had, of course, been corroborated by the commission's own investigative team.

As mentioned, the distinction between transactions involving foreign exchange (such as Sasol's acquisition of Condea) and transactions that involved the straight speculative trading of the rand had, in effect, been separated by the commission's terms of reference. The commission could only investigate certain named transactions involving specifically Sasol, Nampak and M-Cell, along with Deutsche Bank as the common denominator.

Sadly, there was a further distinction. Qunta said that attorneys for Deutsche Bank had 'correctly argued' that the terms of reference required the commission to make a two-stage inquiry. It would establish whether the transactions in question contributed to or gave rise to the depreciation of the rand. Only if the answer was in the affirmative could the commission then go on to make a finding on whether or not the transaction was illegal or unethical.

There had been no conclusive finding on the first stage, and, therefore, the commission refrained from making a finding on the second stage.

However, according to Qunta,

both counsel for the Reserve Bank and Deutsche Bank make a factual error in asserting that there was no evidence before the commission that the transactions had an impact on the exchange rate. In response to a question by Deutsche Bank's counsel, Mr Grove from the Reserve Bank stated that he was not able to state that the transactions had an impact on the exchange rate of the rand. This is quite different from stating that it had no impact and no such assertion was made by the Reserve Bank.

***

'If the American people ever allow private banks to control the issuance of their currency, first by inflation and then by deflation, the banks and corporations that will grow up around them will deprive the people of all their property until their children will wake up homeless on the continent their fathers conquered.' – Thomas Jefferson

It is worth going back to 10 May 2002, when Caroline Southey, under the guise of an 'Editor's note', published the following in the *Financial Mail*:

So Judge John Myburgh has met his deadline and delivered his interim report to the president on the reasons behind the collapse of the rand late last year. But we, the public, are unlikely to see it.

There's a strong case to be made for Myburgh's report to be placed in the public domain, particularly given the dodgy basis on which the inquiry was called in the first place. The reputations of individuals and institutions are at stake. They, and we, have a right to know what has been unearthed.

The credibility of the entire exercise would also be given a significant boost if the judge forced SACOB CEO Kevin Wakeford to name the source behind his letter to the president which sparked the inquiry. Myburgh has the same legal powers as a High Court judge. He has the discretion to decide whether a witness has answered questions 'fully and satisfactorily' and, if not, to find the witness in contempt and impose a fine or prison sentence. Why Myburgh hasn't forced the issue remains a mystery. The naming of the source matters. What if, as rumours suggest, the source works for (or used to work for) a bank that would benefit from the reputation of one of its chief competitors being damaged?

The other consideration is that innocent individuals are being fingered. The rumour machine is once again being stoked. Denials from affected individuals are as emphatic as they were from James Cross, whose name was also bandied about but who was able to make a statement to the inquiry. Others are less fortunate. They are suffering unfairly and unduly and are powerless to do anything about it. Myburgh should put an end to the nonsense.

For one thing, Southey was categorically clear that she would have been happy, if not delighted, to see Wakeford permanently removed from any noticeable function in society. This was one of Southey's least fanciful inventions.

It is of note that when the Reserve Bank, in evidence to the commission, stated that Sasol and Deutsche Bank Johannesburg had contravened exchange-control regulations, Southey was silent, along with the vast majority of the press. When Deutsche Bank capitulated and agreed to initiate R800 million worth of transactions that would create conversions of foreign currency into rands, Southey was as silent as a lamb. As ever, she remained obsessed with the identity of Wakeford's source, despite overwhelming evidence that delinquency in the currency markets was known, and specifically by the Reserve Bank, long before Wakeford had opened his mouth. If Southey had been just 1 per cent alive to proceedings at the Rand Commission, she would have been aware that James Cross later handed in a statement in evidence to the commission. Southey, indeed, referred to Cross in her editorial.

But she only referred to the quaint notion that Cross had denied being Wakeford's source. Cross had given other information that was of serious importance to understanding the rand market during 2001; Southey completely ignored this information. There was no reason to believe that the press would ignore, or perhaps did not comprehend, one of the most crucial issues unearthed during the Rand Commission hearings: the damage wrought by the Reserve Bank's circular published on 14 October 2001.

Even the majority report singled out the Reserve Bank as contributing to the rand's steep plunge, specifically when it issued the circular that called for immediate compliance with all exchange-control rules and regulations. The circular read in part: 'The Reserve Bank stands ready to take appropriate firm steps against trading activities inconsistent with existing rules and regulations.'

The circular also stipulated that all currency trades would have to be supported by documentary proof that there was underlying trade or investment transactions. The circular outlawed the financing of short-term rand positions in the currency market – in other words, borrowing rands to sell for dollars. It was already illegal for non-residents to borrow rands to play the currency markets. The October statement reinforced a prior rule that was either not properly implemented or was being abused. This much was also reflected in the evidence given by the various bank treasury bosses who had testified before the commission.

More than one piece of evidence mentioned that many players in the foreign-exchange markets found the 14 October Reserve Bank circular to be confusing. But there was a lot more to the story. Mark Parker of Nedcor Bank gave monumentally insightful evidence at the Rand Commission. He was questioned at length, under oath in public testimony:

'You say that there were certain existing rules which had not been strictly enforced by the Reserve Bank. To your knowledge, were there rules, and do you have any information to back up that statement?'

'Yes, the rules that we are referring to specifically relate to the requirement of authorised dealers to determine whether there is an underlying transaction before quoting a foreign bank a dollar-rand rate. It was a matter of asking if there was an underlying transaction and getting confirmation; yes, before quoting this became impractical and those who tried to do it strictly would then be bypassed by the foreign banks seeking rand prices. So essentially it was a measure that had fallen into disuse as a result of market practices, it was not practical to do that in the normal course of trading.'

'You would merely ask verbally from the counterparty whether there was an underlying transaction and based on the answer given by that counterparty, it would then be accepted as correct without checking whether in fact there is one?'

'That is correct. It may on occasions be verbally, alternatively it would be through the electronic dealing mechanism of Reuters where you would have asked that question and had it on record.'

'And then, as you say, it sort of fell away because of the market exigency?'

'That is correct.'

'Now it then means that authorised dealers did not comply with exchange-control regulations, is that what you say, strictly?'

'The answer to that is yes but with the knowledge of the central bank of the impracticalities of applying that specific requirement.'

'Did you communicate then to the Reserve Bank that you are not able to enforce the exchange-control regulations with regard to the underlying commitment?'

'I believe the central bank was aware of the issues relating to that specific—'

'No, that was not my question; my question is, did Nedcor inform the Reserve Bank that it was not able to comply with that particular rule?'

'Yes, we did.'

'Was that in writing or oral?'

'No, that would have been oral, in discussion around the market.'

'And what was the response from the Reserve Bank?'

'I do not recall their specific response on those discussions; I would have to consult with colleagues of mine who had been at those specific discussions. I think the answer was that it would have been noted and that is subject to confirmation.'

So it was categorically clear that a number of players in the markets had alerted the Reserve Bank to possible mischief in the market, as early as August 2001, when outsiders had made contact directly with James Cross. Once again, this emphasised not only that Kevin Wakeford was anything but a lone-wolf whistle-blower, but that there was widening knowledge of misconduct in South Africa's foreign-exchange markets, although that knowledge was most certainly not in the public domain.

The questioning of Parker continued:

'The actual statement now – if we could come to the statement of 14 October. We heard evidence from the governor of the Reserve Bank, Mr Mboweni, that the reason for the statement was that they had begun, in fact from Mr Bruce-Brand too, that they had been, the Reserve Bank, had been informed by players in the market that exchange-control regulations were not being enforced properly and that there were in fact problems in that regard and as a result the Reserve Bank felt it was important to restate its intention to enforce such exchange control and in the course of that evidence Mr Mboweni indicated that while it is possible, as you have indicated and several other banks, that the effect of that statement, intended or not, was to reduce liquidity in the market. But he has also given an indication that he thinks it may have gone the other way, that players who were engaging in speculative activities without underlying commitments, a whole range of other practices, once they discover that the Reserve Bank would in fact enforce those regulations, they exited the market. Would you have a comment on that?'

'You know I am not sure as to the reasons why they would have exited the market. I think they were perhaps not happy with the compliance requirement and our statistics illustrate the response to that. I think there was confusion as to specifically what was allowed and I think in the early stages just after that was communicated verbally a number of participants understood that spot trading even was not allowed. It in fact turned out that spot trading was allowed, there was no restriction on that, which was subsequently clarified. So it was just a function of additional confusion in the market, and I guess, perhaps, not just for compliance reasons, but maybe for risk reasons, certain participants elected to withdraw.'

'Did Nedcor attend the meeting that the Reserve Bank called on Sunday the 13th, I think it was 13 October. We have heard evidence that a meeting was called where the senior people, I think the heads of treasury, were called by the Reserve Bank to explain the import of their statement that was going to be issued the following day. Was Nedcor present at that meeting?'

'Yes, we were.'

'And the issues you have raised here with regard to the circulars, did you raise any objection or any concern with the Reserve Bank at that stage?'

'Not at that meeting.'

'Did you understand the rationale for the circular?'

'Yes, we did.'

'And was Nedcor part of the authorised dealers who the Reserve Bank worked with to draft a circular to clarify exactly what was contained in that statement?'

'Yes.'

'Which then went out, I believe, to the foreign banks. Were you part of the drafting of that?'

'Yes, we were.'

'Just a last question – are you, as Nedcor, are you involved in both the inter-bank market and you also trade on behalf of clients, would I be correct?'

'We participate in the inter-bank market and we provide a service to clients in terms of foreign exchange.'

'Would you comment on what transactions you consider that may be not illegal but unethical?'

'I think, it is a difficult question to answer, but any form of price manipulation probably falls into the category of unethical. We have seen instances of rumours being started by participants in the market to get a move going specifically relating to the rand that happened on a number of occasions during the last few years. We would deem that to be highly unethical. Possibly front running of large orders, although that is difficult to pin down specifically. Dealing on incorrect rates and holding a counterparty to that would be deemed to be unethical behaviour and the same applies to holding patently incorrect rates, holding brokers to that, that is covered in the code of conduct, advising of customers, giving them wrong information to induce them to deal would also fall into the category of unethical. As it happens, unethical could also be that in thin markets where stop-loss orders have been left with a bank to try and force the market in a direction to trigger those stop-loss orders. Those are the instances, the examples, that come to mind.'

So the Reserve Bank's rules had become 'impractical', and authorised dealers who tried to enforce them 'strictly' were bypassed by certain foreign banks. The Reserve Bank's 14 October 2001 circular followed a 'long period' during which exchange-control regulations had been allowed to fall into disuse – with the knowledge of the Reserve Bank. While South Africa's authorised foreign-currency dealers were required to ensure that all rand trades by foreign banks were backed by real underlying transactions, the rules had in some cases not been clearly enforced.

After the infamous circular had been released, many players fled the rand market, creating illiquidity. Parker emphasised that foreign banks were unhappy about the 'confusion' created by the circular, and that some had left the market, never to return. The circular required authorised dealers to obtain certificates of compliance from non-resident banks to the effect that all rules and regulations had been observed. Parker said that only 35 per cent of 165 foreign counterparties contacted by Nedcor had acknowledged compliance.

This was crucial evidence and, of course, it was buried in the press, if mentioned at all. The only interpretation was that while there were many foreign players in the rand market, the majority were trading at the margin, like buskers. As in many foreign-exchange markets, there were a few big players, and most of them had a presence in South Africa, allowing further and specialised access to the most intimate details of the rand currency market. Above all else there was an atmosphere, if not a culture, of non-compliance. There was a certain degree of compliance, but the majority of players were non-compliant. The corollary was that the few big players could flex the biggest muscles, but could also do so within a relatively polluted system, and, most importantly, could undoubtedly move the market, especially when the trend line was intensifying in a certain direction.

***

'Therefore, based on the commission's definition of what constitutes a breach of the spirit of exchange controls, the transactions ran contrary to the spirit of exchange controls in that there was a lack of up front and complete disclosure with regard to the transactions and the foreign reserves were depleted to the extent that rand was exchanged for foreign currency in the local forex market.' – Rand Commission majority report

The Rand Commission was closed down in mid-July by minister of justice Penuell Maduna. Paul Setsetse, spokesman for Maduna, said that the two Rand Commission reports would be released in late July. Christine Qunta would issue a dissenting finding, recommending, inter alia, further investigations leading to possible prosecutions. Wakeford interpreted the closing date of the commission as premature. He had further concerns:

It was obvious that the commission failed to conduct widespread investigations and limited its efforts to certain areas. Although the two executive summaries differ on some of their findings and recommendations, both reports refer to elements of delinquency in the markets. It is important to note that the commission did *not* investigate the possibility of collusion and manipulation in the markets.

Whereas the Enron and WorldCom scandals, among others, triggered one of the most comprehensive rounds of corporate reform in the US, and spurred reforms in a number of other countries, it seemed that South Africa was absolutely determined to cover up as much as possible in and around the rand market, especially during 2001. During the hearings, Qunta had asked, 'Mr Chairman, but surely we should be looking at other evidence in relation to what Mr Wakeford is saying?'

Wakeford recalls:

I gave my evidence, and I reminded them at the commission – I'm not a prosecutor, I'm not a forensic investigator. I was given critical information in the context of the financial crisis. I called for a commission of inquiry. It is your duty to establish the facts. Why are you trying to criticise what I've given you when I'm merely handing over information I've received? What is the story here?

But clearly what they were trying to do, they knew they could discredit me. In the press the next day *Business Day*'s front page led with the headline: 'Wakeford's damp squib'. Yet a few weeks later, after George Papadakis had led evidence, backed by forensic investigators together with lawyers, it was a very different story. And that's when *Business Report* had the headline 'Deutsche falls on sword'. Deutsche fell on the sword for those three companies because the companies, the corporations involved, their view was, we were taking advice from corporate financiers, we don't understand this stuff.

According to Wakeford, the moment the Rand Commission was closed, his exit as CEO of SACOB had to be orchestrated. He knew this, counterintuitively, because the powers that be at SACOB 'begged' him to stay on. Wakeford's contract expired in June 2002. He said: 'Gentlemen, I think it's time I leave.' Christoph Köpke and his board conveyed a simple message to Wakeford: 'You stay. We want you to stay.' SACOB, however, wouldn't give Wakeford a new contract – he went onto rolling employment, month to month. Wakeford recalls: 'Even Mandela's office phoned me to congratulate me that I'd been asked to stay on.' Zelda la Grange had left a message on behalf of Mandela. He also recalls that at the closing of the commission by Maduna, the press were told that the commission had been instigated by Wakeford and nobody else. Maduna's attitude regarding Wakeford came across as hostile and irritated, and he then knew he was truly on his own: the multiple reports received by government and their agencies had mysteriously evaporated.

Despite the findings of the Rand Commission and, more importantly, the devastating evidence given by the likes of Mark Parker, as well as Deutsche Bank's R800 million capitulation, the long knives remained out for Wakeford. A number of companies – indeed, a growing number – were withdrawing as members of SACOB. Worse, perhaps, various chambers of commerce were also pulling out. In due course, exits would be announced by the Cape Town Chamber, the Durban Chamber and the Johannesburg Chamber, the three biggest metropolitan chambers in the country. All had been pressurised by heavyweight corporate members rather than the rank-and-file family businesses that represented the vast majority of SACOB's members but in aggregate lacked the membership revenue that flowed from the mighty corporates at local and national level – a metaphoric reminder of South Africa's skewed ownership patterns. In a democracy, numbers should count, but seemingly, if not demonstrably, it is the quantum of revenue that holds far greater power.

Many nerves were still raw. On 17 September 2002, Sasol chairman Paul Kruger launched what *Business Day* journalist John Fraser described as 'a vitriolic attack' on Wakeford. Fraser wrote:

Explaining for the first time Sasol's recent decision to pull out of Sacob, Kruger has also turned up the heat on the organisation over its support for Wakeford, accusing it of being an accomplice to his 'contemptible' behaviour. Kruger's comments, which appear in advertisements in some SA newspapers this morning, form part of his chairman's statement in Sasol's annual report.

Kruger says that instead of distancing itself from Wakeford's 'unfounded and defamatory allegations', Sacob stood by him and renewed his contract. The rand inquiry had since 'exonerated Sasol from any misconduct'. It was 'most regrettable' that the chamber did not publicly distance itself from the allegations made by its CEO, 'implying a degree of complicity' with them.

But Sacob officials said some of Sasol's claims could be debated. 'Wakeford did not go public with his allegations – he wrote a private letter to the president,' one official said. 'And the reports from the Rand Commission did not completely exonerate Sasol, as Kruger suggests – they concluded that the spirit of forex legislation had been contravened, if not the letter.'

Wakeford had no comment on Kruger's remarks, but said he would issue a statement soon. Kruger's criticism of Wakeford is the latest in a string of complaints that have made his tenure at Sacob a turbulent one. The Johannesburg Metropolitan Chamber of Commerce withdrew its affiliation to Sacob last year, citing its failure under Wakeford's leadership to meet members' expectations on the provision of services.

A corporate Sacob member, commenting on condition of anonymity, said yesterday Wakeford had severely compromised his position through his backing of a merger between Sacob and the National African Federated Chamber of Commerce (Nafcoc). The merger is on hold ahead of the faction-racked Nafcoc's annual general meeting this weekend.[2]

***

'Politics is the art of controlling your environment.'
– Hunter S. Thompson

The fires continued to burn. Reserve Bank Governor Tito Mboweni was as impetuous and petulant as ever. Wakeford recalls that Mboweni's stance had been 'quite antagonistic. At the end of the commission he called for a public apology from me to him and the Reserve Bank.' Wakeford requested a meeting with Mboweni. The reply was that he could meet with Mboweni's legal advisor, but not with Mboweni. Wakeford said that he would not meet with the legal advisor, and that was the end of the matter.

Prior to the Rand Commission, Wakeford had had a number of scuffles with Mboweni. On the subject of inflation targeting, Wakeford had said that 'time will tell whether it works or not'. Wakeford and many of SACOB's smaller members believed that inflation targeting was a useless instrument in attempting to control or temper inflation, as most price pressures were exogenous and currency-related. Inflation targeting merely pushed up the cost of capital for small business and the consumer, through excessively high interest rates relative to South Africa's trading partners, and pushed up inflation to higher levels, as small business passed on the high cost of capital as a critical input cost in their businesses. Consumers were, in effect, paying a 'tax' for inflation targeting. It could also be argued that South Africa's interest rates were maintained at high levels to attract 'carry trades' as the country's imports increasingly exceeded its exports, and the trade account deficit grew and grew. On this argument, consumers were paying two kinds of taxes implicit in South Africa's high interest rates.

The elites were having none of it, naturally. Mboweni had literally red-carded Wakeford – interviewed by a television station, the governor took a red card out of his pocket and flashed it symbolically at Wakeford. Mboweni is on public record as having described Wakeford as an 'opportunist' and a 'populist'.[3] Mboweni had been unable – or unwilling – to explain what had happened in the rand market during 2001, but he certainly had focused ideas on what he wished for Wakeford. Central bank governors are most becoming when they play the ball, not the man. When they play the ball, they fade into the background.

∗∗∗

'A man is never more truthful than when he acknowledges himself a liar.' – Mark Twain

Kevin Wakeford had long sensed that he was being hunted down. At one gathering, Christoph Köpke said: 'Kevin, I've been under pressure to get rid of you by my boss, but I've managed to defend you.'

On the day Köpke asked Wakeford to resign, 30 September 2002, Wakeford was returning from a visit to KwaZulu-Natal. He had been visiting the Pietermaritzburg Chamber. He recalls:

I said at the meeting over my last cup of coffee in Pietermaritzburg – because another chamber had just resigned – 'Gentlemen, when I get back I'll be asked to resign.' I walked into my office. Köpke was sitting there and my PA, Marius Louw, former acting ambassador to Argentina. It was almost like a working metaphor. Spinning around in my chair with a big smile on his face, Köpke asked him to remove himself; he closed the door and said, 'Kevin, I think you must resign. I'm under too much pressure now and there could be an impact on me personally.' And I knew straight away he was referring to Jürgen Schrempp because Schrempp sat on the board of Sasol, et cetera, and he'd been lobbied by the CEO of Nampak. Nampak had phoned him and basically implied that I should move on as well. These were big corporate members of SACOB.

Who was Schrempp exactly? This is where one of the most problematic issues surrounding the Rand Commission demands close examination. Outside SACOB, Köpke was executive chairman of DaimlerChrysler South Africa; he also had some responsibilities over DaimlerChrysler assets elsewhere in the southern hemisphere, including Brazil. And here we go ... Köpke's boss was Jürgen Schrempp, CEO of DaimlerChrysler International.

Schrempp was on the advisory board of Deutsche Bank, which had been named by Wakeford. Schrempp was also a non-executive director of Sasol, which had been named by Wakeford. If this was not enough, Schrempp sat on Mbeki's investment council. Schrempp seemed to think highly of South Africa and had bought himself a game farm there. Köpke, likewise, had rural property in South Africa. No matter how it is sliced and diced, Köpke had a conflict of interest: who was he serving first and foremost? Was it SACOB or was it Schrempp? Köpke could easily have removed himself from the equation, by resigning from SACOB, or at least standing aside from matters concerning the Rand Commission. He chose, instead, to remain very much in control of SACOB.

On 11 October 2002, the *Financial Mail*'s Michael Coulson, normally an astute journalist, lamented Wakeford's departure:

The business world will be duller without Kevin Wakeford. In retrospect, the resignation of the Johannesburg Chamber of Commerce and Industry from SACOB spelt the beginning of an attrition that could have only one ending. Wakeford did himself no favours with his intemperate handling of the great forex saga that turned into a damp squib; and the subsequent trenchant attack on him by Sasol's Pieter Cox and actual or threatened defection of other regional chambers were simply final straws.

On 2 October 2002, Moneyweb's Belinda Anderson recalled the original 'Randgate' story that had appeared in March 2002:

> The resignation of SACOB CEO Kevin Wakeford marks a bleak day for SA, according to Barry Sergeant, the freelance journalist who penned a theory, published in *Finance Week*, of how the alleged 'Randgate' deals were structured around the time of the Rand Commission.
>
> Sergeant said it was sad because 'the one person who was prepared to risk everything on speaking up on the calamitous fall of the rand last year has been marginalized from society'.
>
> SACOB chairman Christoph Köpke said earlier that Wakeford's resignation was due to 'personal reasons', and was not directly linked to Sasol's resignation from the business chamber. But, the stance of one of SA's biggest companies could not have increased Wakeford's score in the popularity stakes.
>
> Wakeford sent a letter to President Thabo Mbeki in January that resulted in a commission of inquiry into the rapid depreciation of the rand late last year. Mbeki has yet to pronounce his verdict on the findings, released in two separate reports, one by Advocate John Myburgh and the other by commission member Christine Qunta.

Wakeford's resignation from SACOB had predictably profound consequences for the man, as he recalls:

> I'd never felt more lonely than I felt then. Strangely enough, later in the year *Time* magazine would award its Person of the Year to three women who were whistle-blowers. They were all middle-level people, small

people in relation to the big scheme of things. Probably very similar to me because I didn't represent big business, I represented in many cases family and small business. The majority of my members were independent operators who couldn't hedge their balance sheets offshore.

Wakeford feels that elite powers hijacked the Rand Commission, that the process was ultimately about big claws digging into the system, and having it renavigated. The compass was reset and the mind of government on the matter was reset, using the fear factor. Mbeki had always been sensitive, at every given moment, to the overall issue of globalisation, how it was going to impact on South Africa and Africa, and the power of international markets and capital flows.

Months before the Rand Commission had started, Wakeford managed to get a new message across: the rand was recovering; the crisis was over; the poor could once again afford to buy food. It's possible that Mbeki took a view and told minister of justice Penuell Maduna something along the lines of: 'Let's just shut this thing down. I'm not going to fight you if you shut it down, but you shut it down because I can't, because I started it.'

Wakeford was very disappointed in Mbeki as a person, and Mbeki's immediate helpers:

> I was disappointed in Wiseman Nkuhlu, I was disappointed in Smuts Ngonyama and I was disappointed in Bheki Khumalo, as they assured me at the time that the Presidency was also aware of delinquency in the currency markets, and that Mbeki would not relent on this matter. Perhaps more so than anyone, I was disappointed in Mbeki because he was the guy who took the cudgels in the midst of a crisis and perhaps could have remedied the soul of the nation in the economic sector for years to come if he had been more decisive and if he had pronounced on the outcome of the commission and perhaps initiated a further process. But he didn't do that.

Whether or not Mbeki decided to close the commission prematurely, the commission's work had touched nerves at the highest levels. In Wakeford's view, at some stage 'a grouping of very powerful people' gathered:

I don't know who that grouping was, and I'm not a conspiracy theorist, but I think people argued it as follows: 'This is bad for the country, it's bad for our financial markets, it's bad for the economy, it's bad for the business mood.' There were obviously strong political relationships between the private and public sectors as well. I think the likes of Jürgen Schrempp must have used a bit of his elbow grease on President Thabo Mbeki and hence through the Investment Council perhaps – but in the more informal gatherings of that council when the international players came in to consult with Mbeki, where he consulted them. Even Sakumzi 'Saki' Macozoma, strangely enough a former neighbour to Theo Qabaka in KwaZakhele township and close confidant to Mbeki on matters of business, and leading light on the board of Standard Bank, could also have argued against sustaining an exposé in South Africa's capital markets.

After all, Jacko Maree, the CEO of Standard Bank, had made his distaste known concerning Wakeford and the establishment of the commission of inquiry.

The interconnectivity of the elites prevailed in every direction. Wakeford had been to see Jeff Radebe, whom Wakeford greatly respected and still does, and who was a minister at the time. Radebe said, 'Kevin, you've been a bit hard on my friend', to which Wakeford replied, 'Who's your friend?' The answer, of course, was Martin Kingston, chairman of Deutsche Bank Johannesburg. Wakeford felt that Radebe was not au fait with the process: 'I didn't stand in judgement of him; I just laughed it off and left it there.'

Wakeford also saw Ben Ngubane, the then minister of arts and culture, about another matter, to lobby him, because, as Wakeford put it, he 'spent a lot of time in Pretoria lobbying government ministries'. Even Ben Ngubane 'kind of looked' at Wakeford and said, 'I don't agree with what you've done.' However, Dullah Mohamed Omar, who was a cabinet minister from 1994 until his passing in 2004, told Wakeford that under no circumstances should he apologise to Tito Mboweni. Omar, who had been minister of justice from 1994 until 1999, was switched to minister of transport by President Mbeki. Omar is generally ranked among the top politicians and ministers of South Africa's democratic era, a man with a fierce independence of thought.

A number of fine people said that Wakeford would be unemployed for the rest of his life. More than a few power-mongers said that Wakeford would never again find a job.

For Wakeford, the outcome of the Rand Commission was far from complicated:

> We all know that the commission never fulfilled its mandate. It did not fulfil even 20 per cent of its terms of reference. If you go through the official terms of reference, the commission headed by John Myburgh knew nothing about currency markets or finance. The commission was not meant to investigate my cases – that wasn't the purpose of the commission. The commission was to use those case studies and then to investigate a larger pattern and trend in the markets – which it never did. What they did was to focus on my cases that I'd handed over, in order to discredit me. When they called me to the commission, they didn't know that I knew the evidence was already there, that in fact the information that I'd given them was correct. And their attitude that day was to discredit me.

Wakeford's argument was always that his case – or at least his source's case – involving Deutsche Bank, Sasol and others, was just the tip of the iceberg:

> It was rumoured at the time that at one of our major banks many screen savers in its currency trading rooms had 'Fuck The Rand' displayed on them. Apparently, Deutsche Bank in Joburg had a picture of my face inlaid in a shark head on their screen savers at the time. I received a postcard with the caption *Deutschland über alles!* I guessed it came from them. I was past being unnerved by such antics and rumours. What really got to me, though, was when I got news of my daughters, Jessica and Bayla, being targeted at school, clearly by kids that had heard their parents lamenting about me and how much they had lost offshore. When both my rear tyres burst on the way to the airport – my car was being driven by friends at the time – I really started worrying. I even made myself a makeshift mirror on a piece of wire and would routinely check under the vehicle when returning to the airport parking from other parts of the country – perhaps

they would end my misery with a bomb. I was a little paranoid at the time.

I attended Caroline Southey's husband's funeral sometime after the commission and discovered on my departure that one of the Deutsche Bank elite had parked next to me. He proceeded to hurl untold abuse at me – I grinned and rode off. Clearly the poor lad was less grieved by the death than I was, and perhaps more inclined to grieve his personal situation at the bank.

There had always been a high degree of public interest in the Rand Commission – or, more correctly, in finding out why the rand had been trashed in 2001. From early in 2002, Wakeford had received hundreds of letters, emails and other messages, overwhelmingly in favour of the decision he had taken to call for a commission of inquiry. Despite the beating that Wakeford had taken at the hands of South Africa's elites, many ordinary people articulated a clear understanding of 'the rand story'.

Rosemary Wilson of Port Elizabeth put it so, in a letter to *Business Day*:

On 2 April 2002, Chamber of Business CEO Kevin Wakeford gave testimony at the rand devaluation commission about 'dubious financial methods' which contributed to the rand's crash late last year. There has been much public scepticism and criticism about his credibility.

The Reserve Bank gave evidence verifying virtually everything in Wakeford's testimony.

It fingered the exact companies and bank Wakeford did.

It confirmed an investigation had found structured deals and non-compliance [with] regulations.

It stated that if Deutsche Bank had properly explained all the related and subsequent hedging transactions, it would not have approved the now controversial deals.

It seems to me that Wakeford, the man who blew the whistle, has been deadly accurate.

8

The horses of hazard

The horrors of moral hazard ... The horrors of Fannie Mae ... The Occupy Wall Street campaign ... 'Organised greed defeats organised democracy' ... Law enforcement and the Reserve Bank turn a blind eye to Kebble's defalcations ... The horrors of broad-based black economic empowerment in South Africa.

'South Africa experienced its biggest financial crisis in 2001.
It is therefore essential that the reasons for the collapse of the
currency be investigated in more detail than this commission has
been able to. It is therefore recommended that a further investigation
takes place which will investigate the crisis that occurred in 2001.
In view of the serious problems of confidentiality, such an
investigation should not be a public one in order to meet some of
the legitimate concerns of confidentiality of persons and institutions
who may be the subject of investigations.' – Christine Qunta

'Royalty are not my people; that is what I have learned, royalty of any
colour. These guys are my enemies. These are people for whom dinner
means roast duck or nothing. For four years they have been hunting me.
Not one person has lost money from anything they're accusing me of.
Compare that to the rand's collapse, a national disaster dealt with in
four months by technical guilt and minor punishments.' – Brett Kebble

Big money was made during the rand's epic collapse in 2001. Money was made in various markets – be it currency, equity, bonds or derivatives. No doubt more money was made in side bets in dealing rooms, bars and restaurants. For those in the know, the rand had become one almighty joke.

To this day, the identities of most of those who profited so heavily have been carefully shielded. Yes, Deutsche Bank paid a fine for 'technical' infringements, but that was only scratching the surface. It was not the first time, and would by no means be the last, that astonishing profits were produced by market delinquency. By the same token, it was not the first time, and definitely would not be the last, when regulators, law enforcement and policy-makers would turn a blind eye.

This raises the question of whether or not the world has in effect, unofficially of course, created new classes of crimes that are rarely prosecuted. This, in turn, raises the underlying and broader question of whether bloodless crimes are special. One useful concept that can be raised in a discussion of this nature is known as *moral hazard*. Legal systems have yet to find a coherent, never mind effective, way to deal with moral hazard, a notion developed many years ago to describe a situation where an individual is shielded from the consequences of particular actions that he or she takes. Published academic Paul Krugman has defined moral hazard as any situation in which 'one person makes the decision about how much risk to take, while someone else bears the cost if things go badly'.[1] In simple terms, moral hazard is about power without any responsibility, or with only limited responsibility.

The most extreme cases often involve lending institutions: if things go badly, bailouts come by way of government intervention, in one way or another – that is, by way of taxpayers. Over the past two decades, nearly 100 banking crises around the world have been rescued by government intervention.

It is also widely accepted that moral hazard lay at the root of the subprime mortgage-bond crisis in the US. Consumers were offered dirt-cheap home financing. Such actions have a societal impact, and can be deemed 'moral'. The problem was that the vast majority of these consumers had next to nothing, in the material sense, and nothing to lose. As mentioned, the subprime mortgage bonds were bundled and sold as hybrid securities: subprime mixed with high-quality mortgage bonds. These products were rated as 'investment grade' by credit-rating agencies and were then sold to investors across the US, and also widely outside the US. After consumers started defaulting, especially on the subprime portion of the hybrid products, the system failed, and eventually the entire market collapsed. The meltdown degenerated into potential systemic failure, forcing the US federal government to step in.

The subsequent conduct of the federal government was haphazard and contradictory, illustrating the mercurial nature of moral hazard. In March 2008, when Bear Stearns, once a hallowed Wall Street name, failed, a private-sector bailout was authorised. But six months later, when Wall Street's Lehman Brothers failed, no bailout of any kind was authorised. When AIG, a giant insurance company, which had 'insured' billions of dollars in toxic subprime products, failed, it was bailed out by the US government: tens of billions of dollars were coughed up. This was the first time that rescue packages were extended not only to banks, but also to related sectors. The US even coughed up for corporates outside of financial services, not least for parts of the auto sector. Amid the panic, the system had lost itself. Leading US policy-makers made it clear that the country was going to be saved, whatever it took. Ben Bernanke, chairman of the Federal Reserve, and an expert on the causes and effects of the Great Depression of the 1930s, led in formulating the US's response. Compared to those bad old days, however, the US and the world were facing an unprecedented crisis. It was as if hazard had finally triumphed over morals.

What did the US's reaction tell us about our basic, underlying nature as humans? One answer is that we regard financial institutions as super-special – innocence is presumed; prosecution will be applied only in the most extreme cases. Take, for example, the US's Fannie Mae and Freddie Mac, two government-sponsored enterprises, long mandated to operate in the mortgage-bond market. These were both nationalised by the US government in September 2008, which was described as one of the most sweeping government actions ever seen in private markets. The federal government offered a package that included up to $200 billion in additional capital. Fannie Mae and Freddie Mac had been deeply sucked into the vortex of the subprime mortgage-bond market. In 2006 alone, the two institutions insured 24 per cent of all subprime mortgages granted during the year.

The loop was complete. On the one hand, poor consumers had been bombarded by cheap mortgage bonds, which carried no risk for the consumers in the event of default. On the other hand, lending institutions had comfort that any woes arising on their books would be mended by whom- or whatever. When the hazard turned into grim reaper, the taxpayer became overwhelmingly the victim. The mandarins of Wall Street survived;

the US's poor were worse off than ever before. There was no blood shed in the normal sense of crime, but there was blood in every direction.

The US subprime crisis has been discussed and analysed in no uncertain detail. One of the most accomplished works on the subject, which includes many dots previously not joined, was published in 2011 – *Reckless Endangerment: How Outsized Ambition, Greed and Corruption Led to Economic Armageddon*, by Gretchen Morgenson and Joshua Rosner. The authors explore a considerable amount of detail that may have been overlooked in previous works. The focus is on Fannie Mae. For most of the 1990s, this institution was run by James Johnson, described as 'tall, charming and politically shrewd'.

The highly detailed book shows how Johnson spent more than $100 million of Fannie Mae's money lobbying Congress, including offering sweetheart mortgage bonds to key political figures. At the same time, Johnson moved to the moral high ground by promoting a broad policy of 'increasing home ownership'. Substantial sums were also spent by Fannie Mae on currying favour with local community groups and charities. The second pillar of Johnson's strategy was to eviscerate regulators, mainly by lobbying on Capitol Hill. Fannie Mae developed into something more resembling a hedge fund. Criticism of the institution was rejected. Fannie Mae was not unknown to attack certain individuals as 'mentally unbalanced'. Fannie Mae was also increasingly active in courting mortgage lenders. Countrywide's Angelo Mozilo was once said to remark that Johnson was so slick that 'he could cut off your balls and you'd still be wearing your pants'. And, if it need be mentioned, Fannie Mae treated the press like a lackey. For its part, the press had missed the story anyway.

The self-serving Johnson was successful in more ways than one. During his nine-year career at the helm, his remuneration from Fannie Mae was close to $100 million. As everyone knows by now, Fannie Mae was one of many financial institutions in the US that gave a new meaning to 'risk taking'. The final tab for bailing out Fannie Mae is yet to be calculated, but could top $100 billion.[2]

In the final analysis, the broader subprime crisis involved herd behaviour on an unprecedented scale. For all those feigning ignorance, it has been convincingly shown that some specialist investors, among others, had predicted the subprime meltdown years before its actual manifestation.

As mentioned in Chapter 1, Paulson & Co. Inc. made hundreds of millions of dollars by betting against a subprime-derived product that was literally designed to fail. In his book *The Big Short: A True Story*,[3] Michael Lewis documents how a collection of 'misfits, renegades and visionaries' saw that the biggest credit bubble of all time was about to burst, and made a killing on their bets.

In 2007 and 2008, Paulson & Co. ripped gains of $3.7 billion out of the system, betting against (mainly US) banks. When the fund faced daylight and more competitive markets, it lost billions. Paulson & Co. reportedly lost 51 per cent of its funds valuation during 2011, mainly on the bet that the Eurozone would take a serious beating. Similarly, bets on gold bullion and certain listed gold stocks were also ill-timed.

***

'What you need to know is the big picture: if America is circling the drain, Goldman Sachs has found a way to be that drain – an extremely unfortunate loophole in the system of Western democratic capitalism, which never foresaw that in a society governed passively by free markets and free elections, organized greed always defeats disorganized democracy.' – Matt Taibbi[4]

The concept of moral hazard is generally thought to have originated from the experiences of insurance companies, and is broadly based on what has been described as 'hidden' actions or conduct. An example is where a person driving an insured motor vehicle behaves recklessly or carelessly, sensing – if not knowing – that damages from a potential accident will be picked up by the insurance company. If the insurer knew more about this individual's hidden conduct, it may elect to cancel the policy, or at least increase the premiums. But moral hazard can be found everywhere. In business and politics, it can arise when someone at the top of the pecking order occupies the position following a process of nepotism. If underlings step out of line, they will be punished in one way or another. At the same time, such underlings have less reason than normal to refuse to engage in conduct that may be immoral, if not illegal. Taken to the extreme, a discussion of this nature can also refer to the depressing issues examined at the Nuremberg Trials.

The subprime mortgage-bond crisis has left a bitter taste and a foul smell that have continued for years. It has also led to street-level protests, such as the Occupy Wall Street campaign. This extended expression of activism can be traced to the Canadian *Adbusters* Media Foundation, which publishes *Adbusters*, an advertisement-free, anti-consumerist magazine. In mid-2011, *Adbusters* hatched the idea of presidential commissions mandated to separate money from politics. This led, in turn, to campaigns, including the Occupy Wall Street movement, which aimed to 'occupy' New York City's Lower Manhattan, focusing on Zuccotti Park. Activists and participants have often identified themselves as 'the 99 per cent'. This may have been a wry reference to the Hell's Angels, who have long described themselves as 'one percenters', but it is, in the modern sense, a reference to the significant percentage of wealth controlled by just 1 per cent of the US population.

The Occupy Wall Street demonstrations, which spread across the US and to countries outside the US, have been likened by some participants to the protests that precipitated the so-called Arab Spring, such as the peaceful occupation of Tahrir Square, Cairo, which eventually toppled the Egyptian government in 2011. There were similar-minded protests in several other countries, such as Spain's Indignants movement. By October 2011, analysts had counted demonstrations in about 70 cities across the world, involving more than 600 communities. If it is possible to distil the demands of the protesters, inequality probably tops the list of complaints. It is clear that citizens are sick and tired of organised greed, as tirelessly exhibited by the corporate and banking sectors.

In searching for universal themes, there seems to be little question that people are more organised than ever. Social media has become a real force. The surprise is that the enemy, at least the underlying enemy, is to be found less in political systems than in how such systems continue to support the growing wedge between the haves and the have-nots.

'Swinging doors' dominate this landscape: mountains of cash are regularly moved from the corporate and banking sectors to fund the lobbying of governments, thereby sustaining the vicious circle. Where prosecutions were made, it was only when specific evidence was available, as found in the case where Goldman Sachs settled after disgorging more than half a billion dollars. This particular case would have been as compelling with or without the subprime crisis. It was, however, opportunities arising from the subprime crisis that precipitated the covert creation by Goldman Sachs of the product known as Abacus, which, according to ACA Financial, a bond insurer, 'was designed to fail'.[5] Paulson & Co. Inc., also directly involved in the Abacus product, took an easy bet and profited to the tune of hundreds of millions of dollars.

However, perhaps the fuller significance of the SEC suing Goldman was that the US's political elites had finally conceded – unofficially of course – that things had gone too far. When big money runs amok, one way to send a strong signal is to slap its flagship member with a fine of more than $500 million.

Beyond organised group greed, looking at individual foulness, the insider-trading case against hedge-fund manager Rajaratnam (mentioned in Chapter 4) was similarly based on specific conduct. Financial malfeasance is never easy to prove. In this case, for the first time in an insider-trading case, federal law-enforcement agents used wiretapping, a technique usually associated with investigations into organised crime syndicates and drug traffickers.

The biggest markets tend to produce the most egregious cases of insider trading, leading, in turn, to prosecutors who are more determined and better equipped than usual to see the guilty serve time. Three capital markets dominate the global landscape: New York, London and Hong Kong account for around 70 per cent of global trade in equities, and are home to many of the investigators and prosecutors who possess the ambition and wherewithal to close down the canniest insider traders, and to prosecute them if warranted. And the cost of enforcement is no small affair: the SEC has requested a system that would allow it to police equity and derivatives markets in real time – a system that could cost an estimated $1 billion.

While insider trading is typically criminalised by specific legislation, it is by nature an activity that violates common law. Rajaratnam was convicted of 14 counts of insider trading and conspiracy. Yet as evil as greed and recklessness may be, whether or not individuals who stand accused of money crimes are indeed guilty remains a grey and elusive area, and one that agonises the senses.

In South Africa, moral hazard among the country's elites may have reached a breaking point. The country's democratic era has been character-ised by people with little relevant experience being appointed to positions of enormous power. There are exceptions to this rule, but in the main, government has not shown any convincing ability to conduct itself in a sustainable, cohesive way. As ever, the unemployment rate provides the key litmus test. South Africa may rank as the world's 25th biggest economy, but it ranks first in terms of unemployment levels. This crisis is progress-ing to the point where it will infamously become multigenerational, if it has not already been reached.

Government's weaknesses extend to lacking credible policy responses for dysfunctional systems for basic health, basic education and basic ser-vice delivery for the impoverished. Relative to the size of its population, South Africa now ranks as the world's biggest welfare state, further aggra-vating chronic unemployment.

Government's general maladministration has created opportunities for people short on scruples. Where there is power without responsibility, moral scruple tends to fade and, in the face of a weakened law-enforcement system, becomes lifeless. Among the case studies that can be cited, it is arguable that the most egregious instance – in the public domain, any-way – involves the core part of Brett Kebble's career of looting.

Reports published in the public domain by forensic experts JLCO show that from 2002, 24.6 million shares in Randgold Resources were looted by Kebble, with some minor assistance from one or two of his sidekicks. The shares had been owned by Randgold & Exploration (Randgold). Randgold (listed in Johannesburg and the US) had established Randgold Resources in 1995, which was listed in London in 1997 and in the US in 2002.

From 1997 Randgold Resources was therefore a foreign stock. Rand-gold, the parent company, was required to obtain permission from the Reserve Bank in respect of pretty much any decision that Randgold made about its holding in Randgold Resources. Because Randgold Resources was a foreign-listed stock, Randgold's interest in it fell to be regulated by South Africa's draconian exchange controls.

Given Kebble's permanent state of cash deprivation, he had every reason to sell down Randgold's stake in Randgold Resources. The story goes as follows: Kebble started selling Randgold Resources shares for cash and immediately stole the cash to use in his other activities – which included bribing all kinds of people, not least the erstwhile police commissioner Jackie Selebi.

None of the stolen cash generated by selling Randgold's investments went back to Randgold. The JLCO forensic reports show that in aggregate, Kebble raised R1.59 billion in cash by stealing and selling stolen Randgold Resources shares (plus an additional R300 million by selling other shares owned by Randgold). JLCO's forensic reports, which have never been challenged, show, as mentioned, that Randgold had been looted to the tune of 24.6 million shares that it once held in Randgold Resources.

Within the context of the currency markets, it is worth tracing one thread of transactions. On or about 6 June 1995, the Reserve Bank's exchange-control department, Excon, approved an application by Randgold for the formation of Randgold Resources as a private non-South African company to hold all of Randgold's non-South African exploration interests. There were strict conditions: Randgold was not allowed to dispose of its interest in Randgold Resources without the specific approval of Excon. Share certificates representing Randgold's shareholdings in Randgold Resources were to be lodged with the Standard Bank of South Africa and held to the order of Excon.

On or about 27 September 1996, Excon approved an application by Randgold for the establishment of Randgold Resources Holdings (RRH) as an offshore company and wholly owned subsidiary of Randgold, to hold its interest in Randgold Resources. The application was approved on condition that all income of RRH had to be repatriated to South Africa. The original share certificates of RRH were to be lodged with Standard Bank and held to the order of Excon. Crucially, Randgold was not allowed to dispose of its interest in Randgold Resources without the prior approval of Excon.

On or about 27 March 1997, Excon approved an application by Randgold for the listing of Randgold Resources' shares in London on condition that Randgold was obliged to retain a minimum of 50.1 per cent shareholding in Randgold Resources. On or about 14 March 2002, Excon approved an application by Randgold for the dilution of its shareholding in Randgold Resources to 36 per cent, on the condition that a further reduction of Randgold's shareholding in Randgold Resources required Excon's prior approval.

On 20 July 2004, SocGen Johannesburg, a subsidiary branch of France-based Société Générale, applied to the Reserve Bank for confirmation that Randgold had legitimately handed 6.65 million Randgold Resources shares as collateral for a certain facility granted by SocGen. The facility was in favour of JCI – Kebble's mother ship – and not Randgold. In other words, Kebble was in effect stealing 6.65 million shares in Randgold Resources. As mentioned, SocGen's application was necessary by law because Randgold Resources was classified as a foreign-listed stock. In the event of a default, SocGen would have wanted to cash in the Randgold Resources shares. What has become clear, with hindsight, was that Kebble, from day one, intended to default on the facility.

On 27 July 2004, SocGen's application to the Reserve Bank was declined.

In due course, as Kebble and his companies defaulted, SocGen sold off millions of shares in Randgold Resources. It was as if the country's exchange controls had never existed.

A separate transaction involved Investec Bank UK (IBUK), since renamed Investec Bank plc, part of the Investec group. In the so-called IBUK transaction, there has also never been any evidence that IBUK was given permission to sell 5.46 million Randgold Resources shares. Once again, these Randgold Resources shares had been stolen.

Like SocGen, Investec and IBUK have always strenuously denied any knowledge that the relevant Randgold Resource shares were stolen. What is clear, however, is that in both the SocGen and IBUK transactions, the cash raised from selling the stolen shares was, as mentioned, not directed back to Randgold, the owner of the stolen shares. The apparent violations of Excon's rulings by SocGen, IBUK and Investec were investigated by the Reserve Bank, which appointed as consultants KPMG Services, the forensic division of KPMG. The investigations died a quiet death. The Randgold Resources shares, which Excon had ordered to be held by Standard Bank as agent for Excon, were gone, as if Excon's rulings had never been made. KPMG was also auditor at Standard Bank, Investec, SocGen South Africa and T-Sec, the Johannesburg-based stockbroker that had laundered more than R1 billion of the cash stolen by Kebble.

Looking just at the foreign-exchange angle, it seems to be fair to conclude that South Africa's exchange controls are applied on a selective basis, thus compromising and polluting the entire system. This is a system that cannot be trusted. It is a system that breeds uncertainty and contributes heavily to blotting South Africa's reputation as an investment destination. It is frightening.

It would be impolite to mention that South Africa has a long way to go before it even challenges situations where moral hazard has run out of control. Until then, it is set to continue malfunctioning as a cruel and brutal playground for elites, who expect to be respected as among the world's most virtuous and righteous.

***

If moral hazard translates as 'power without responsibility', then it is fair to say that South Africa has developed its own special home-brew version. In South Africa, the political elites publicly espouse the values enshrined in the country's Constitution. In private, though, the accumulation of loot, with considerable assistance from private-sector elites, remains the supreme objective of personal constitutions.

Ultimately, this is power without responsibility – and power exercised with impunity.

The most tortuous case studies can invariably be found in the beguiling area of so-called broad-based BEE, and especially in mining. The various ministers complain incessantly that white miners are not doing nearly enough to transform mining. From time to time, the Department of Mineral Resources (DMR) complains along the lines of 'the continued negligible social investment in communities proximal to mines and fetid living conditions under which most mineworkers are subjected to',[6] yet utters not so much as a whisper when a handful of individuals become worth billions of rands overnight.

BEE mining deals are, with apologies to Churchill, riddles wrapped in a mystery inside an enigma. The deals are structured by big law firms – though, it should be pointed out, not all are involved. The deals are signed off by big firms of accountants and auditors. Again, to be fair, not all are involved. The deals are then presented as puffballs, beautiful objects of empowerment art, designed to benefit millions and save the world. In reality, the deals are designed to benefit a tiny number of elites.

The minutiae of the deals are rarely studied, and less understood, by the press and even by professional investment analysts. Opposition politicians seem equally unaware of the innards of the deals. As a result, the deals bypass meaningful scrutiny. It is possible, however, to disembowel each deal – not fully, but certainly to the point where a fair representation of the real deal can be presented.

The net result is that the see-through quintessence of BEE mining deals, and most other kinds of BEE deals, never makes it into the public domain. South Africans are deprived of the chance to form an opinion on the deals, let alone debate their merits. Elites in both the public and private sectors have done one hell of a job.

Zwelinzima Vavi, general secretary of COSATU, the South African trades union congress, has expressed indignation, attacking the country's 'corrupt political elite'. He famously announced: 'We're headed for a predator state where a powerful, corrupt and demagogic elite of political hyenas are increasingly using the State to get rich.'[7] Unfortunately, however, Vavi and COSATU have been unable to articulate specific cases of such corruption in the public domain. The main reason, as explained, is that the transactions are conceived and executed in swathes of deception.

If one were to examine far behind the smoke and mirrors of the BEE mining deals, it would show that they are explicitly aimed at enriching just a handful of people. There have been cases where some individuals have benefited to the tune of R1 billion – and more. Individual benefits of more than R100 million are not uncommon.

A brief tour through a few BEE deals provides some insight into the inner workings of South Africa's elites, almost in the manner of observing moving violations, which were very much the hallmarks of the rand market during 2001.

Imperial Crown Trading

One of the few BEE cases that gained widespread press attention involved Kumba Iron Ore (a subsidiary of Anglo American) and Imperial Crown Trading (ICT), one of those entities that magically fell out of the sky. The reason for the attention was not so much the details, but because politically connected individuals were explicitly named as parties with – purported – shareholdings in ICT.

Until 30 April 2009, a 21.4 per cent mining right was held in Sishen Iron Ore Company (SIOC), a highly profitable world-class mine in the

Northern Cape, by ArcelorMittal South Africa (AMSA), a unit of Arcelor-Mittal, a transnational steel company. The majority of the mining right in SIOC was held by Kumba, which has always operated the mine. Inexplicably, AMSA allowed its rights in SIOC to lapse. Kumba lodged an application for the right. On all the evidence available, ICT lashed together a similar application – almost too similar to be true – over the weekend starting 1 May 2009 (a Friday and the first day of the Easter weekend).

Immediately, there were signs that various officials at the DMR were up to no good. The DMR awarded ICT the rights. ICT paid a few rands for a 'prospecting licence' to an area where, in fact, a mine had already operated for many decades. On 10 August 2010, AMSA offered to buy ICT for R800 million. On the same day, AMSA announced a R9.1 billion broad-based BEE transaction. Named 'beneficiaries' in the deal included Sandile Zungu, Oakbay Investments (a unit of the Gupta family), Jagdish Parekh (a Gupta associate) and Mabengela Investments (led by Duduzane Zuma).

Duduzane Zuma, a son of President Jacob Zuma, was seemingly so embarrassed that he soon announced in a strange meeting with some journalists that he would 'give away' 70 per cent of the value in Mabengela, estimated to be worth more than R1 billion.

On 24 January 2011, Sandile Nogxina, director general of the DMR, informed SIOC in writing that its application for AMSA's prior 21.4 per cent part of the mineral rights in SIOC had been rejected, as the application made by SIOC was 'submitted prematurely and in an irregular, misleading and fraudulent manner'.[8] It was not uncommon for the DMR to make decisions with only feeble footing in the law and, for that matter, the facts.

Nogxina, an advocate by training, seemed unwilling or unable to bring his professional skills to the fore. Instead, he seemed to almost relish the many court cases that the DMR became embroiled in. As a rule, the DMR loses in court. In some cases, the court would express surprise that the case had made it to court in the first place.

On 21 December 2011, a High Court judgment ruled that upon the conversion of SIOC's old-order mining right relating to the Sishen mine properties in 2008, SIOC became the exclusive holder of a converted mining right for iron ore and quartzite in respect of the Sishen mine properties. The High Court held further that, as a consequence, any decision taken by the DMR after such conversion in 2008 to accept or grant any further rights to iron ore at the Sishen mine properties was void. The High Court also reviewed and set aside the decision of the minister of mineral resources or her delegate to grant a prospecting right to ICT. Once again, the DMR and the minister had suffered heavy losses in the courts. The DMR appealed to the Supreme Court of Appeal. The case was waiting to be heard at the time of writing.

Mining disinvestment

In recent years, there has been a slow momentum building up in disinvestment from South Africa by mining companies, not that it is possible to have this phenomenon confirmed – in the public domain – by anyone. Look, instead, to what mining companies are doing, rather than what is being said. To take one example, in November 2010, Coal of Africa (CoAL), a firm listed in Johannesburg, London and Australia, announced that it was buying Rio Tinto's South African coal-mining assets. What caught the attention of specialists is that CoAL, which operates in South Africa, was paying just $75 million for the assets. CoAL was also given relatively easy repayment terms.

The apparent prize in the assets purchase by CoAL was the Chapudi Coal Project, which holds a proven resource of 1 billion tonnes of coking coal. This type of coal is not only relatively rare in South Africa, but it also ranks as one of the world's most profitable minerals, along with iron ore and copper. Coking coal, used in the reduction of iron ore to pig iron, sells at up to three times the price of more common steam coal used to fire power stations.

Rio Tinto, the world's third-largest mining company, waited little more than a month after selling its South African coal assets before announcing a A$3.9 billion bid for Australia-listed Riversdale Mining, mainly for its 65 per cent stake in Benga, a coking-coal project in Tete, a province of Mozambique. There seems little question that Benga sits on more than a billion tonnes of coking coal, but Rio Tinto's willingness to 'switch' so radically from South Africa's Chapudi to Benga makes a telling point. Rio Tinto subsequently announced that it intends investing in the development of Benga – not just the mine, but also transport, logistics, port facilities and possibly even a power station.

Benga is the second-biggest coal-mining development in Tete Province. The first, Moatize, is under the hand of Brazil's Vale, the world's number-two mining company. Vale has so far spent billions of dollars on development of the mine, along with all the attendant infrastructure and logistics needed to transport the coal by rail from inland to the coast, onto ships, for delivery to Asian customers. Vale has shown little interest in becoming involved in South Africa.

The general informal view of mining executives on this situation is that South Africa is regarded as on hold and of little, if any, interest for the foreseeable future. This may have been confirmed in an ironic way in January 2013, when Rio Tinto announced that it would be taking a $3 billion impairment on the coal assets it had purchased in Mozambique. The cynic would say that Rio Tinto was so keen to get out of South Africa and into Mozambique that it was prepared to overpay by billions of dollars for the opportunity.

As mentioned, few, if any, mining executives are prepared to speak openly about the negative investment climate that has built up in South Africa. There was something that amounted close to an exception to this in December 2012, when Cynthia Carroll gave a speech in Johannesburg. As the outgoing CEO of Anglo American, it seemed that she was prepared to go a little further than usual. Carroll was diplomatic, as always, but at the same time she went as far as someone in her position could go in expressing frustration with the investment situation in South Africa. There were some barbs in her speech – tiny but very sharp:

Mining is at the heart of the South African economy. It has a critical role to play in supporting the aspirations of the New Growth Path and the objectives of the National Development Plan. And it is an industry with long-term horizons. When making investments, mining companies have to think decades ahead. They need certainty as to the rules under which they will operate. They will not invest if there is a fear of arbitrary and unpredictable regulatory change.

The regulatory debate in South Africa has been going on for a very long time. And it is still not completely resolved. The spectre of nationalisation has been laid to rest. But the need to guard against damaging regulatory changes remains.[9]

Until South Africa reins in its elites, the entire country will continue to perform well below its potential. The underlying drivers of the horribly destructive forces deployed by the elites – deceit, hubris and utter selfishness – dominate the political and business landscapes. A commonality of purpose can be identified in major incidents, ranging from the rand market in 2001 to the debilitating case of ICT.

International investors are increasingly sceptical about South Africa, and suspicious of the intentions of the ruling party, seen as bent on enforcing an unworkable political system – driven by ideology – that continues to drive an ever wider wedge between the elites and the tens of millions who remain mired in poverty.

Driven perhaps more by guilt – and grotesque salaries and perks – than anything else, government continually rolls out new aggregated wish lists, such as the National Development Plan, unveiled amid great ceremony during 2012.

The country's overall status quo is far from what a famous economist once described as 'animal spirits'. In *The General Theory of Employment, Interest and Money*, published in 1936, John Maynard Keynes used the term 'animal spirits' to describe a general human exuberance that drives consumer confidence and at the same time inspires trust between people. Keynes believed that animal spirits were crucial in motivating people to take positive action. South Africa's animal spirits have long fled the borders. It will need miracles to get them back.

Like so much of the world, if not all of it, South Africans are victims of media hucksterism, which has only intensified in the recent era. This leaves precious little time to reflect, never mind analyse, the bigger picture. It is of little comfort that this bigger picture shows that since the 2001 rand debacle, the conduct of South Africa's loosely knit elites has continued to deteriorate to the point where an increasing number of concerned citizens are sensing desperation.

This is a country where power is exercised with impunity. As mentioned, Krugman defined moral hazard as any situation in which 'one person makes the decision about how much risk to take, while someone else bears the cost if things go badly'. In South Africa, the elites are prepared to take on any amount of risk, smug in the comfort of knowing that the rest of the population takes the punishment.

9
Hooves of thunder

In South Africa, whistle-blowers are treated as vermin ... South Africa's
policy of selective prosecution ... From Phoenix to Malema ... Mbeki's
intractable taste for bad people ... More from Mark Parker's illuminating
insights ... The horrible truth: South Africa's exchange controls are in a
sad mess ... Mbeki clashes with Wakeford on democratising business ...
Mboweni goes ballistic ... South Africa's elites fib to themselves, to South
Africans and the world ... The strange jabbering of Russell Loubser.

'It would take wild horses to get me to talk.' – Gene Scott

When *Time* magazine gave its Persons of the Year award for 2002 to
Cynthia Cooper of WorldCom, Coleen Rowley of the FBI and Sherron
Watkins of Enron, it carried an extensive number of articles. In an over-
view, *Time* had this to say:

These women were for [2002] what New York City fire fighters were
in 2001: heroes at the scene, anointed by circumstances. They were
people who did right just by doing their jobs rightly – which means
ferociously, with eyes open and with the bravery the rest of us always
hope we have and may never know if we do. Their lives may not have
been at stake, but Watkins, Rowley and Cooper put pretty much everything else on the line. Their jobs, their privacy, their sanity – they risked
all of them to bring us badly needed word of trouble inside crucial
institutions. Democratic capitalism requires that people trust in the
integrity of public and private institutions alike. As whistle-blowers,
these three became fail-safe systems that did not fail. For believing –
really believing – that the truth is one thing that must not be moved
off the books and for stepping in to make sure that it wasn't, they have
been chosen by *Time* as its Persons of the Year for 2002.[1]

Watkins was already on the lecture circuit, earning up to $25 000 for an appearance. She had also been offered $500 000 as an advance to co-author a book. In South Africa, whistle-blowers are regarded as vermin. No matter what truth a whistle-blower may know, or the truth that a whistle-blower intuitively knows is somehow there, they are regarded as worthless in this country, as people to be immediately thrown on the scrap heap of society.

South Africa is run by a group of elites in the political, business and banking sectors. From time to time, individuals in these elite groups silently and invisibly pass the baton on to the next member of the elite. This tradition was established by President Thabo Mbeki, primarily by fostering the creation of a black elite. South Africa's much vaunted broad-based BEE strategy has been nothing more than a cynical way of creating an upper echelon of oligarchs. As a result, the poor have been increasingly marginalised to the point where South Africa has the worst so-called Gini coefficient in the world. This measure, first outlined and defined by Italian sociologist Corrado Gini in his 1912 paper 'Variability and mutability', measures the inequality among values of a frequency distribution, such as national income distribution. A Gini coefficient of one (100 on the percentile scale) expresses maximal inequality among the values measured – for example, the case where a single person earns all the national income. There are other useful measures that may be mentioned in this context. In 1906, Vilfredo Pareto conducted an analysis of Italian wealth distribution and found 20 per cent of the population owned 80 per cent of the land, hence the so-called Pareto principle. This continues to be applied today; it is more commonly known as ABC analysis or the 80/20 principle.

Apart from the new black elite, South Africa's societal structure has changed but little – especially since 1994. As Brett Kebble deftly put it, 'South Africa's big error was that the political deal left the old guard untouched. That was short-sighted, and shocking. The old-order fuckwits had made money out of slave labour, and were allowed to continue as if nothing had changed.'[2] The Big Men in the private sector and the Big Men in politics have weakened South Africa's democracy at every opportunity. For example, the elites regard law enforcement as something to be whipped into subservience, rather than something to be respected.

In the financial arena, the Financial Services Board (FSB) has become a sad rendition of a regulator long lost and woefully emasculated. The FSB, which oversees the JSE Securities Exchange, turned a blind eye to the biggest fraud in South African history: the Kebble era. The main reason, no doubt, was that Kebble himself had tossed money into the dirty hands of all kinds of people – mainly in the public sector.

The JSE has also pretended that the Kebble era was some kind of fictional story that took place on some distant planet. This is despite the presence in the public domain of forensic reports that show in detail how Kebble stole shares from Randgold and sold them for cash – R1.9 billion in aggregate. The forensic reports show that more than R1 billion of the stolen cash was laundered through a stockbroker, Tlotlisa Securities (T-Sec), a member of the JSE. No action was taken against T-Sec, not by any regulatory or law-enforcement authority. As mentioned, the Reserve Bank also turns a blind eye when the Big Men are in town.

South Africa's intolerance – if not hatred – of whistle-blowers is deeply rooted. The elites in ruling politics, business and banking have more to hide than to show, and cannot afford to be revealed in full daylight. In the evolution of these horrors in the political system, it is useful to note that Thabo Mbeki had a habit of appointing very disappointing people to his cabinet and to other important positions, and of stubbornly refusing to fire them when they failed.

It was Mbeki who appointed Selebi as commissioner of police. When it became clear that the then head of the NPA, Vusi Pikoli, wanted to arrest Selebi, Pikoli was hurled in front of a commission of inquiry. He was cleared, but he lost his job anyway. Selebi's prosecution ranks among the highest level of its sort in South Africa's democratic era. Selebi was also head of Interpol. There is a strong possibility that Pikoli had an ulterior motive in pursuing Selebi. Pikoli's former boss, minister of justice Penuell Maduna, demonstrably had some kind of hold over Pikoli, and Maduna had certain scores to settle with Selebi. Either way, of the dozens of people in the private sector, government, law enforcement and elsewhere who received illicit cash or benefits from Kebble, either directly or indirectly, not one was arrested, never mind prosecuted. Selebi was the only exception, which means that his case was, simply, a freak.

***

'I see in the near future a crisis approaching that unnerves me and causes me to tremble for the safety of my country. Corporations have been enthroned, an era of corruption in high places will follow, and the money-power of the country will endeavour to prolong its reign by working upon the prejudices of the people until the wealth is aggregated in a few hands and the Republic is destroyed.' – Abraham Lincoln

Selective prosecution – and, of course, non-prosecution – is institutionalised in South Africa, although detailed scholarly analysis of this sensitive subject is not available. The problem, which is either ignored or misunderstood by the media, is systemic to the point where almost everyone is involved, if not by commission, then by omission. The most common form of big-money fraud is, without question, tender fraud. From time to time, various estimates are made by various parties as to the cost of such fraud, and the general estimates run into tens of billions of rands a year. However, given the kind of bigwigs involved, prosecutions are all but extinct.

At least one voice from time to time vents its frustration with tender fraud: that of the higher courts. In some ways, the Phoenix case ranks as the low-water mark of tender-fraud analysis. Judge Jonathan Heher used choice words in the judgment in *Minister of Social Development* v. *Phoenix Cash & Carry*: 'Unfortunately, as experience in this Court proves, the high standards that the Constitution sets seem to be more honoured in the breach than in the observance … The award of public tenders … is notoriously subject to influence and manipulation.'[3]

The case in question ranks as truly astonishing, a microcosm that illustrates the mechanics of how tens of billions of rands are being stolen via tender fraud in South Africa. The complainant in the case, Phoenix Cash & Carry, sued the then minister of social development, Zola Sidney Themba Skweyiya, and three of the entities that had won the tender in question, Snotho Trading, MDC Catering and Pfula Mbokoto Consortium.

Previously, Phoenix had held a contract to supply food hampers to dreadfully poor families in KwaZulu-Natal and the Eastern Cape. Contract renewals were called, with the closing date set for 30 March 2005, with the aim of appointing local service providers and consortiums to supply food items to about 150 000 destitute families. Phoenix submitted a bid, which included all the required documents – letters from Standard Bank, Newcastle Branch, a letter from Messrs Khan, Salejee & Company Chartered Accountants, letters from six proposed commodity suppliers, and so on.

In October 2005 Phoenix learnt that the tender had been awarded to other entities. The Department of Social Development supplied certain information, showing, for example, that tender prices per parcel from those companies that had been awarded the tender ranged from R269.10 to R299.69. The prices per parcel for the two options offered by Phoenix were substantially less: R187.00 and R180.70. Phoenix litigated and won its case in the High Court.

Remarkably, the matter was taken on appeal to the Supreme Court of Appeal. Clearly, the fraudsters feared nothing, and were annoyed about having been sued by a real business, Phoenix. From the start, the circumstantial evidence suggested that at least some of the fraudsters were sitting inside the government department – not that the court pronounced on this point.

Judge Heher wrote:

the initial reasons furnished to Phoenix by the Department were, to say the least, seriously misleading. They created the impression that its tender had been evaluated and rejected on its merits, which was far from being the case. No explanation for the compilation of those reasons was ever furnished. In a proper case such a failure might justify an inference of *mala fides* [bad faith].[4]

The representative of the department, one Ms Phemba, was unable to supply Phoenix's attorneys on request with the addresses of Snotho and Pfula. As such, these parties could not be served or given notice of the court proceedings that Phoenix initiated. 'Yet,' Judge Heher noted, these parties 'were represented by counsel when the matter came to court'. This also was unexplained. The learned judge does not ask the question, but it would be equally interesting to know who paid legal costs for Snotho and Pfula.

According to records from the Companies' Office annexed to the court papers, Snotho was a close corporation, but one that had only been incorporated after the closing date of the tender. 'Prima facie,' stated Judge Heher, 'that rendered its bid invalid ... One perforce asks how Snotho could have satisfied the requirement of providing evidence of readily available financial resources ...'

Judge Heher found that the merits of Phoenix's tender were 'so manifest and the grounds of its exclusion so flimsy that doubts are necessarily raised as to the reliability and credibility of the procurement process employed by the Department'. Counsel for Phoenix informed the Supreme Court of Appeal that duly served notices calling on Snotho and Pfula to disclose particulars of proprietors or partners were neither followed up nor answered. 'The unsatisfactory result,' Judge Heher stated, 'is that counsel representing those entities asked this Court to make orders in favour of those respondents without knowledge of their *locus standi*, their true nature or the faces behind them.'

Judge Heher said that 'certain general observations are demonstrated as true' by the Phoenix case. First, a tender process, which depends on uncertain criteria, lends itself to the exclusion of meritorious tenderers. Second, a process that lays undue emphasis on form at the expense of substance 'facilitates corrupt practice by providing an excuse for avoiding the consideration of substance'.

After the judgment was handed down, confirming the High Court decision in favour of Phoenix, I asked the Department of Social Development for comment and was met by a wall of silence. The modus operandi of fraudsters of the type who tried to usurp Phoenix aim to win tenders illegally. When the deal is done, the fraudsters will then approach a party or parties that can fulfil the terms of the tender. The fraudsters take a 'turn' on the price of each unit, which has been awarded at levels way above a competitive level.

As such, tender fraud requires little in the way of skills, and zero ability to supply the goods or services tendered. There appears to be little, if any, interest by law-enforcement authorities to prosecute tender fraud. The fact that the Phoenix case involved tens of thousands of literally starving widows and orphans was clearly irrelevant.

Tender fraud is also a horribly powerful political weapon against those who have fallen out of favour or perhaps have even progressed to the status of enemy. In 2012, Julius Malema, who had been expelled as a member of the ANC and fired as president of the ANC Youth League, was arrested on allegations relating to misconduct involving certain tenders. That was one thing. However, he was subsequently notified that he would be charged on various counts of money laundering. Later he was told that he would also be facing charges of racketeering. Both money laundering and racketeering are governed by the Prevention of Organised Crime Act (POCA), which was passed in 1998.

According to Section 3 of the Act, any person convicted of racketeering 'shall be liable to a fine not exceeding R1 000 million, or to imprisonment for a period up to imprisonment for life'.

A fine of up to one billion rands? Up to a life sentence in prison? The penalties for money laundering are equally eye-popping. The Malema case was due to be heard later in 2013.

For years, as leader of the ANC Youth League, Malema had constructed a populist power base. On the one hand, he was going to deliver South Africa's poor from poverty; on the other, he lived a life of high-end luxury, which could never have been explained by his modest salary as a politician. As Malema's apparent popularity grew, he became more abusive of power in the ANC, and he eventually started going after President Zuma. More a product of the media than anything else, Malema ran way beyond any talent he may have had. He launched tirades of personal and racial attacks, seemingly randomly in many cases. During interviews, he was inarticulate and dull, and unable, for instance, to explain in any vaguely passable manner the reasons that the ANC Youth League was demanding the nationalisation of mines.

Malema's treatment can be compared with that of those who managed to remain in favour with the elites. On 31 May 2005, Schabir Shaik, an associate of Jacob Zuma, was found guilty of corruption and fraud in the High Court. He was sentenced to 15 years in lock-up, and in due course was released on medical parole. The judgment in the case was awash with transfers of cash and other benefits that Shaik had made to Zuma.

On 18 December 2007, Zuma was voted in as president of the ANC. He would in due course be sworn in as South Africa's president. On 27 December 2007, Zuma was indicted on a number of charges, including fraud and corruption, but, most tellingly, on charges of racketeering and money laundering.

On 6 April 2009, the NPA withdrew charges against Zuma on the basis that there had been flaws in the prosecution. Various so-called spy tapes had indicated the possibility of a political conspiracy against Zuma. The acting head of the NPA, Mokotedi Mpshe, said that the withdrawal of charges against Zuma did not amount to an acquittal. The legality, or otherwise, of the spy tapes has never been completely clarified.

On 18 December 2012, Zuma was again voted in as president of the ANC.

***

Where whistle-blowers in South Africa are not tossed out with the garbage, they are simply ignored. Mbeki appointed Manto Tshabalala-Msimang as his health minister in 1999, a position she held until 2008. Tshabalala-Msimang faithfully followed Mbeki's inexplicable and bizarre notion that HIV does not cause AIDS. She was extremely reluctant to adopt a public-sector plan for treating AIDS with antiretroviral treatments. Instead, she promoted the benefits of the likes of beetroot, garlic, lemons, beer and African potatoes, along with good general nutrition.

The more she was ridiculed and lampooned in South Africa, and across the world, the more Mbeki dug in his heels and refused to fire her. She was an alcoholic and on 14 March 2007 received a liver transplant. The operation took place in a private hospital – the public hospitals that fell under her ministry were clearly not up to her royal standards.

According to a *Sunday Times* whistle-blowing article titled 'Manto: A drunk and a thief', published on 19 August 2007, she was a convicted thief who had stolen items from patients (while under anaesthetic) at a hospital in Botswana, and had been deported from Botswana and declared a prohibited immigrant. Tshabalala-Msimang was not included in Zuma's first cabinet, announced on 10 May 2009. She passed away in a private clinic on 16 December 2009.

It is entirely possible that whistle-blowers simply have no place in modern South Africa. Take, for example, South Africa's long-term electricity crisis. Alex Erwin, who served as minister of public enterprises from 29 April 2004 to 25 September 2008, and who had a busy career in and around the trade union movement, indicated a strong immunity to many things, not least reality. His competence was seen to be at its height in January 2008, when South Africa's monopoly power supplier, Eskom, plunged the country into darkness.

Experts who became whistle-blowers had from the mid-1990s warned the South African government that the country's power-generation capacity had to be upgraded to meet rising demands. Baseload power stations take years to commission and build. The warnings were ignored until the absolute crisis that emerged in January 2008.

Given the suboptimal status of whistle-blowers in South Africa, Kevin Wakeford's attempt to uncover the truth about the rand market in 2001 was not so much a case of David taking on Goliath, as one of a modern-day Sisyphus. As a reminder, in this tale from Greek mythology, Sisyphus was a king of Ephyra, who was punished by being ordered to roll a huge boulder up a hill, only to watch it roll back down. He was forced to repeat the action forever.

As CEO of SACOB, Wakeford was of some interest to Mbeki. In September 2000, Wakeford was at SACOB's annual convention at the Bellville Velodrome, near Cape Town. The facility, which seats around 6 000, was packed in the seated area and there was a large exhibition with standing space. Mbeki had been invited to address the convention. Then the message came through that there were problems with the presidential jet and in no time, a private businessman agreed that he would organise another jet for the president. During these times, SACOB was especially influential in the national arena: it carried similar clout to that of COSATU in the civil-society arena. After the meeting, Mbeki walked out with his arm around Wakeford.

Mbeki, always the busybody, had at least one bone of contention. Wakeford was looking at consolidating business power at the local level, at the grass roots, by promoting the integration of racially divided chambers. He was also looking at harmonising race relations and fostering non-racialism across the business field. Says Wakeford:

I believed that merely unifying the chamber movement at national level in a 'confederal' structure (similar to that of the tricameral parliament of P.W. Botha) would reinforce inequality and separation of organised business and their members' businesses at local level. The sociology of business was wrong – business deals are fostered by relationships and trust – local chambers could become rallying points for racially integrated deal-making and trade. A certain corporate leader from the Afrikaanse Handelsinstituut said to me during the business-unity talks, 'We have sold out the politics of South Africa, and we certainly are not going to allow you to sell out the economic sector.' Mbeki too had raised the option of the state funding the chamber movement with myself and Köpke in a meeting at the president's offices in Cape Town. My response was defiantly quick and to the point: 'Do you want to castrate us as an independent actor in the broader political economy?' Mbeki giggled and moved on to the next topic.

Deeply fearing the potential political consequences of this business manifestation of democracy, Mbeki, and big business, wanted consolidation on a top-down basis.

One of Wakeford's ambitions had seen the light of day: the creation of the South African Federated Chamber of Commerce, a staggered merger – over 36 months – of SACOB and the National African Federated Chamber of Commerce and Industry (NAFCOC). This posed a huge threat to Mbeki's elitist system and the creation of a black elite. After all, why would one require high-level crony BEE deals if all the natural energy of non-racial deal-making were to be induced across the country at local level? That is when long-time multibillionaire Patrice Motsepe and his henchmen stepped in to wreck the process.

This was a task performed with clinical precision and backed by big resources. NAFCOC was initially split into two and then the small guys were evicted like rats who had sold out their high-and-mighty peers. Local black business, which resembles micro-enterprise, simply had to wait its turn – no matter how indefinite that wait may be. The feeding frenzy for the black elite was not over: they wanted to remain as the gatekeepers of NAFCOC for as long as it took to remain at the trough. Motsepe was often seen with Mbeki at business-related trade-and-investment missions, and was a known supporter of the president at the time.

Wakeford was never opposed to deracialising the corporate sector, but continuously warned against crony capitalism, and encouraged a broad-based approach to BEE that did not exclude local integration of chambers. As it turned out, Wakeford's approach was far too idealistic and generous, in that it envisaged creation of a playing field in the economy that promoted non-racial integration at the most basic levels of the market system.

In Wakeford's view, had his plan been allowed to go through, the economic environment would not be the arena of conflict and contest that it is today:

> The markets would now be beginning to reap the rewards of greater participation by all and the barometer of discontent and relative deprivation would not be at boiling point. Chambers in most areas to this day are racially based and separate. NAFCOC continues to operate out of a spaza-shop environment whilst the South African Chamber of Commerce and Industry (formerly SACOB) and the Afrikkanse Handelsinstituut continue to host sophisticated and relatively well-resourced chambers. Inequality continues to pervade the business space and threatens the ongoing credence of the market system in South Africa while the elite, both black and white, look on dispassionately while Rome burns.

Jethro Goko, deputy editor of *Business Day* at the time, said that organised business had not yet grasped the incredibly important role that Wakeford had carved out for it in the broader political economy. Goko said Wakeford had given business credibility and that there was an aura of redemption and relevance among the broader citizenry. Goko said he was not sure whether 'they' had grasped the strategic importance of this valuable asset called Kevin Wakeford.

'They' would truly miss Wakeford at the sacrificial altar of expediency.

Financial Mail editor Caroline Southey, ever the agent of The Big and the Beautiful, attacked (naturally) the merger on 19 October 2002:

> For the past two years, the merger has been dogged by fierce resistance from within SACOB and NAFCOC, and from further afield ... Other ominous clouds hung over the launch. President Thabo Mbeki had been invited to make the keynote address. He wasn't there. Nor did government send a replacement.
>
> Those behind this week's launch believe passionately that a non-racial business organisation is key to generating economic growth in SA. By assisting, building and fostering small and medium-sized businesses from Gariep to Gauteng, the new business chamber will help

generate new economic energy, as well as wealth for individuals, and for the country.

Detractors argue that those bent on the merger have sown more division than they have nurtured unity ... There are also accusations that SACOB's leaders (Christoph Köpke as president and Kevin Wakeford as CEO) set a marching pace quite out of step with their members, many of whom are disaffected and angry ... Critics also argue that neither of the two merging entities is sufficiently representative to form a coherent new chamber. NAFCOC is a shambles. SACOB has suffered defections.

Long before the Rand Commission was even heard of, Wakeford's attempts at reform in the business sector were being frowned upon. As such, after Wakeford was forced to resign from SACOB, organised business reverted to type – the 'Big Man' syndrome.

Wakeford was offered the job of running the Eastern Cape Development Corporation. He took it up, and was astonished and completely shocked when he was settling in to find himself confronted by two certain individuals on the board of directors. They set on Wakeford like two crazed bulldogs that had overdosed on something illegal – mescaline, perhaps.

Wakeford resigned. He is convinced to this day that Mbeki set the pair on him, to somehow teach Wakeford a lesson, particularly after his criticism in his *Business Day* column of the political agendas driving the criminal-justice system.

There must also be a running chance that Mbeki had been seriously upset by what Wakeford 'discovered' – no matter how inadvertently and indirectly – about how the administration of exchange controls had become polluted on Tito Mboweni's watch. When Wakeford blew the whistle on the rand, he suspected that something in the system was rotten. Although he had specific names, such as Deutsche Bank and Sasol, these were incidental in his attempt to unearth a far broader picture. When he started out on his quest early in 2002, he had no idea about what was really going on inside the Reserve Bank. By the same token, he had no idea of what was going on inside the banking community.

The evidence about what the Reserve Bank was doing – and what it wasn't doing – was devastating. The list was long, and included the Reserve

Bank ranking as a net buyer of dollars during 2001. The bank also made it clear that it would not intervene to support the rand. But the most disturbing evidence had nothing to do with what was happening in the currency markets: it was about what *wasn't* going on in the currency markets. The Reserve Bank had been in dereliction of its duties. Mark Parker, executive general manager, treasury, at Nedcor Bank, was asked during the Rand Commission's hearings about recommendations Nedcor had made regarding the administration of exchange control. This is his reply:

In our opinion, the problems are as follows:
- Divergent interpretations of authorised dealers in respect of certain aspects of Reserve Bank rulings.
- The competitive nature of the marketplaces and authorised dealers at risk of losing client business in the event of overly strict interpretation of certain rulings.
- Lack of transparency of exchange-control-related information between Reserve Bank and authorised dealers, pertaining to specific approvals granted to multi-banked customers.
- The current requirement for the presentation of paper-based documentation to support cross-border payment transactions is not necessarily effective and is open to abuse. Such documentation is easily replicated.
- Initiatives to improve processing efficiencies through automation in the relevant back-office environments are restricted by the current high-cost, manual, paper-based exchange-control requirements.
- The difficulty of enforcing compliance with South African exchange controls against foreign banks.
- The accurate matching of multiple debit transactions against credit transactions of CFC accounts can be problematic. This is further complicated where clients maintain multiple CFC accounts at more than one authorised dealer.
- As I have already stated, paper-based supporting documentation is open to abuse and fraudulent replication.[5]

It is therefore recommended that compliance with exchange-control regulations be based on the electronic monitoring of trade and payment

transactions wherever possible. This would require the alignment/
integration of databases of the relevant parties involved in trade transactions, i.e. South African Revenue Service, South African Reserve Bank
and authorised dealers. The level of compliance could be improved by
placing more emphasis on the accountability of customers who hold
CFC accounts.

A process similar to the current 'Letter of Undertaking' for import
and export clients could be used for these account holders. Restrictions
could also be placed on the movement of funds between CFC accounts
held by persons at different authorised dealers. We have made reference
to the difficulty of monitoring funds held in such accounts.

In addition to the abovementioned specific recommendations, we
would suggest that a representative forum be established to review existing and/or planned future exchange controls, agree on procedures/
processes which will ensure high levels of compliance and ultimately
improve the effectiveness of such controls.

We would like to reiterate our willingness to cooperate with the
commission at all times and assist the relevant authorities where appropriate with regard to these matters.

It seemed truly unbelievable that exchange controls were still paper-based,
as when the system was first introduced more than 80 years ago. But this
was almost trivial within a system that had progressively become polluted
under the Reserve Bank's watch.

Was this the Rand Commission's 'Watergate moment'? If it was, then
the commission had been let off the hook by its terms of reference: it was
not mandated to look beyond the three transactions named by Wakeford.
By the same token, however, there was no reason for the commission to
ignore the Reserve Bank's regulatory and other failures. Instead, the Reserve
Bank's weaknesses, governance failures and ill-begotten policy decisions
were brushed to the side, and only mentioned in passing.

The lead agent promoting this agenda was the governor of the Reserve
Bank. It would have been an understatement to say that Tito Mboweni
flew into a rage. In one public speech, he launched a broadside at banks
that had sent their 'heads of treasuries', rather than CEOs, to testify at the
Rand Commission. The criticism was nonsensical: currency trading is a

specialised and technical area that bank CEOs delegate to those with long and successful experience in the currency markets. (In rare cases a CEO, like Goldman Sachs's Lloyd Blankfein, may rise from the trading pits.) This was one of Mboweni's many red herrings, no doubt aimed at distracting from the real issues at hand.

In this speech, Mboweni went so far as to use the word 'dishonest' in connection with South Africa's private-sector banks. Adopting the Big Man approach all over again, he patronisingly said: 'When I was a boy, I was told not to bite the hand that feeds you.' The meaning of this, intended or otherwise, was enough to terrify anyone in South African banking – and beyond. Mboweni appeared to be saying that banking licences in South Africa were at his pleasure, which translated into an automatic requirement of silence on the part of the banks.

The silence had been broken. Mboweni, paternalistic beyond measure, seemingly expected the world to crawl in front of him. His stinging criticism continued: 'Privately the chief executives of banks said we should not criticise each other, but they were doing it through their heads of treasuries.'[6] Whether the evidence had been given by CEOs or heads of treasury would have made no difference to the substance of testimony under oath. Had the CEOs testified, it is likely that their testimony would have been less articulate, but it would have been the truth. This was, after all, a judicial commission. Mboweni was somehow suggesting that because the banks had given him some kind of an undertaking, their evidence given under oath to the commission should somehow have been different – and would be most likely to include major omissions. If this was the case, then it indicated that Mboweni had an interesting attitude to the law.

Mboweni had long conducted a campaign against anything that he found even vaguely unpleasant. He had driven the fear of something really awful into the press in South Africa. It may not have surprised Mboweni that he was sometimes compared with Idi Amin, referring not only to Mboweni's impressive size.

On 29 May 2002, Mboweni wrote a long letter to *Business Day*, which appears to have been published in full. The content provides an astonishing insight into an imperious mind, glimpsed not so much in the highfalutin discussion that Mboweni disgorges on monetary policy, but in his attitude as to how the world should regard him, the governor of the Reserve Bank. In the letter, Mboweni patronisingly refers to 'open-mouth operations', which apparently is a jargonised reference to words that may be uttered from time to time by governors of central banks. Mboweni also refers to a specific meeting at which *Business Day* reporter Lukanyo Mnyanda was present. Mboweni bluntly portrays himself as an esteemed member of a national and international elite: 'I welcome debate and discussions on issues of national importance, such as monetary policy.'

As to the reference to 'national importance', Mboweni was no doubt adamant that he would never be seen as sequacious by anyone, and the 'I' seemed to include governors of central banks around the world.

Mboweni's tirade against Mnyanda includes some of the most pernicious and cruel sentences ever strung together: 'If your Mnyanda tried to do some reading, he would have known that OMOs [open-mouth operations] are not irregular in international banking. But what we have here is a glorification of utter and complete ignorance when a reputable financial daily publishes articles such as Mnyanda's. We are willing to assist your journalists if only they would ask.'

Mboweni adopts the Big Man approach, mixed up with some inscrutable sarcasm: 'I won't respond to the other jumbled up things in the second part of Mnyanda's article. It is difficult to work out exactly what he is saying. Maybe that is why the article is under the heading "Dismal Science".'

If this characterised Mboweni's discourse with a fellow human being, then there would be no surprise if he treated other humans with similar contempt. Mboweni's message, in a nutshell, was that Mnyanda was incurably inferior, and that Mboweni was irreversibly superior. This was, of course, the new South Africa.

The Rand Commission's Watergate moment had another inbuilt shield: racism. If anyone had accused the Reserve Bank of dereliction of duty, whether or not it was true, the accuser would have been branded a 'racist'. If the accusation of incompetence had been voiced, then, equally, the racism card would have been played.

Mboweni's intemperate conduct only seemed to deteriorate as the years went by. In an entry under his name in Wikipedia, the following is noted:

In his final years as Governor of the Reserve Bank (2007–2009), Mboweni was noted for his poor level of facilitation of the Bank's annual general meetings where shareholders were prevented from questioning the governor on basic corporate governance infringements and confusing financial reporting.

Mboweni was further mired in controversy when he insulted and accused a shareholder of being racist in a public meeting. Ironically, this led to Mboweni being brought before the Equality Court (2010) on charges of racism and prejudicial conduct.

Seen in the broader South African context, it should have been no surprise that the administration of exchange controls at the Reserve Bank was in a mess. There are few, if any, sectors of the public service, or within the universe of state-owned enterprises, that have not experienced major problems, especially over the past decade. By now, everyone is surely familiar with South Africa's catastrophic problems in education, healthcare and service delivery. Technically, the Reserve Bank is privately held, but it is very much controlled, like any central bank, by government. Much along the lines of the judiciary, central banks are deemed and treated as independent entities, but the appointment of officials is a choice only the government of the day can make.

Mboweni survived as governor well beyond Mbeki's years. He shared with Mbeki – and later, Jacob Zuma – the talent of being able to flip and rage in the public domain. Racial issues have inevitably ranked among the most demeaning and divisive of such unbecoming rants. In October 2004, Mbeki made an attack on commentators who argued that violent crime was out of control in South Africa, calling them 'white racists' who want the country to fail. He said crime levels were falling, but that even so, some journalists – and it was hardly a secret who he was thinking of – 'distorted reality' by depicting black people as 'barbaric savages' who liked to rape and kill.[7] Mboweni's conduct during his tenure as governor of the Reserve Bank created the impression of a man with mediocre talents, a man overwhelmed by an ambition to box way above his weight. The Rand Commission made no findings on the conduct of the Reserve Bank. Had it done so, there is no doubt that Mboweni would have been plunged into a deep and vicious depression, and he would have exploded, sooner or later, into hysterical attacks on anything he could drown with words.

In 2001 Mboweni was awarded a doctorate of economics, *honoris causa*, by the University of KwaZulu-Natal. This was not the first, and would not be the last, time that he was honoured. This raises questions over the analytical abilities – and even common sense – of the institutions that have chosen to hold Mboweni in such high regard. This can be upgraded into a far bigger and wider inquiry. It would be unfair to tar the entire nation with a single brush, but it is fair to say that South Africa's elite have developed into a pack of accomplished calumniators, muttering gibberish wherever they go. They hustle themselves, they hustle each other and they hustle the world.

It should be mentioned that in the *Global Competitiveness Report 2012–2013*, published by the World Economic Forum, South Africa ranked 52nd out of 144 countries included in the survey. But consider that South Africa ranked first in the world in the 'regulation of securities exchanges'. If that were not enough, South Africa was ranked first in the world in terms of 'strength of reporting and auditing standards'. In terms of 'soundness of banks', it was ranked second in the world.

The South African contributors to the survey are listed as Business Leadership South Africa (Frieda Dowie, director, and Thero Setiloane, CEO) and Business Unity South Africa (Nomaxabiso Majokweni, CEO, and Joan Stott, executive director, economic policy). These learned people are living in some kind of warp, beyond the extreme reaches of cloud cuckoo land. If South Africa deserves any number-one ranking, it would be in a category that could loosely be headed 'collusion in covering up stinky money-grubbing plots that harvest crops of unimaginable bounty'.

The Kebble saga, which burst into life when Brett Kebble was murdered on 27 September 2005, never involved the banking system as such. Bank accounts were used extensively in the Kebble frauds, and he was close to certain banks, too close. But that is different to imperilling the banking system. Likewise, Kebble was not involved in any active way in the 2001 trashing of the rand. Mountains of exhaustively researched evidence have shown that the Kebble saga was about market abuse, fiscal abuse, breaches of exchange control and straightforward corruption in all its many guises.

There were many elements of insider trading, which rank, however, as small in the overall scheme of things.

The criminal investigation into South Africa's biggest-ever fraud died a quiet death. The main reason was the number of people in high places who had benefited from Kebble's largesse: there had to be a cover-up. And the cover-up was engineered and implemented by a number of parties, including certain banks, and a good number of accountants, lawyers and other hustlers.

Kebble may have had a number of private-sector entities and individuals tied to his nether regions, but, equally, there were political, law-enforcement and intelligence-community figures also tied to those nether regions.

In the private sector, the mandarins at the JSE showed no hesitation in joining the cover-up. If this were not enough, the JSE showed little hesitation in picking off easy targets, and, in some cases, simply propagating plain nonsense. In an interview on 19 October 2011, Russell Loubser, who was to retire after 15 years as the CEO of the JSE, craftily juggled his lofty financial balls: 'Here in South Africa our credo is there are only two parties who count in my game which is the issuer and investor, the issuer being the listed company and the investor being, of whatever nature, short term, long term, speculative, non-speculative, local, and foreign. Those are the only two parties that count in South Africa ...'[8]

Investors in Randgold, a listed company, were defrauded of more than 90 per cent of the value of their asset, and the JSE did nothing. Neither the JSE nor the Financial Services Board treated the Kebble era and its aftermath as anything more than a fleeting freak flash that lit the markets in 1997 and then disappeared, like a rodent on tequila, never to be seen again. The smug and consistent posture has paid off well given the number-one ranking that South Africa occupies in the World Economic Forum survey. One day, however, the truth will out.

Epilogue

Deutsche Bank Johannesburg ... Martin Kingston ... Niall Carroll ... The Watson brothers ... Jürgen Schrempp ... Christoph Köpke ... Raymond Parsons ... Maria Ramos ... ABSA and Barclays ... Sasol ... Mandla Gantsho ... Penuell Maduna ... John Myburgh ... Sasol (again) ... Trevor Manuel ... Tito Mboweni ... Caroline Southey ... Brett Kebble ... South African Airways ... Kevin Wakeford ... The press ... Christine Qunta ... George Papadakis.

'The banker must at all times conduct himself so as to justify the confidence of his clients in him.' – J.P. Morgan, Jr

Deutsche Bank Johannesburg was never quite the same. It seemed that someone or something, most likely the Deutsche Bank head office in Frankfurt, had read the Johannesburg branch some kind of riot act. If so, it was carefully orchestrated to make personnel changes appear to be relatively smooth. There were also carefully crafted changes of personnel at Deutsche Securities Johannesburg.

Generally, Deutsche Bank moved effortlessly from one scandal to another. At the risk of trying the reader's patience, please allow this contemporary update to suffice, from Jonathan Weil, published by Bloomberg on 1 February 2013:

> The first people to tell the public that the world's oldest bank was cooking its books weren't the bank's executives, its outside auditors at KPMG, its regulators at the Bank of Italy, or anyone else who had a duty to keep the place honest.
>
> They were journalists with a good source: a stack of documents from another bank that helped craft the scheme. About two weeks ago, *Bloomberg News* reporters Elisa Martinuzzi and Nicholas Dunbar broke the story that Deutsche Bank AG designed a derivative in December 2008 for Banca Monte dei Paschi di Siena SpA that hid the Italian

lender's losses before it sought a 1.9 billion euro ($2.6 billion) taxpayer bailout in 2009.[1]

Banca Monte dei Paschi di Siena, the world's oldest surviving bank, dating from 1472, was bailed out by the Bank of Italy to the tune of €3.9 billion on 26 January 2013.

Martin Kingston lost his plum job as chairman of Deutsche Bank Johannesburg in 2003. It was all quite hushed. Kingston had first visited South Africa in 1990 and moved to the country in 1995. Sometime during 2003, he returned to the UK and announced the formation of his own advisory firm, Longcross Capital. Later he returned to South Africa. He was soon marketing himself as heading the local office of N.M. Rothschild. In this capacity, Kingston and his team peddled itself as having 'significant experience in and understanding of local markets and their regulators'. Kingston's focus moved to 'broad-based black economic empowerment' and 'facilitating dialogue between clients and the various stakeholders'. The drivel continued: 'We were the first advisory house in South Africa to implement an empowerment transaction, and our involvement in BBBEE transactions includes those of Anglo American, Anglo Platinum, Anglo Coal, Xstrata and Palabora Mining Company.'

What follows has been touted as one of Kingston's favourite quotes: 'Whatever I do, I am committed to continuing to play whatever role I can in implementing sustainable transformation in SA.'[2] Thankfully, that sustainability did not extend to what happened to the rand back in 2001. As for making a new life in broad-based BEE, it was perhaps no coincidence that increasing calls were made for the complete abolition of broad-based BEE. The policy had not created broad-based anything. It had not created jobs; if anything, jobs had been lost. But it had certainly empowered a tiny elite. It was in and around this group that Kingston found himself, on the hunt for the next big money ball.

On 29 February 2004, Deutsche Bank Securities Johannesburg's **Niall Carroll** quit and moved to an executive job at the Royal Bafokeng Nation. During the Rand Commission, Carroll had played a highly significant, and ineffective, role in press relations on behalf of Deutsche. He was close to a number of journalists. He lacked any real charm or personality, relying instead on his job title. In March 2012, Carroll quit his job at Royal Bafokeng Holdings.

The Watson brothers, who had felt the evils of the apartheid system in Port Elizabeth, went on about their family businesses as ever. For Wakeford, the Watsons are

> still close friends to this day and I continue to respect and appreciate all that they have done in contributing to my life. Even after my alienation as a result of the outcome of the commission into the rapid depreciation of the rand, they stood with me and assisted me immeasurably – even in securing me business opportunities when it was extremely difficult to put bread on the table and where doors kept closing on me.

The Watsons give white South Africans genuine credibility, a sense of redemption. Yet so many whites remain deceived as to who the family really are and what they truly stand for. The propaganda against the family has been sustained to this day, possibly as a reminder to most whites of what living non-racialism is truly about. Over many years, I have encountered, and held discussions of various kinds with, Valence, Ronnie and Gavin Watson, and I await the day when I can chew some fat with Cheeky Watson. His son, Luke, a world-class rugby player, has not escaped the ongoing controversies associated with the Watsons.

Jürgen Schrempp, the architect of the global merger between Daimler Benz and Chrysler, looked increasingly disconsolate as the deal continued to degenerate, which it had done from day one. It had always been one of the silliest mergers in the history of the global auto industry. Schrempp, who was hailed as a genius at the start of the process, was hoisted by his own petard. It couldn't have happened to a nicer guy – however that's said in German.

On a different level, Schrempp found himself in a bit of a storm upon the announcement of the Daimler–Chrysler merger, when he suggested that his career was a greater priority than his wife. Schrempp made waves after he went to a company party where he was said to have departed carrying his female assistant, Lydia Deininger (now his wife), over his shoulder. Apparently he had a bottle of champagne in his other hand.[3]

Christoph Köpke kind of faded away and grows flowers for foreign and domestic florists in the Pelindaba area, west of Pretoria, while spending time in Germany for half of each year. He was around during the latter parts of 2012, but refused to take my calls or respond to text messages.

Raymond Parsons, even today, perhaps ironically, still has an executive role in organised business, irrespective of his relationship with reality, or otherwise. He is, however, very in tune with the games elitists play; hence the prevailing tolerance of his continued tenure at Business Unity SA.

Maria Ramos moved from director general of South Africa's Treasury to CEO of Transnet, the state rail, port and pipeline monopoly, in January 2004. In 2009 she became CEO of ABSA, and a member of ABSA parent Barclays plc's executive committee. Barclays had bought a 55.5 per cent stake in ABSA during 2005.

In July 2012, the global banking sector, seemingly determined to climb into deeper and deeper holes, was again exposed in the LIBOR (the London inter-bank offered rate) scandal. Barclays was then first mover among the culprits. Hoping for soft punishment, it agreed to pay fines and penalties of $453 million, and promised full cooperation with authorities in the UK and the US.

Barclays, and perhaps 20 other global banks, had acted to manipulate global benchmark interest rates, of which LIBOR is the most important. The scam was first uncovered in an investigation initiated in 2008 by the Commodity Futures Trading Commission (CFTC), a US regulator. CFTC chairman Gary Gensler described the rate-rigging scandal as 'historic'. He explained that LIBOR 'underpins so many different financial transactions that the effects of tampering with it could be hard to fathom'. Gensler said the LIBOR rate is 'embedded in ... many of your mortgages, your credit card loans, and anything that you borrow against'.[4]

David Meister, the CFTC's director of enforcement, remarked that 'the American public and our markets rely upon the integrity of benchmark interest rates like LIBOR and Euribor because they form the basis for hundreds of trillions of dollars of transactions and affect nearly every corner of the global economy'.

In pronouncements on its settlement with Barclays, the CFTC said that Barclays had 'attempted to manipulate and made false reports concerning two global benchmark interest rates, LIBOR and Euribor, on numerous occasions and sometimes on a daily basis over a four-year period, commencing as early as 2005'.[5] The investigation into LIBOR and related scams has extended to as many as 20 of the big banks in an increasing number of countries, including, besides the US and the UK, Canada, Japan, the EU and Switzerland. It seemed that Barclays did not deny guilt. Bob Diamond, who resigned as the CEO of Barclays on 3 July 2012, told staff in a memo that 'on the majority of days, no requests were made at all' – to manipulate LIBOR, that is.[6] As *The Economist* commented, 'this was rather like an adulterer saying that he was faithful on most days'.[7]

Ramos, who had so far sat on the Barclays executive committee for two and a half years, told the Johannesburg-based *Sunday Times* that 'it's important for us to know what we're about. We're about integrity and honesty, trustworthiness and fairness. And I know that Barclays is about that.' Ramos said she was 'not concerned that ABSA's image would be contaminated by its close association with Barclays'.[8]

In the great South African tradition, Ramos just brushed the LIBOR story aside, as if Barclays was not the majority shareholder in ABSA, and as if she did not sit on the Barclays executive committee. CFTC chairman Gensler may have disagreed with Ramos's sentiments: 'The real problem with the LIBOR scandal is that it erodes public trust in a financial system already regarded with suspicion.'[9]

Sasol played a truly amazing role in the wake of the Rand Commission. Mandla Gantsho, who, like Kevin Wakeford, originated from Port Elizabeth, and who, along with John Myburgh, delivered the majority report of the Rand Commission, was appointed a director of Sasol in 2003. He was also appointed a director of, among others, the South African Reserve Bank. One or two cynics asked whether the appointments were some kind of 'reward' for the stance Gantsho had taken at the Rand Commission. At one point, some such comment from Moneyweb infuriated Gantsho to the point where he seemed to be considering taking legal action. The lawyers instructed by Gantsho were none other than Bowman Gilfillan, a firm in which Penuell Maduna was now a partner.

Penuell Mpapa Maduna, the justice minister who presided over the Rand Commission, appeared in a Sasol announcement on 1 July 2006. This was a broad-based black economic empowerment transaction, in which Tshwarisano acquired 25 per cent of Sasol subsidiary Sasol Oil for R1.45 billion. According to Sasol, 'Tshwarisano, which means "pulling together" in Sesotho, comprises many historically disadvantaged groups around the country. Its chief promoters are Dr Penuell Maduna, Ms Hixonia Nyasulu and Mr Reuel Khoza.'[10]

Maduna was also seen as a favoured partner in a number of other BEE deals. It may be recalled that in 2007, nine individual founding shareholders in Eland Platinum innocently scored a debt-free R2.3 billion gain on occasion of the cash bid for the company by Xstrata. The biggest individual gain was notched up by Loucas Pouroulis, at R819 million – pre-tax, of course. Eland Platinum's BEE partners were mysterious, but Maduna's name appeared, no matter how obliquely.

Maduna played an extraordinarily ambiguous role as the minister of justice. In 2003 he was to indirectly cross paths with Kevin Wakeford, who, during and after the Rand Commission, inspired whistle-blowers across the country. The case of Mike Tshishonga was perhaps the most dramatic. In October 2003, Tshishonga, then a justice department deputy director general, levelled serious accusations at the then justice minister, Penuell Maduna. Prior to going public at a press function held at a hotel in Pretoria, Tshishonga had consulted extensively with Wakeford and, to some extent, with me. When the news was in the public domain, I published a series of articles on the subject on Moneyweb. This was another story that the press had no appetite for; once again, Moneyweb took it on.

Tshishonga, who was also MD of the Master's Business Unit, which oversees liquidations in the private sector, accused Maduna of conducting a 'nepotistic' relationship with a liquidator who went by the name of Enver Motala, a shady character who was part of an extensive web.

In October 2003, Tshishonga's concerns were dismissed as 'rumours'. Vusi Pikoli, who had from 1999 served as Maduna's director general in the justice department, said: 'I was never informed of the allegations ... The first time I heard about it is when I saw it in the newspaper [in October 2003].'[11] Pikoli later testified that he did not believe what he had heard, and therefore did not order an investigation. Tshishonga had accused Maduna of being involved in 'exploitation and abuse of state apparatus and the infrastructure and staff of the Department of Justice and Constitutional Development ... for the purposes of advancing his personal interests and agendas'.[12]

Earlier in the year, on 28 January 2003, Maduna had called Tshishonga and stated: 'You are the first casualty ... I have decided to remove you as the head of the Master's Business Unit. As to where the director general will put you, I don't care; he will see where to put you.'[13] Maduna, unable to dispose of Tshishonga in any vaguely normal way, had simply emasculated him. The next day, Pikoli wrote to Tshishonga: 'It is with sadness that I have to convey to you the Minister's telephonic instructions ...'[14] Pikoli again wrote to Tshishonga on 19 February, giving him a new job where there was no job to be done.

Rewind to the end of 1999, when Oliver Powell, one of the country's leading liquidators, was 'bust' by Maduna, as justice minister. Maduna stated that 'possible prosecutions for alleged corruption at the Pretoria Master's Office were expected as early as next month'. To this day, no such prosecutions have ever been launched, but within a short space of time, back then, Powell was vanquished; his reputation was ruined forever. Enver Motala, who represented himself as a liquidator, emerged from the *platteland* as the self-confessed 'no. 1' in the national sector.

The liquidations sector is a big nut with a very thick shell, and a beautiful soft and sweet centre. Liquidators are paid a percentage of the assets recovered, rather than by the hour, which applies to most professional jobs. In South Africa liquidators are not required to have any qualification, even a matric, which can be earned at the end of senior school. There has never been any evidence that Motala holds so much as a matric. One of the earlier liquidations in which Motala secured an appointment was in the so-called RAG case, the Retail Apparel Group. The assets under the chop were estimated to be worth around R1 billion. This meant the liquidators – Motala was one of five – stood to earn up to an aggregate of about R100 million.

Maduna reacted to Tshishonga by publicly calling him a 'dunderhead'. Both Powell and Tshishonga won case after case in defending their innocence.[15] Maduna never once bothered to show his face in Tshishonga's hearings – that grubby job was handled by Pikoli. In February 2004, the Labour Court ordered Tshishonga's reinstatement as MD of the Master's Business Unit, subject to the outcome of his disciplinary hearing (he had been suspended in October 2003). Tshishonga was cleared on all counts in July 2004, under whistle-blower's legislation. Pikoli refused to reinstate Tshishonga, as ordered by the court. In jurisdictions that profess to follow the rule of law, this is known as contempt of court.

Move to 24 August 2009, when Motala was looking famous at a press conference at the luxury hotel in Melrose Arch, Johannesburg. I asked how it was that Motala was appointed as one of the provisional liquidators to the Pamodzi Gold case, already one of the most notorious liquidations in national history. It was, said Motala, by way of the Master's panel in Pretoria. Anyone familiar with the liquidations sector knew that the 'panel' was a euphemism for Ben Nell, acting alone. Motala confirmed that he had been appointed on a discretionary basis – that is, without support from any creditor or trade union.

Asked if he knew Pretoria attorney Henk Strydom, Motala said yes, and that he was in the audience. Your enthusiastic author then asked Strydom if he is and/or was personal attorney to Ben Nell. Under glaring lights, Strydom had no choice but to confirm. Asked how many applications he had brought to have Pamodzi Gold finally dumped into provisional liquidation, Strydom said it was six or seven. In the manner of an ambulance-chaser, Strydom had finally succeeded and Nell appointed Motala to yet another liquidation that would generate tens of millions of rands in fees. It was almost too sweet to bear.

For more than a decade, the various justice directors general and heads of the NPA have ignored, at very best, the outrageous abuses in the liquidations sector, but there has at least been an atom of light. On 5 September 2011, the deputy master of the High Court, Pretoria, wrote a long letter to Motala, telling him that he had been removed from the panel of liquidators, Pretoria.

The office has jurisdiction over liquidators working in the province of Gauteng, which includes Johannesburg. As such, Motala would no longer be selected for any appointments in the country's smallest but most prosperous – and populous – province. The letter to Motala stated, inter alia, that:

> On 17 August you attended at the Master's office and gave evidence under oath. In the course of the sworn testimony you
>
>> 9.1 denied that you have ever been convicted of theft or fraud;
>>
>> 9.2 stated that you had no idea of the identity of the person referred to in *The Citizen* article as sharing your identity number;
>>
>> 9.3 had no idea of the offences allegedly committed by that person;
>>
>> 9.4 did not know who Enver Mohamed Dawood is; and
>>
>> 9.5 knew nothing of the convictions of theft and fraud attributed to Dawood.
>
> On 17 August 2011 the Master wrote to you and informed you that the Master's investigations had revealed that:
>
>> 10.1 one Enver Mohamed Dawood had been convicted of theft and 93 counts of fraud;
>>
>> 10.2 Dawood (who coincidentally has the same first two names as you) is the person who shares with you the identification number as referred to in the article published in *The Citizen*;
>>
>> 10.3 both you and Dawood were born on 20 September 1953;
>>
>> 10.4 documentation from the Department of Internal Affairs disclosed that Enver Mohamed Dawood and Enver Mohamed Motala are the same person more particularly in that on 23 June 1981 the Department had consented to Enver Mohamed Dawood changing his name to Enver Mohamed Motala; and
>>
>> 10.5 an application made in your name to the South African Police on 30 July 1992 for a firearm licence disclosed an acknowledgement by you of convictions which appear to accord with those attributed to Enver Mohamed Dawood.[16]

Motala had been given ample opportunity to explain himself, according to the Master's Office. He had failed to do so, and had thus been removed from the panel. As usual, Motala unleashed a small army of lawyers to battle for him all over again.

Back on 2 July 2004, the Serious Economic Offences Unit, an elite division of the South African Police Service, had arrested Motala on allegations of fraud and corruption. During the early parts of 2004, I sat down to a long meeting with Jackie Selebi, the then commissioner of police, to discuss a number of issues, including Enver Motala's unconscionable conduct. A few months later, Motala was arrested. As is to be expected within South Africa's weak law-enforcement and prosecutions environment, so it was that in due course, the case disappeared into thin air.

During my meeting with Selebi, the police commissioner had expressed astonishment over Maduna. Selebi said that he had spent his years in exile with Maduna, and that when they returned to South Africa, neither of them had a 'damn thing'. Selebi mentioned that he had recently visited Maduna at his 'mansion' in Bryanston. By the time the South African legal system, such as it is, had caught up with Motala in 2011, the man who had been convicted of dozens of counts of white-collar crimes had spent more than a decade as a liquidator and had earned fees of more than R100 million. Healthy chunks of this fouled booty had gone, in turn, to the baffling number of lawyers Motala deployed for any number of reasons. The names of these lawyers, which include a prominent senior counsel, are well known. If any of them return to earth in their next lives, they would undoubtedly all be whelped at the same time as a pack of vampire hyenas.

While Maduna was justice minister, he went to extraordinary lengths to protect Motala. The facts about Motala, as put to Motala by the master of the court in September 2011, were equally available to Maduna and Pikoli back in 2003, when Tshishonga had accused Maduna of a number of serious inadequacies in his relationship with Motala. Pikoli, a Marxist, had defended Maduna 'through thick and thin'.

Sadly, the system rumbles on, degenerating by the day. On 2 March 2012, the *Mail & Guardian* reported that Enver Motala had 'secretly applied for a presidential pardon for fraud and theft – apparently as part of a bid to overturn the decision by the master of the High Court to blacklist him. And he has drafted ANC heavyweights to support him, including Winnie Madikizela-Mandela and party security boss Tito Maleka.'

It was of no small import that during his long reign as number-one liquidator, Motala had forged close links with the Scorpions, the then investigative unit of the NPA, and was described in some parts of the press as the 'Scorpions liquidator'.

Pikoli would famously become head of the NPA on 31 January 2005, replacing Bulelani Ngcuka. It was Pikoli who would indict police commissioner Jackie Selebi on charges of corruption. Pikoli was eventually fired for his efforts. Selebi was found guilty and sentenced to 15 years in the slammer. Shortly after starting his service, he was released on medical parole.

Something seemed a little weird: Pikoli had protected Maduna regardless of the facts that were easily available to Pikoli, and yet Pikoli had chased down Selebi with a fervour that bordered on obsession, going so far as to lose his job. To me, it was entirely possible that Selebi was being punished for having dared to arrest Motala. If so, it was a grim outcome, reflecting heavily on a country that has completely lost its moral compass, if not its head. Was this not another glaring case of public law enforcement being used to pursue private agendas?

After Pikoli was sent packing from his job as head of the NPA, he was replaced by Menzi Simelane, who moved up from director general of justice. Archbishop Emeritus Desmond Tutu described Simelane's new appointment as 'an aberration'.[17] This observation gained heavy traction in 2008, when Simelane gave testimony to the Frene Ginwala inquiry into Pikoli's fitness to head the NPA. Ginwala was quoted as saying that in general, Simelane's 'conduct left much to be desired. His testimony was contradictory and without basis in law ... In cross-examination on his role, the DG was asked whether he had sought legal opinion from senior counsel on the responsibilities of the responsible accounting officer ... Having initially denied doing so, he finally admitted that he [had] sought such an opinion.'[18]

The Democratic Alliance, the official opposition, instituted a court case against Simelane on the basis that he was not fit to head the NPA. Simelane lost the case and his job.

It is of note that Brett Kebble had followed the 'career' of Enver Motala in great detail and with great interest. The extent to which Motala was protected, and by whom, convinced Kebble that justice in South Africa was vulnerable to the influences of unseemly people driven by personal agendas. Kebble was inconsolably astonished by a system that allowed a convict with nearly 100 white-collar criminal convictions and a 'new' name to operate so brazenly in the open, and with the clear support of top-end bureaucrats and politicians.

It seemed that **John Myburgh** was also fondly remembered by Sasol and the banking sector. After the Rand Commission, he was appointed chairman of the board of directors of the Ombudsman for Banking Services, a position that he served in for many years. It was a nice, soft job.

From August 2002 to March 2003, Myburgh was appointed to conduct a review of the corporate governance of the five biggest South African banks. He was appointed chairman of the Sasol Accident Trust, where he served from 2006 to 2009. In 2009 he was involved in the review of Sasol's competition-law compliance.

Sasol, meanwhile, found itself at the receiving end of a number of lawsuits. Among the more impressive, on 1 October 2008, after an investigation by the European Commission, the European Union found that members of the European paraffin-wax industry, including Sasol Wax GmbH, had formed a cartel and violated antitrust laws.

A fine of €318 million was imposed by the European Commission on Sasol Wax GmbH. According to the decision of the European Commission, an infringement of antitrust laws had commenced in 1992 or even earlier. In 1995, Sasol became a co-shareholder in an existing wax business located in Hamburg, Germany. In July 2002, Sasol acquired the remaining shares in the joint venture and became the sole shareholder of the business.

Sasol said it 'was unaware of these infringements before the European Commission commenced their investigation at the wax business in Hamburg in April 2005'.[19]

On 15 December 2008, all Sasol companies affected by the decision lodged an appeal with the European Union's General Court against the decision of the European Commission on the basis that the fine was excessive and should be reduced. Sasol separately warned that 'as a result of the fine imposed on Sasol Wax GmbH, it is possible that customers may institute court proceedings against Sasol Wax for compensation of damages'.[20]

Sasol has been at the receiving end of a number of antitrust cases. Without stretching the point, Sasol in some ways resembles so many banks in the way it seems to prefer to play by its own rules, knowing that, at worst, it may one day face fines – no matter how substantial.

Trevor Manuel went on to become the longest-serving finance minister in the world, according to some reports. He then moved into a special ministerial position in the president's office.

Manuel, who is not shy about shooting from the hip, in his 2002 budget speech gleefully sprang a truly stinging attack on the private sector. He told Parliament:

> The Enron debacle has brought into sharp relief a number of key issues – weak or non-existent governance structures, the fiduciary responsibility of directors, negligent and sometimes reckless management, ineffective auditing, independence of auditors and conflicts of interest arising from inadequate separation between auditing and consultancy.[21]

As time would show, Enron was far from being a creation of accountants, contrary to what many, including Manuel, seemed to have immediately concluded. For Manuel, this was another gaffe, vaguely in the same arena as his intemperate remark on 'amorphous markets'. Manuel had little, if any, hard-core experience in the international arena, or in markets.

Manuel was silent on the extensive evidence given to the Rand Commission, which had shown the Reserve Bank's administration of exchange controls to be scandalously short of acceptable. For Manuel, the private sector and the markets were a far easier target.

No matter how impressive his track record as South Africa's minister of finance, Manuel has to live with the reality that the country's economy has for years grown at suboptimal rates. And this is likely to persist.

Tito Mboweni, eighth governor of the South African Reserve Bank, from 1999 to 2009, was appointed to the board and as chairman of AngloGold

Ashanti on 1 June 2010. Mboweni was also appointed non-executive chairman of Nampak, one of the companies under investigation at the Rand Commission. He was also appointed as 'an international advisor' to Goldman Sachs.

It may be recalled that on 15 July 2010, the SEC in the US boldly announced that 'Goldman, Sachs & Co. will pay $550 million and reform its business practices to settle SEC charges that Goldman misled investors in a subprime mortgage product just as the US housing market was starting to collapse'. So far, this has been the biggest settlement in Wall Street history. Goldman naturally denied any wrongdoing.[22]

In a tribute in its 2011 annual report, AngloGold Ashanti said that Mboweni, as labour minister from 1994 to 1998, 'was the architect of South Africa's post-apartheid labour legislation which today continues to provide the basis for the mutually respectful labour relationships central to AngloGold Ashanti's operational approach in South Africa'. During 2012, South Africa experienced some of the most violent and disruptive labour strikes in the country's history. One of them was the tragic event known as the Marikana massacre, in August 2012.

In its *Global Competitiveness Report 2012–2013*, the World Economic Forum ranked South Africa 52nd overall out of 144 countries surveyed. Among the subcategories, South Africa ranked 144th for 'cooperation in labour–employer relations'; 140th for 'flexibility in wage determination'; and 143rd for 'hiring and firing practices'.[23] This suggests that Mboweni's legacy as labour minister left nothing to the imagination.

Caroline Southey moved on from the *Financial Mail*. Early in 2001, she had invited Wakeford to a dinner in the cellar at The Saxon, an upmarket establishment in Johannesburg – the same venue chosen by Lady Gaga in 2012, put together by an insurance tycoon, Douw Steyn. Also present at the dinner were Jacko Maree, the CEO of Standard Bank, and no less than Tito Mboweni. The dinner was hosted by Southey. In the months ahead, when he was awarded 'businessman of the month', Maree would say that he was embarrassed to accept the honour because a few months before, the award had been made to Wakeford.

After Southey moved on from the *Financial Mail*, she was given a plush executive job at Standard Bank. During 2010, she really moved up in the world, when she moved from Standard Bank to ABSA and took up the position of specialist: chief executive of communications. Southey's new boss was none other than ABSA CEO Maria Ramos. Revolving doors? Most certainly, but of the Congo, not Washington, type.

One of **Brett Kebble**'s biggest-ever transactions, which went down on 13 December 2001, almost at the rand's lowest point, was not so much mentioned at the Rand Commission. Western Areas, which was building the ultra-deep South Deep gold mine, west of Johannesburg, had defaulted on debt that it owed to Investec. Western Areas was significant to Brett Kebble, in that it represented his single most important personal investment. It was a listed company, and he ranked, indirectly, as the single biggest individual shareholder. As the CEO of Western Areas, Kebble authorised and signed a 'hedge book', which came into effect on 13 December 2001.

It was no coincidence that Investec was a one-third counterparty on the other side of the Western Areas hedge book, as one of three 'hedge banks'. Seen in context, it is reasonable to suspect that Investec played a significant role in strong-arming Western Areas into signing onto a hedge book that no sane person would ever have agreed to. The Western Areas 'hedge book' was never any such thing. It was a reckless, brutal, naked-assed cash-raising exercise.

Publicly, the hedge book was marketed as nirvana. In December 2001, $104 million in cash rolled into Western Areas. The cash was converted to rands. The debt that Western Areas owed to Investec was immediately repaid.

While the hedge book meant that Western Areas received a significant cash injection, the flip side was a horror. Western Areas had, among other things, sold call options of over 1.8 million ounces of gold at an average strike price of around $300 per ounce for gold that would be produced over more than the next decade. This is no misprint: the call options were done at around $300 an ounce.

In other words, for more than a decade, Western Areas would be forced to sell a portion of its gold production for $300 an ounce, regardless of the spot price for gold bullion. The Western Areas hedge book would prove to be one of the most toxic in global gold-mining history: over the decade ahead, gold bullion would easily clear the $1 000-an-ounce mark and later, during the latter parts of 2011, push on in an attempt to breach the $2 000-an-ounce level.

The Western Areas hedge book was finally closed down in January 2007, when its new owner, Gold Fields, paid an astonishing $528 million in cash to kill the hedge book once and for all. The beneficiaries were the three hedge banks. Investec cashed in on huge benefits. All told, Gold Fields paid $3 billion to buy South Deep and close down its hedge book.

Kebble took a double negative whammy when he signed off the Western Areas hedge book in mid-December 2001. The rand was at historic lows, which meant that any gold sold forward from Western Areas would translate to fewer rands, all else being equal. Second, the hedge book was signed at a time, more or less, when the dollar gold-bullion price was at multi-decade lows. Seen as a cocktail, it was going to be like downing litres of battery acid.

South African Airways (SAA) had nothing to do with the Rand Commission – or did it? Some of its mega-transactions could well have been around in the background during 2001. According to SAA, the company's most important and material risk is that the airline's net exposure to dollars is negative. In other words, its dollar inflows fall short of covering its foreign outflows. The exposures arise mainly from entering into long-term (i.e. 10 to 12 years) dollar-denominated financing; operating lease contracts; short-term fuel exposures; and dollar contractual obligations for the acquisition of aircraft and equipment. Consequently, SAA executes a hedging programme.

Hedging, properly designed and executed, is a form of insurance. A well-designed hedge book can cope with extreme fluctuations, both on the upside and on the downside. A hedge book should be properly managed by an expert agent, such as a specialist division of a bank. Monitored minute by minute, a properly managed hedge book can limit its losses by executing 'cover' transactions during the life of the hedge book.

In practice, the beneficiaries of a hedge book tend to say and do very little when the client hits a well. Sometimes, the hedge book goes the other way – where the client profits. And so it was that on 31 March 2002 the total hedge portfolio of SAA reflected a positive mark-to-market value of R2.3 billion. In other words, there were excellent unrealised profits sitting in the hedge book.

What happens next is seriously rotten. Given the collapse of the rand during 2001, SAA, as soon became apparent, had implemented a hedge book based on the notion that the rand would continue going south.

On 31 March 2003, the mark-to-market value of SAA's hedge book had reversed by a massive amount: it was sitting at a negative R4.5 billion. This represented a swing of nearly R7 billion from the positive position a year before. SAA's hedge book continued to deteriorate at a rapid rate. There were signs that the hedge book was not being actively managed, and that it had been designed with few, if any, stop-losses. The position deteriorated to far beyond crisis point and SAA had no choice but to implement a decision to kill the entire hedge book – something that would require billions in cash.

Hedge books are a zero-sum game: for every R1.00 loss, someone, or something, out there receives R1.00. The two add up to zero. Hedge books, along with other kinds of derivatives, always include an expiry date – when the initial contract terminates and the parties must settle. In some circumstances, where the debtor has substantial financial muscle, the creditor may agree to 'roll over' the contract, but sooner or later the contract will terminate and, after settlement, the net value of the instrument will be zero.

On 30 June 2004, something, or someone, was given a cash cheque by SAA to the tune of R5.958 billion. The hedge-book liabilities were settled with sums of R2 billion (the balance on SAA's 2003 share issue), plus proceeds of R4 billion, raised by issuing a compulsory convertible loan to SAA's parent, Transnet, a state-owned enterprise. SAA had been fed and had eaten a vicious lemon of a hedge book.

Kevin Wakeford picked himself up and continued with his life after the Rand Commission and his subsequent departure from SACOB in October 2002. For him, blowing the whistle on the rand was a 'defining moment'. His view of the Rand Commission is that it turned into 'a lame duck'. He is convinced that it was closed down too quickly:

> It looked into the case studies that I'd presented, it didn't look too
> much broader than that; in my view, if it had, I believe a lot more

would have come out. The rand at that time had gone to R13.84 to the dollar and about R20 to the pound. After the commission, the rand went all the way to around R5.70 to the dollar and at the end of 2012 was sitting where it was more than 10 years ago.

I'm quite happy that this in a sense has vindicated what I did at the time. It illuminated the markets and I think when there's illumination and light, darkness recedes and a lot of the skulduggery stopped. I'm not saying it stopped completely, it will always be there in the markets, you're going to have your foxes in the marketplace, as Clem Sunter calls them; they're there.

If I look back, I would do exactly the same thing; I don't think I would have done anything differently. I possibly would have been less naive and perhaps a little bit more – as we say in Afrikaans – *vasberade*, and I would have been far more aggressive in taking on some of those issues.

For instance, when the commission closed perhaps it should have been challenged in a court of law and the findings, particularly the minority report, which pointed to the need for prosecution and further investigation, I think perhaps it would have been more prudent of me then to institute some kind of class action against those who had shut it down for whatever reason they had. One small consolation was that President Thabo Mbeki thanked and acknowledged those who sounded the alarm on the rand in his speech at the ANC elective conference in December 2002 in Stellenbosch.

Facing a new life in the closing months of 2002, Wakeford sold properties that he owned and traded in his vehicle for a cheaper one. He went back to 'some really earthly living'. Wakeford recalls his time after leaving SACOB as one where he had 'a number of very, very tough years. I think there were a lot of people who sympathised with me, a lot of people who identified with what had happened, but the character and nature of the business realm is that you stay away from anything that's perceived as controversial.'

In 2003 and 2004, Wakeford was assisted by one of his business mentors and a close friend Gerald John, who facilitated seed capital for Growth Africa, a firm that Wakeford had set up with radio presenter Tim Modise, his childhood friend Theo Qabaka, and others. Unfortunately,

Growth Africa was dead in the water. Doors simply closed. The company was liquidated on a voluntary basis. Eventually, in December 2004, Wakeford was appointed as interim CEO of the Eastern Cape Development Corporation, and after resigning in 2005, he advised the Eastern Cape premier on economic matters. He also worked as a project advisor for a minister from the Department of Home Affairs on the national turnaround strategy for the department. During that stint, Wakeford met teams that had worked on Homeland Security in the US, for the Netherlands Department of Internal Affairs and the Belgian Department of Home Affairs. In 2009 the Home Affairs turnaround project won the esteemed Princeton University award in the public-sector category.

The Watson brothers, as always, also stood with Wakeford, and through Vulisango Investment Holdings nominated him to numerous listed boards. Gavin Watson also appointed Wakeford as a regular consultant in various companies that he manages and leads. Wakeford often laments what he describes as

> the pathetic and facile attack against Gavin and companies where he is the CEO by the right wing in the press and the criminal-justice system. They are obsessed with destroying a good man because he and his brothers had the guts to stand up against apartheid as far back as 1976. Gavin and his brothers have built a truly non-racial business platform for their shareholders and have hence outsmarted their competitors who are in the main cronies of the group-identity elite and super conservative in orientation. Gavin will prevail and those second-guessing his integrity will be left wanting. Time will tell.

In addition, Simon Koch, a mutual friend, also harnessed Wakeford's talents to market his innovative Convertible Debt Fund at Sovereignty Capital.

Having recently lived through a half-century, Wakeford regards his working life as good for another 20 years. He wants to buy some agricultural land, and possibly farm with indigenous animals such as Nguni cattle and Pedi sheep, and even indigenous goats. Wakeford sees this as a possible growth industry because these animals don't need antibiotics, and only rarely need dipping and dosing. But if this materialises, the farming would only be as a matter of passion, rather than a full-time business.

As for the press, perhaps the less said, the better. The situation was handily captured in a letter to *The Star* penned by Michael Botes of Randburg, Johannesburg:

> There are a few disturbing aspects that came out of the hearings by the Rand Commission that I wish to highlight.
>
> SA Chamber of Business chief executive Kevin Wakeford, after his submission, was lambasted by some sections of the media for acting on hearsay evidence that was unsubstantiated and therefore not credible when presenting his case to the commission.
>
> However, a few days later in evidence to the commission, the parties he named in his submission verified many allegations in Wakeford's submissions. In fact, it was acknowledged by some parties in their submissions that the transactions entered into by them appeared to be murky and that all the details of these transactions were not divulged to the appropriate authorities.
>
> Surely this vindicated Wakeford in what he had to say to the commission?
>
> Lo and behold, the next day, the media comes out saying that nothing new has emerged and that the dealings of the parties concerned did not contribute to the fall of the rand! That after the Reserve Bank acknowledged in its submissions that the parties mentioned by Wakeford did not divulge all the details of their transactions and that they acted in contravention of certain aspects of exchange controls.
>
> The Reserve Bank in its submission acknowledged that if it had known all the details of these transactions it would never have approved them. The bank further agreed that Deutsche Bank in fact had structured deals relating to Sasol, Nampak and M-Cell that were not compliant, and were rand negative.[24]

Christine Qunta's Cape Town-based commercial law practice, which had become well known and highly reputed, fell on very hard times. Qunta now manages a company called Pholosang BEE Resolution Services, where she is executive chairwoman and majority shareholder. Ironically, she focuses on resolving matters of fraud and fronting in the BEE sector and attempting to regain some economic justice for black shareholders who have been ripped off by their white elite buddies.

George Papadakis was ostracised and marginalised after the Rand Commission by the private sector but continued to enjoy much credibility in the public sector. After serving on a number of commissions and curatorships, including the one involved in the scandal at Fidentia, he was recruited by the South African Revenue Service as head of forensics. He is likely to continue to uncover the dark heart of South Africa's private sector.

Postscript

*'The fact of the Watergate cover-up is not nearly as
interesting as the step into making the cover-up.
And when you understand the step, you understand that
Richard Nixon lied. That he was a criminal.' – Bob Woodward*

The meltdown of South Africa's currency during 2001 was apocalyptic –
although, happily, not the end of days. I had put it this way in the 8 March
2002 edition of *Finance Week*:

> Whatever the commission of inquiry ultimately finds in its investiga-
> tion into the rand's collapse last year, it will be scrutinising the use of
> financial products designed to enrich the few at the expense of many.
>
> For here is a Machiavellian plot that brings into question the techni-
> cal competency of the country's governors and leading corporations,
> if not their moral fibre, in respect of the rapid destruction of much of
> South Africa's store of value, its currency.
>
> The rand's latest dive certainly rocked South Africa's foundations
> with key implications for food prices, economic growth, inflation,
> unemployment and monetary policy.
>
> Now the commission must venture into the private sector's cor-
> ridors of power to examine a product that made billions of rand in
> profit for a select few at the expense of the currency and the country.
> And if no action can be taken against those responsible, based on
> the legality of the mechanics, the necessary law may have to be written
> retroactively in South Africa, with the necessary recourse, and perhaps
> even on an international scale because the actions involved are detri-
> mental in particular to developing nations but can harm any country
> open to trade, in shares, bonds and currencies.
>
> The product that gave rise to what is becoming known as Randgate,
> in that the scandal is to currency-share trading what Watergate was to
> politics, has been laid at the door of local investment banks, including

Deutsche Bank, the South African arm of Deutsche Bank AG, Europe's biggest bank. Deutsche South Africa has denied any involvement in the rand's fall.

With investment banking in South Africa under pressure for some time – commissions earned from institutions, especially for equity dealing, have declined since the JSE deregulated in 1995 – brokers have been desperately seeking new money-spinners.

As it turned out, the words that resonated longest and loudest were 'the technical competency of the country's governors and leading corporations'. This encompassed the official fiscal cluster – Treasury and Reserve Bank – along with the banks and corporates, especially large entities.

At the core of the rand's meltdown was the inability – or unwillingness – of the Reserve Bank to do its job properly. Its failures opened the door during 2001, and before, to an environment where market players identified opportunistic niches where monumental amounts of 'one-way' money could be made. The Reserve Bank was negligent in the execution of its duties; only the degree varies, depending on how the analysis is applied. More pointedly, the Reserve Bank had abrogated its primary mandate, firmly rooted in South Africa's Constitution: 'The primary object of the South African Reserve Bank is to protect the value of the currency in the interest of balanced and sustainable economic growth in the Republic.'

And yet the Reserve Bank had continued buying dollars during 2001 to reduce the net open forward position (NOFP). There was no question that it was imperative to eliminate the NOFP, over the longer term. At the same time, the Reserve Bank was under no obligation to reduce the NOFP on a vanilla basis – by simply buying dollars incessantly until the NOFP was eliminated. In the interests of market hygiene, the Reserve Bank had every reason to implement contrary trades from time to time, to keep the market on its toes. A parallel policy would have been to lay off the market for extended periods and to implement 'hiccup' trades designed to confuse market players, without disrupting the market. Instead, to aggravate the situation, the Reserve Bank took the unbelievable decision during 2001 to make it clear that it would not intervene in markets to protect the rand.

Worse still, there is no evidence that the Reserve Bank managed any kind of meaningful market-intelligence activities. On the contrary, in August 2001, certain market players brought to the attention of the Reserve Bank that certain asset-swap deals, either done, in play or proposed, could have impacted or would impact negatively on the rand. The record shows that on 13 October 2001, a Sunday, the Reserve Bank called in the heads of treasury of banks active in the currency markets, and voiced its concern over the possibility that certain exchange-control rules and regulations were not being observed. The next day, the Reserve Bank issued a circular which immediately, without any phasing-in period, re-implemented rules and regulations that had long been in place – supposedly anyway.

According to testimony made by heads of treasury of various banks at the Rand Commission, various exchange-control rules and regulations had fallen into disuse, and in some cases were even being abused. The sledge-hammer 'Big Bang' approach adopted by implementing the 14 October 2001 circular was devastating. More than half of the foreign entities that participated in the rand market immediately withdrew from the market – in the words of one banker, 'never to return'. Also in October, Telkom announced that its listing on the New York Stock Exchange would be delayed until 2002. Had the listing proceeded as planned, South Africa would have experienced a fairly heavy inflow of dollars during the latter parts of 2001.

Far from protecting the value of the rand, the Reserve Bank had played a measurable role in plunging the rand market into a full-blown crisis. Over the next two months, the rand would be punished as never before – or since. Various players in the currency markets which had taken bets on the rand being savaged made absolute fortunes. Many of the dodgy deals in the rand currency market took place offshore. And without inside evidence, these deals remained untraceable. On the other hand, all that was required was to identify a single trader in Johannesburg, or London or New York City, who had the inside track on the delinquency. The Rand Commission had powers of subpoena. These were never used, not in the sense of digging out unwilling witnesses.

There was also overwhelming evidence that the forces responsible for trading the rand were playing a much bigger, but intimately related, game in the equity markets. Any trader who had a running bet on the rand falling could have taken positions in the equity markets. When the rand falls, especially heavily, there is a virtual certainty that the prices of 'rand hedge' stocks will rise. This includes practically all resources stocks, from the mines to the likes of Sasol. The Rand Commission did not conduct so much as a cursory investigation into what kind of mischief had taken place in the equity markets during 2001. By the same token, speculators with knowledge – real or imagined – that the rand was going to tank could have exploited South Africa's bond markets.

Just one person, Kevin Wakeford, was the only real counterforce to the trashing of the rand. For his efforts, he would be victimised and targeted by bullies at the top end of South Africa's crony elites. But as the record shows, the rand was the decisive winner: it appreciated heavily over the next three years. South Africa was back in business. Today, more than a decade later, the rand has depreciated, in line with South Africa's long-term inflation rate vs major currencies, but even so, the rand trades nowhere near the lows it experienced during the fourth quarter of 2001.

The Rand Commission's very narrow terms of reference produced all kinds of counterproductive outcomes. Key among these was that the commission made no finding on the role – or lack of it – played by the Reserve Bank, the ultimate custodian, in terms of the Constitution, of the rand. From the outset, Governor Tito Mboweni had campaigned against the very existence of the commission. When various negative details emerged in evidence at the commission, Mboweni expressed more than anger; he flew into an intemperate rejection of any criticism and went further, attacking those who had done nothing more than testify under oath, done nothing more than tell the truth. It was the Greek dramatist Aeschylus who was attributed with the words, 'In war, truth is the first casualty'. For Mboweni, this was war – a war to preserve Mboweni's reputation as a central bank governor – one who had never worked in banking.

Seen in its fullness, the Rand Commission was more significant for what it omitted than anything else. For the observer who was wide awake, the commission in its many omissions in effect disclosed much about South Africa's dysfunctional elites. It needs to be asked, for example, whether or not one or more of these elites played a role in formulating the commission's terms of reference. As was graphically shown, the terms were narrow in the extreme, immunising the vast majority of the rand currency market, never mind related markets, from the commission's investigations.

Despite all the commission's failures, including cover-up by omission, the 2001 rand apocalypse and its aftermath will in time be more fully understood as a fundamentally significant event in South Africa's history. After more than a decade of digesting the crisis and its aftermath, I have had more than enough time to place the events, as known, in some kind of context. Sometimes, it felt that the savaging of the rand was simply a story too large to digest, a cascade of events that took place in an imaginary hell. Had the rand trend line of 2001 remained in place, South Africa would have been plunged into a hell, created by unknown and faceless greed vampires.

The word 'apocalypse' is not used lightly here. The word is from the ancient Greek ἀποκάλυψις, and for a long time meant 'revelation', as in the Revelation of John. The revelation as seen by John is of the ultimate victory of good over evil. The battle is self-contained. Sadly, the broader war between good and evil is never-ending. Revelation is an excellent benchmark for what *could* be. For those who encounter the savage and often vicious clashes between good and evil, Revelation is an excellent patch of refuge.

The Book of Revelation is also about the end of the present age. Since 1175, this has become the primary meaning of the word 'apocalypse'. In modern times, apocalypse refers to prophetic revelation, or so-called end-time scenarios, or to the end of the world in general.

Many of us are aware of these forces, but have only limited access to experiencing the titanic meeting of good and evil. We find it difficult to articulate these experiences, no matter how limited. The rand crisis hinted at some meanings hidden from the vast majority of us by falsehood and misconception. As the year 2001 weaved its way through time, South Africa looked increasingly into the face of financial Armageddon, which would have soon spilt over into every conceivable part of life. The process of trying to unravel what had happened – something the Rand Commission vaguely attempted and failed to do – brought South Africans face to face with the disclosure of negative elements, hingeing on devious and unconscionable conduct by a relatively small number of people in Johannesburg – and no doubt elsewhere. It is even possible that certain people in the City headed the list.

The 2001 rand crisis often felt like a new chapter of Revelation. Some people out there were making mountains of money, making a mockery of anything and everything, like scenes of devils, resplendent with all the potent, almost baroque, imagery. The devils were not alone. Ultimately, this was about the forces of good attacking the multi-headed monsters of evil.

On this score, there was something peculiar about the rand crisis taking place in the year that Islamist extremism terrified most of the world with the attacks on two of the most iconic buildings in New York City. This was the biggest-ever onslaught on US soil and it was no surprise that the country's administration reacted in a hysterical and angry manner.

What has happened over time is that freedom of every kind has come under attack. This is arguably a case of *silent enim leges inter arma* (for among [times of] arms, the laws fall mute). It is completely understandable that the US, as the world's superpower, would go to extraordinary lengths to root out terrorists, but what has happened in practice is that the White House has transformed into a centre of power that appears to fear no oversight. Where an underlying issue overlaps, even ever so slightly, with terrorism, conflation inevitably rules. Acts and omissions associated with terrorism, no matter how vaguely, if at all, can be, and often are, met with forms of retaliation that can be, and often are, illegal.

In practice, almost all information about poor and even illegal behaviour on the part of the US government, following the 2001 attacks, has come from whistle-blowers. The White House has unofficially declared a war on whistle-blowers. A collateral theme is that individuals who have broken the law are treated as immune from any kind of law enforcement. In plain and simple terms, many acts that are simply illegal are in effect condoned, but people who so much as mutter anything about such illegalities will be hunted down. The US has long claimed to be the leader of the free world; as such, the US's treatment of those who want the truth out is crucial to understanding the direction of the modern world.

In 2005 the *New York Times* carried an article headed 'Bush lets US spy on callers without courts':

Washington, Dec. 15 – Months after the Sept. 11 attacks, President Bush secretly authorized the National Security Agency to eavesdrop on Americans and others inside the United States to search for evidence of terrorist activity without the court-approved warrants ordinarily required for domestic spying, according to government officials.

Exactly the same happened with revelations by the *New York Times* of the illegal Bush NSA [National Security Agency] warrantless eavesdropping program. None of the officials who eavesdropped on Americans without the warrants required by law were prosecuted. The telecoms that illegally cooperated were retroactively immunized from all legal accountability by the US Congress.

The only person to suffer recriminations from that scandal, as the *New York Times* recounted, was Thomas Tamm, the mid-level Department of Justice official who discovered the programme and told the newspaper about it. His life was ruined by 'vindictive investigation'.

Among others, Bradley Manning, who was suspected of passing on classified material to WikiLeaks, was arrested in May 2010. He was due to go on trial in June 2013, on charges that included the possibility of a death penalty, although prosecutors have indicated that a lesser sentence would be sought, should a conviction be secured. None of the illegalities exposed by Manning were subject to any kind of investigation.

Then there was John Kiriakou, a former CIA analyst, who, completely out of sorts and financially exhausted by legal bills, on 22 October 2012 pleaded guilty to disclosing classified information about how the US used waterboarding, which Kiriakou regarded as torture, against al-Qaeda prisoners. On 25 January 2013, he was sentenced to 30 months in prison. The judge said that if she had not been bound by the plea-bargain arrangement, she would have sentenced Kiriakou to 10 years in prison. He had lost his job along with his house and pension. The terrible irony of the case was that the US, by definition, admitted that it was using illegal torture practices. But not a single individual involved in practising such illegal torture has been prosecuted.

Under President Barack Obama, the US administration has scored a dubious new record, as reported on 18 October 2012 by the Bloomberg news agency:

Eric Holder, Attorney General under President Barack Obama, has prosecuted more government officials for alleged leaks under the

World War I-era Espionage Act than all his predecessors combined, including law-and-order Republicans John Mitchell, Edwin Meese and John Ashcroft.

The indictments of six individuals under that spy law have drawn criticism from those who say the president's crackdown chills dissent, curtails a free press and betrays Obama's initial promise to 'usher in a new era of open government'.

The targets, to reiterate, are never those involved in illegal activities.

The White House finds itself involved in a growing web of abuses, not least those at the Abu Ghraib Prison in Iraq; the extra-legal activities at Guantanamo Bay (which the US leased from Cuba on a permanent basis from 1903); the Obama-hosted television footage showing the killing of Osama bin Laden; the secret 'black ops' conducted by the CIA, including the use of 'black sites'; significant pressure by the US to halt German and Spanish investigations into US torture abuses; the video of a US Apache attack helicopter gunning down journalists and rescuers in Baghdad; and persistent stinking lies about 'non-killings' of innocent civilians in a number of countries.

The response of the Obama administration has been weak and ambiguous, in that explanations are never given for allowing illegal acts to go unpunished. The US Justice Department, says spokesman Dean Boyd, 'does not target whistle-blowers in leak cases or any other cases … An individual in authorized possession of classified information has no authority or right to unilaterally determine that it should be made public or otherwise disclose it.' In practice, this means that illegalities can be cloaked under secrecy provisions. According to Danielle Brian, executive director of the Project on Government Oversight, Obama does not see 'the world of national security as being part of open government'.

In an article published in the UK newspaper *The Guardian* on 27 January 2013, Glenn Greenwald suggested that the Obama administration's abuses were motivated by a selfishness and cynicism that reeked of vanity and self-delusion:

The Obama administration does not dislike leaks of classified information. To the contrary, it is a prolific exploiter of exactly those types of leaks – when they can be used to propagandise the citizenry to glorify the president's image as a tough guy, advance his political goals or produce a multi-million-dollar Hollywood film about his greatest conquest.

Leaks are only objectionable when they undercut that propaganda by exposing government deceit, corruption and illegality. Speaking of the Obama administration's propensity to leak classified information for propagandistic and other political purposes, numerous senators have indicated their intent to investigate whether the CIA and other officials passed classified information about the bin Laden raid to the makers of *Zero Dark Thirty* in order to influence the film.

If you have any doubts about whether this happened, just consider what *ZDT* screenwriter Mark Boal just said in *Time* magazine about this film – and decide for yourself.

Most of the mainstream media in the US, and most of its judiciary, have become subservient to the jackboot-style strategy and tactics dished out by the Obama machine.

The 11 February 2013 edition of *Time* magazine ignores the citing of sources, a very basic requirement of journalism, as it goes out of its way to glorify the wonders of the US's new killing machines:

[Drones] have certainly transformed the US military: of late the American government has gotten very good at extending its physical presence for the purpose of killing people. Ten years ago the Pentagon had about 50 drones in its fleet; now it has some 7,500. More than a third of the aircraft in the Air Force's fleet are now unmanned. The US military reported carrying out 447 drone attacks in Afghanistan in the first 11 months of 2012, up from 294 in all of 2011. Since President Barack Obama took office, the US has executed more than 300 covert drone attacks in Pakistan, a country with which America is not at war.

In this context, today it seems incredible that for what was in essence a string of wiretapping cases, the Nixon administration was slowly dismantled, and that nearly 50 senior White House staff were convicted.

As mentioned in Chapter 5, on 22 December 2012, the US Partnership for Civil Justice Fund announced that it had obtained documents, pursuant to the Freedom of Information Act, showing that from its inception, the FBI treated the Occupy Wall Street movement as 'a potential criminal and terrorist threat',[1] even though the FBI itself acknowledges in documents that organisers explicitly called for peaceful protest and did 'not condone the use of violence' at the protests. This is an explicit and crass example of the Obama administration aligning itself with big money under the catch-all mantle of terrorism. It is also yet another example of public law enforcement being used to selectively protect vested private-sector interests.

It may be recalled that Richard Nixon and H.R. Haldeman tried to bully the CIA into telling the FBI that the Watergate issue was a matter of national security. They were rebuked, and history was made when the US's democratic machinery resolved that a special prosecutor be appointed to handle the Watergate scandal. The first special prosecutor appointed to the case was Archibald Cox. He took leave from Harvard Law School to get on with the job. Those were the days all right.

***

'To whom do lions cast their gentle looks?
Not to the beast that would usurp their den ...
The smallest worm will turn being trodden on
And doves will peck in safeguard of their brood.'
– Henry VI, Part 3

Beyond what was disclosed – and not disclosed – during and around the Rand Commission, and leaving aside the sad story of the Reserve Bank's role, the major technical failing was brushing over an examination of dollar-linking. The dollar may be fiat money, but it continues to rank as the world's reserve currency. Beyond the euro, the yen, sterling and the Swiss franc, virtually any currency that free-floats is asking for trouble – sooner or later.

Take, for example, Zimbabwe, which has over the past two decades experienced one of the world's most spectacular socio-economic, never mind political, failures. Zimbabwe was also home to the world's most recent bout of currency insanity, where the exchange rate had been 24 Zimbabwean dollars to the US dollar in 1998. To cut a terrible story very short, Zimbabwe almost reinvented fiat money: in January 2009, it introduced a new Z$100 trillion banknote.

Finally, on 29 January 2009, in an effort to counteract the madness, it was announced that Zimbabweans would be permitted to use other currencies, such as sterling, euros, rands and US dollars. On 2 February 2009, the Reserve Bank of Zimbabwe announced that a further 12 zeros were to be taken off the currency, with 1 000 000 000 000 Zimbabwean dollars being exchanged for one new, or the 'fourth', Zimbabwean dollar.

In practice, Zimbabwe abandoned its currency in April 2009. The US dollar has become the principal currency of choice in Zimbabwe. Beyond its status as the world's leading currency, it is made of high-quality cotton, and can be washed and recirculated more times than most currencies. If anyone needs proof that good old cotton is superior to today's increasingly synthetic banknotes, all they need do is find some US dollars that have been through a thousand hands in Zimbabwe.

Zimbabwe has become an infamous case of illustrating the reality that a country can print as much money as it wants, but that, sooner or later, the economy will plunge into hyperinflation and outright disaster. It has been noted that since the country abandoned its own currency, economic growth has shown positive signs for the first time in many years.

Any extended examination of currencies would be remiss without considering the remarkable record of Korekiyo Takahashi, who served as Japan's finance minister from 1927 to 1936. Takahashi has been described by Ben Bernanke, the current chairman of the US Federal Reserve, as the man who 'brilliantly rescued' Japan from the Great Depression. Takahashi ripped up the rule book and implemented a series of radical monetary and fiscal reforms. In 1931 he severed Japan's links with the gold standard and, to stimulate economic activity, opted for Keynesian budget deficits. Some have described Takahashi as having launched a 'new deal' blitz even before Franklin Roosevelt took the US president's office. During a period of 100 days, commencing on 4 March 1933, Roosevelt successfully sponsored major legislation and signed a long list of executive orders instituting the 'New Deal' – a number of programmes aimed at reducing socio-economic hardship, such as government jobs for the unemployed, economic recovery stimuli, and reform, mainly by amending the regulation of Wall Street, banks and transportation.

On his home turf, Takahashi compelled the Bank of Japan to monetise debt until the economy was once again up and running. Later, the Bank of Japan sold bonds to private-sector banks, to drain excess liquidity from the economy. As for the yen, that was Takahashi's boldest move: he devalued the currency by 60 per cent against the dollar, and by 40 per cent on a trade-weighted basis. This meant that Japan's exports – mainly textiles, machinery and chemicals – exploded across Asia, prompting a trade war with the British Empire and India. The next part of Takahashi's policy was to implement restraint, which included cuts in military expenditures. That was a bad decision – for him at least – and led to his assassination in 1936. After that, Japan's monetary, fiscal and currency policies completely lost momentum, then disintegrated, and in due course hyperinflation set in.

Takahashi's career as finance minister – including the post-mortem fallout – could be summed up in six stages:

- stagnation (sick, wheezing economy);
- monetisation (liquidity boost, a positive stimulus for economic activity);
- devaluation (boosting competitiveness of exports, restraining imports);
- stabilisation (soaking up excess liquidity);
- retaliation (vested interests revolt); and
- hyperinflation.

Early in 2013, there were strong signs that the new administration in Japan was implementing an amended version of Takahashi's policies, in a desperate bid to stimulate an economy that had staggered along with deflation for more than two decades. This prompted interesting comments from certain central-bank bosses, such as the Bank of England's Mervyn King, who referred to 'actively managed exchange rates'.

It seemed imminently possible that the world was more likely than ever to enter a period of currency wars. By most measures, the yen had been overvalued for years, if not decades, choking the competitiveness of Japan's exports. Only time would tell if the Japan of 2013 could implement the best of Takahashi's policies, and somehow avoid potential fallouts.

For many years, the yen has had peculiar problems, in that when the world economy is expanding, the yen tends to weaken, when Japan least needs it. During tough times, the yen tends to strengthen – undermining the competitiveness of Japan's exports. One of the main reasons is that the yen ranks as one of the world's major currencies, along with the euro, the British pound, the Swiss franc and, of course, the dollar.

Which, in a way, loops back to Zimbabwe. Any country with a free-floating currency is vulnerable to all kinds of risks – known and sometimes unknown. Many countries have long thrown in the towel and implemented three main variations of a link to the world's reserve currency, the dollar. Today Zimbabwe is one of more than 60 countries (besides the US) that adopt the US dollar as legal tender, peg the domestic currency to the dollar or manage the domestic currency exchange rate against the dollar. There is another category, where a currency is managed against a basket of currencies that includes the dollar, as applied by Botswana. Countries in the first three categories include tadpoles such as St Kitts and Nevis, some populous countries like Bangladesh, and mid-level economic powers such as Saudi Arabia. The list goes on: Jordan, Maldives, Belize, the Bahamas and Hong Kong. There are also countries that adopt all kind of negative stances towards the US, yet reference their currencies to the dollar, such as Venezuela – and, of course, Zimbabwe.

By far the most notable member of the dollar bloc is China, which today ranks as the world's second-biggest economy on most counts, and is set to overtake the US well within the next decade. China keeps a very tight rein on its yuan, and has allowed it to slowly depreciate against the dollar, in the face of continual US criticism that the yuan is undervalued, rendering Chinese exports 'supercompetitive' – that is, unfairly competitive. A significant school of thought in the US regards China's currency policy as a form of economic warfare.

China has long made clear its intentions to create its own reserve currency, but remains demonstrably happy with the dollar link. The yuan has become influential in its own right. A recent analysis by the National Institute of Public Finance and Policy in Delhi shows that the yuan already has a material influence on at least 33 currencies.

For reasons unknown, the rand is too 'special' to have any kind of dollar linkage. Had any of the variations of dollar linkage been in force during 2001, there would simply have been no meltdown in the rand. Instead, the rand would have appreciated, however mildly, through 2001. It is again worth remembering that the rand was in effect pegged to the dollar, at $1.40 to the rand, for 21 years from 1961 to 1982. The rand currency market may have been one of the most boring ever, but South Africa's national interests were more than served. Policy-makers, companies, banks and, of course, citizens could go about their business without spending so much as a second worrying about what the currency might do next.

South Africa continues to seem to be happy, if not delighted, with a free-floating currency, with all its attendant costs and vulnerability to manipulation. What this says about the wishes of the country's super-elites is unclear.

Currency exchange rates impact on practically everyone in the world, and will remain controversial, often evoking extremes in interpretation and expression. Try to digest these words from the 22 December 2012 edition of the London-based *Economist*, published under the heading 'All hope not lost: The euro has survived 2012, but it will be a long time before it is cured': 'If it were in Dante's *Inferno*, the euro would have moved from the eighth circle (the penultimate one), where flatterers are immersed in excrement, to the third, where foul stuff rains down on gluttons. Salvation is still a long way off.'

Indeed. But at least we have a vague idea of what it looks like. Sadly, it is a fading idea.

* * *

While we wait for salvation to come back into shape, here are a few points to ponder. The global currency market continues to rank as the single biggest market in the financial system – as a number of governments have found out to their great cost. As even the most developed countries such as the UK and Japan have discovered, it is all but impossible to intervene successfully in big currency markets other than for brief moments in time.

Perhaps the best-known debacle in currency markets – known as Black Wednesday – took place on 16 September 1992, when the British Conservative government was forced to withdraw the pound from the European Exchange Rate Mechanism, following a failure to maintain the value of the pound above an agreed floor – or minimum limit. George Soros, the speculator, infamously made more than £1 billion by short-selling the pound. In 1997 the UK Treasury estimated that the overall 'cost' of Black Wednesday amounted to £3.4 billion.[2]

The potential 'shock and awe' of currency markets has only continued to grow. Currently, turnover in currency markets averages between $4.5 and $5 trillion a day. The global currency system remains unregulated: this is the Wild West of the global financial system.

Even so, currency markets are dominated by four giants. A May 2013 Euromoney Institutional Investor plc survey found that although hundreds of entities participate in foreign-exchange markets, four banks dominate, with an aggregate share of more than 50 per cent Deutsche Bank (15.2 per cent); Citigroup (14.9 per cent); Barclays (10.2 per cent), and UBS – 10.1 per cent.[3]

Can currency markets be regulated? Consider benchmarks, which are set independently. Various regulators around the world are reviewing the integrity of benchmarks, not least derivatives, commodities (starting with crude oil) and swaps, in the wake of three banks (so far) paying fines in aggregate of $2.5 billion for rigging the London interbank offered rate, or LIBOR.[4] There are also benchmarks in currency markets.

It may be all but impossible to successfully manipulate the value of global currencies such as the dollar, yen, pound and Swiss franc, but manipulating currency *benchmarks* may be relatively easy. This profound news hit markets on 11 June 2013, when news agency Bloomberg broke an article confirming, in many ways, what many had long suspected: that currency rates were and are being manipulated – albeit indirectly.

Under the headline 'Traders said to rig currency rates to profit off clients', Bloomberg stated: 'Traders at some of the world's biggest banks manipulated benchmark foreign-exchange rates used to set the value of trillions of dollars of investments, according to five dealers with knowledge of the practice.'[5]

According to Bloomberg, 'the behaviour occurred daily in the spot foreign-exchange market and has been going on for at least a decade, affecting the value of funds and derivatives, the two traders said'.

Employees, said the Bloomberg journalists, 'have been front-running client orders and rigging WM/Reuters rates[6] by pushing through trades before and during the 60-second windows when the benchmarks are set'.

In currency markets, the WM/Reuters rates are king.[7]

The fixing of benchmarks is one of the most important processes in global finance. Fund managers around the world work in a complex labyrinth, and inevitably manage securities – stocks, bonds, property, commodities and cash – across multiple jurisdictions.

As such, the WM/Reuters rates are utilised by fund managers around the world to compute periodic – say, day-to-day – valuations of their hold-ings, and by index providers, such as the FTSE Group[8] and MSCI Inc.,[9] which track stocks and bonds in several countries. The main function of such trackers is to produce data that enables fund managers and investors to measure their performance against the 'average'.

Ironically, while the WM/Reuters rates 'aren't followed by most invest-ors', as Bloomberg put it, 'even small movements can affect the value of what Morningstar Inc.[10] estimates is \$3.6 trillion in funds including pen-sion and savings accounts that track global indexes'. The WM/Reuters rates are among the most sophisticated investor tools available.

In practice, the WM/Reuters rates data are collected and distributed by World Markets Co., a unit of Boston-based State Street Corp.[11] and Thomson Reuters Corp.[12]

According to Tom Kirchmaier, a fellow in the financial-markets group at the London School of Economics, as quoted by Bloomberg, the WM/Reuters rates data is a 'price mechanism' that amounts to no less than 'the anchor of our entire economic system . . . Any rigging of the price mechanism leads to a misallocation of capital and is extremely costly to society.'

Rigging this, rigging that and rigging something else are at the corner-stone of hustling, which sits at the centre of the darkest parts of the human heart. The next time you hold money in your hand, or authorise an electronic payment, consider for a moment, first, the illusion that the money is really all yours and, second, that the money is worth what you so fervently believe.

Notes

CHAPTER 1

1. SACOB's full press statement was issued on 4 January 2002, under the heading 'SACOB calls for currency commission'.

2. From notes made by the author during and after conversations with Brett Kebble, 1996 to 2005.

3. Fiat money is currency that a government has declared as legal tender, despite the fact it has no intrinsic value and is not backed by reserves. Because fiat money is not backed by reserves, it runs the risk of being printed indiscriminately, causing hyperinflation, which in due course renders fiat money worthless. For much of history, gold – the antithesis of fiat money – served in various roles as the ultimate currency. After 1971, when the Bretton Woods system broke down, the world effectively abandoned gold, and unleashed the era of fiat money. Many countries, however, continue to hold gold bullion as part of their national reserves.

4. In modern foreign-exchange markets, the yuan, when expressed in English, refers to China's currency, the renminbi, internationally coded as CNY. Similarly, 'sterling' is often used to refer to the currency of the UK and a number of its territories. Just as the units of sterling are pounds (GBP) and pence, so renminbi is the unit of the yuan.

5. The full indictment can be found at http://www.sec.gov/litigation/complaints/comp18115b.htm.

6. See http://www.investmentu.com/2009/January/letter-to-barackobama.html.

7. The SEC published extensive materials relevant to its case against Goldman Sachs, starting with 'Goldman Sachs to pay record $550 million to settle SEC charges related to subprime mortgage CDO: Firm acknowledges CDO marketing materials were incomplete and should have revealed Paulson's role', dated 15 July 2010. Available at http://www.sec.gov/news/press/2010/2010-123.htm.

8. The SEC's statement of litigation, dated 15 April 2010, can be found at http://www.sec.gov/litigation/complaints/2010/comp21489.pdf.

9. See http://www.sec.gov/news/press/2010/2010-123.htm.

10. Ibid. Of the $550 million to be paid by Goldman Sachs in the settlement, $250 million would be returned to harmed investors through a Fair Fund distribution and $300 million would be paid to the US Treasury.

CHAPTER 2

1. Trevor Manuel was widely quoted on these words at the time. See, for example, Nic Borain, 'Politicians tend to hate markets – for good reason': http://nicborain .wordpress.com/2010/07/19/politicians-tend-to-hate-markets-for-good-reason/.

2. From weekly statistics published by *The Economist*, http://www.economist.com/news/21571953-foreign-reserves. .

3. The Reserve Bank publishes extensive statistics and analyses, including its useful quarterly bulletin. The reference here is to the bulletin for the quarter ending December 2012; see http://www.resbank.co.za/Publications/Detail-Item-View/Pages/Publications.aspx?sarbweb=3b6aa07d-92ab-441f-b7bf-bb7dfb1bedb4&sarblist=21b5222e-7125-4e55-bb65-56fd3333371e&sarbitem=5313.

4. Goldman Sachs allows some of its research to go into the public domain. For this reference, see, for example, http://www.efinancialnews.com/story/2012-12-12/goldman-sachs-top-trades-2013.

5. From weekly statistics published by *The Economist*, http://www.economist.com/news/economic-and-financialindicators/21571915-trade-exchange-rates-budget-balances-andinterest-rates.

6. Journalist Tom Nevin wrote a detailed article on the collapse of the rand, 'Why is the rand falling?' dated 1 February 2002, for *The Free Library*, where he quoted, inter alia, Rob Lee; see http://www.thefreelibrary.com/Why+is+the+rand+falling%3F+(Finance).-a082863420.

7. Trevor Manuel was quoted widely on his thoughts on Zimbabwe; see, for instance, http://www.thepost.co.za/south-africa-isn-t-zimbabwe-says-manuel-1.79241#.UbG1Yc8aKM8.

8. See Tom Nevin, 'Why is the rand falling?'

9. Ibid.

10. For a source on collected utterances and writings on being either 'with us' or 'against us', see http://en.wikipedia.org/wiki/You%27re_either_with_us,_or_against_us.

11. See https://docs.google.com/viewer?a5v&q5cache:C9Mmcm6IkSYJ:www.hsbc.com/news-and-insight/2012/~/media/CFD69C5336204FC4BA24979CCD300883.ashx1&hl5en&gl5za&pid5bl&srcid5ADGEESg4zVycy5MmzWi7RCH4BuGq4sLFSa_I4FjzvjpZLJ8HPhqH9nMDtrXR1yy81_uDbtWL6fy4dqVNjAPX7YeHCl_LHCdsZDpsBILlWGKt47Z5tS-lhRRH-JUVkrJ-XZIJD2Nq4-2v&sig5AHIEtbQLo3Oq745vc2g1SUksKfJ34eua_w.

12. See http://www.forbes.com/sites/marketshare/2012/12/13/hsbc-theworldwide-local-ban-for-money-laundering-and-rogue-nationssome-brand-positioning-huh/.

13. The raid on Deutsche Bank was widely reported in the global media. See, for example, http://www.thegwpf.org/green-mafia-500-police-raid-deutschebank-carbon-fraud/ and http://uk.reuters.com/article/2012/12/12/uk-deutschebank-prosecutors-idUKBRE8BB0NA20121212.

CHAPTER 3

1. See James Lamont, 'South Africa: Gold miners sleep soundly', *Business Day*, 24 December 2001.

2. The rand fell at rates of between 20 and 45 per cent in 1961, 1976, 1984/85, 1998, 2001 and 2008. The biggest fall by far, however, was in 2001.
3. See Tom Nevin, 'Why is the rand falling?'
4. Sworn statement by James Cross to the Rand Commission, read into evidence on 8 April 2002; see http://www.justice.gov.za/commissions/comm_rand/rand_hearings_pdfs/april8.pdf.
5. See http://allafrica.com/stories/200203070483.html.
6. Sworn statement by James Cross to the Rand Commission, 8 April 2002.
7. See *Business Day*, 28 February 2002, 'South Africa: Mboweni attacks Wakeford over rand manipulation claims', where Lukanyo Mnyanda wrote, inter alia, 'Reserve Bank governor Tito Mboweni launched a scathing attack on SA Chamber of Business CE Kevin Wakeford yesterday, dismissing his claims about the cause of the rand's depreciation last year as "populist"'.

CHAPTER 4

1. Sworn expert evidence given by Iraj Abedian to the Rand Commission; see http://www.justice.gov.za/commissions/comm_rand/interim%20report_pdf.pdf.
2. See http://en.wikipedia.org/wiki/Alex_Berenson.
3. Frank Partnoy, *F.I.A.S.C.O: Blood in the Water on Wall Street* (New York: W.W. Norton, 1997).
4. Speech by Alan Greenspan, 'Remarks by Chairman Alan Greenspan at the annual dinner and Francis Boyer Lecture of the American Enterprise Institute for Public Policy Research, Washington, D.C.', 5 December 1996; see http://www.federalreserve.gov/BOARDDOCS/SPEECHES/19961205.htm.
5. Ibid.
6. See http://en.wikipedia.org/wiki/Enron.
7. The Nieman Foundation for Journalism at Harvard; see http://www.nieman.harvard.edu/reportsitem.aspx?id=101334.
8. Ibid.
9. One of the more complete articles on the events at Eland Platinum, by the author, can be found at http://www.moneyweb.co.za/moneyweb-mining/eland-platinum-again.
10. Derived from 'Hell is empty and all the devils are here' (*The Tempest*).
11. See http://www.efinancialnews.com/story/2010-12-03/interviewbethany-mclean-all-the-devils-are-here.
12. Ziegler's infamous quip is embedded deep in history; see, for instance, http://en.wikipedia.org/wiki/Ron_Ziegler.
13. There are numerous sources for Richard Nixon's comments; see, for example, https://en.wikipedia.org/wiki/Watergate_scandal.
14. Hunter S. Thompson, *Hell's Angels* (New York: Random House, 1967). Thompson was an avid reader of newspapers and would clip articles of special interest, some of which are cited by him in the book.

15. The Lynch Report was cited in diverse news reports; beyond those mentioned, see 'The motorcycle gangs: Losers and outsiders', *The Nation*, 17 May 1965: http://www.thenation.com/article/motorcycle-gangs.

16. See 'California: The wilder ones', *Time*, 26 March 1965: http://www.time.com/time/magazine/article/0,9171,841749,00.html.

17. For the FBI's account of this chapter of Mafia history, see 'Mafia takedown: Largest coordinated arrest in FBI history', dated 20 January 2011: http://www.fbi.gov/news/stories/2011/january/mafia_012011.

18. For more detail, refer to the FBI's public release, 'Ninety-one leaders, members, and associates of La Cosa Nostra families in four districts charged with racketeering and related crimes, including murder and extortion; total of 127 individuals charged in Brooklyn, N.Y.; Manhattan, N.Y.; Newark, N.J.; and Providence, R.I.', dated 20 January 2011. Available at http://www.fbi.gov/newyork/press-releases/2011/91-leaders-members-and-associates-of-la-cosa-nostra-families-in-four-districts-charged-with-racketeering-and-related-crimes-including-murder-and-extortion.

19. See William K. Rashbaum, 'Nearly 125 arrested in sweeping mob roundup', *New York Times*, 20 January 2011: http://www.nytimes.com/2011/01/21/nyregion/21mob.html?_r=0.

20. For more detail, see 'Attorney General Eric Holder speaks at the press conference on organized crime arrests', Brooklyn, N.Y., 20 January 2011: http://www.justice.gov/iso/opa/ag/speeches/2011/ag-speech-110120.html.

21. For more detail on what Giovanni Falcone said, see http://en.wikipedia.org/wiki/Sicilian_Mafia#cite_ref-2.

22. See materials from the US's Permanent Subcommittee on Investigations, including 'U.S. vulnerabilities to money laundering, drugs, and terrorist financing: HSBC case history', 17 July 2012: http://www.hsgac.senate.gov/subcommittees/investigations/hearings/us-vulnerabilities-to-money-laundering-drugs-and-terrorist-financing-hsbc-case-history.

23. See the New York State Department of Financial Services litigation statement against Standard Chartered Bank, 'Consent order under New York Banking Law § 44': 'Whereas, on August 6, 2012, the Department of Financial Services (the "Department") issued an order pursuant to Banking Law § 39, charging Standard Chartered Bank ("SCB"), a wholly owned subsidiary of Standard Chartered plc, with certain apparent violations of law and regulation, and directing that SCB appear before the Department on August 15, 2012 to explain those charges (the "August 6th Order")', and so on; available in full at http://www.dfs.ny.gov/about/ea/ea120921.pdf.

24. See the US's National Public Radio, 'Ex-hedge fund boss sentenced to 11 years in prison', 13 October 2011: http://www.npr.org/2011/10/13/141311454/u-s-seeks-record-sentence-for-ex-hedge-fund-boss.

25. See Peter Lattman, 'Galleon chief sentenced to 11-year term in insider case',

New York Times, 13 October 2011: http://dealbook.nytimes.com/2011/10/13/rajaratnam-is-sentenced-to-11-years/.

26. For more on the speech, as revised, by Joseph Yam, CEO, Hong Kong Monetary Authority, 'International capital flows and free markets', at the Credit Suisse First Boston Asian Investment Conference, reprinted in the *HKMA Quarterly Bulletin Issue* No. 19, 26 March 1999, see http://www.hkma.gov.hk/eng/key-information/speech-speakers/jckyam/speech_260399b.shtml and http://www.justice.gov.za/commissions/comm_rand/rand_final_minority_report/part_2a.pdf.

27. Personal letter to Kevin Wakeford.

28. Personal letter to Kevin Wakeford.

29. Byron Kennedy 'Corporates next on finger pointing hit-list', *Moneyweb*, 8 March 2002: http://www.moneyweb.co.za/moneyweb-historical-news-news/corporates-next-on-finger-pointing-hitlist?sn=Daily news detail.

30. Alec Hogg, 'Viva, Rand Commission, viva', *Moneyweb*, 10 March 2002: http://www.moneyweb.co.za/moneyweb-historical-news-news/viva-rand-commission-viva?sn=Daily news detail.

31. The Rand Commission's full terms of reference can be found at http://www.justice.gov.za/commissions/comm_rand.htm.

32. The letter is published with the permission of Kevin Wakeford.

33. Carolyn Pritchard provided the author with a copy of the work she completed in South Africa.

CHAPTER 5

1. As recollected by the author from various meetings and experiences with Brett Kebble over the period 1996 to 2005.

2. A reference to a small coin.

3. From notes made by the author during and after conversations with Brett Kebble, 1996 to 2005.

4. Ibid.

5. Kebble's full statement can be found at http://www.jci.co.za/default.asp?pathid5investor_centre/announcements/company_news/display.asp&ID548.

6. The Partnership for Civil Justice Fund (PCJF) published the expose 'FBI documents reveal secret nationwide Occupy monitoring' on 22 December 2012; see http://www.justiceonline.org/commentary/fbi-files-ows.html.

7. Among the pages released by the PCJF to the FBI, the page referring to snipers is numbered 61, and can be located in full at http://www.documentcloud.org/documents/549516-fbi-spy-files-on-the-occupy-movement.html#document/p61. The implications of the redacted material were examined by but few in the mainstream media. An analysis by *Russia Today* is available at http://rt.com/usa/fbi-assassination-ows-sniper-227/. A full run of the documents obtained by the PCJF from the FBI may be found at http://www.justiceonline.org/commentary/fbi-files-ows.html#documents.

8. As recalled by Kevin Wakeford.
9. See Roger Pitot, 'The South African automotive industry, the MIDP and the APDP presentation', NAACAM, October 2011: http://www.automechanikasa.co.za/pdf/2013-docs/NAACAM-Presentation.pdf.
10. Ibid.

CHAPTER 6

1. The news about the email from Neil Morrison to Maria Ramos arose in sworn evidence given by Niall Smith of Deutsche Bank to the Rand Commission on 5 April 2002; see http://www.justice.gov.za/commissions/comm_rand/rand_hearings_pdfs/april5.pdf. Some journalists, such as Vernon Wessels of *Business Report*, were able to obtain further information regarding the email, along with additional information. A comprehensive report, 'Stage is set for clearing murky waters on foreign exchange control policies: Reserve Bank to reflect on Deutsche deals', was published in *Business Report* on 8 April 2002.
2. See Vernon Wessels, 'Adjournment spices commission session', *Business Report*, 8 April 2002.
3. A copy of the letter, addressed to SACOB and dated 8 April 2002, was handed by Kevin Wakeford to the author.
4. See http://www.justice.gov.za/commissions/comm_rand/final%20report.htm.
5. Deutsche Bank's 'confidential settlement agreement' with the Reserve Bank, dated May 2002, was published by the Rand Commission and is available at http://www.justice.gov.za/commissions/comm_rand/prs/may_28_rand_settlement_2002.htm.
6. The deal would result in Deutsche's London branch selling short dual-listed shares to long-term foreign investors, either through London- or South African-registered stock or American Depositary Receipts. Deutsche London would then borrow the shares it sold, receive the foreign exchange and convert this into rands. The rands would be loaned to Deutsche Securities in South Africa to buy stocks on the JSE Securities Exchange. These JSE shares would be bought forward by London. Deutsche London would continue to replace its remaining Sasol and Nampak shares with investors.
7. See 'South Africa: Perceptions baffle brains', *Business Day*, 26 July 2002.
8. See Vernon Wessels, 'Letter attributed to Sacob chief Kevin Wakeford over plot to knock rand stirs hornet's nest: Deutsche, Sasol deny collusion', *Business Report*, March 2002.
9. Sworn statement by James Cross to the Rand Commission, 8 April 2002.

CHAPTER 7

1. Mark Langley, in sworn testimony to the Rand Commission on 5 March 2002; see http://www.justice.gov.za/commissions/comm_rand/rand_hearings_pdfs/5march.pdf. See also Vernon Wessels, 'SA banking is shady, rand probe hears',

Business Report, 6 March 2002: http://www.iol.co.za/news/south-africa/sa-banking-is-shady-rand-probe-hears-1.82899?ot=inmsa.ArticlePrintPageLayout.ot.

2. See John Fraser, 'South Africa: Sasol turns up the heat on Sacob, Wakeford', *Business Day*, 17 September 2002.

3. Kevin Wakeford heard from more than a few people who had seen Tito Mboweni 'red-carding' him on national television. Wakeford recalls his disappointment, at the time, that the Reserve Bank governor could have treated an apparently serious matter in such a trivial manner.

CHAPTER 8

1. See http://en.wikipedia.org/wiki/Moral_hazard.

2. Gretchen Morgenson and Joshua Rosner, *Reckless Endangerment* (New York: Times Books, 2011).

3. Published in 2010 by W.W. Norton & Company.

4. Matt Taibbi, 'The great American bubble machine', *Rolling Stone*, 5 April 2010: http://www.rollingstone.com/politics/news/the-great-american-bubble-machine-20100405.

5. On 4 January 2013, ACA Financial filed a second amended complaint naming Paulson & Co and its hedge fund Paulson Credit Opportunities Master II Ltd as defendants in a US$120 million lawsuit it brought against Goldman in 2011. ACA Financial alleged, inter alia, that 'Paulson and Goldman conspired to market a structured finance product, known as ABACUS, which was designed to fail so that Paulson could reap huge profits by shorting the portfolio and Goldman Sachs could reap huge fees'. See http://www.aca.com/press/pdfs/2013/ACA%20Adds%20Paulson.pdf. A Reuters article providing a wider context can be found at http://www.reuters.com/article/2013/01/31/paulson-abacus-aca-goldman-idUSL1N0B0A5020130131.

6. See, for example, https://docs.google.com/viewer?a5v&q5cache:Z84cE4g-9ZcJ: www.dmr.gov.za/publications/finish/198-ministerspeeches-2012/840-address-by-minister-susan-shabangu-at-theafrica-down-under-conference-perth-australia-29-august-2012/0.html1&hl5en&gl5za&pid5bl&srcid5ADGEESh7VtklasIGLk1X 0t2YyCMjuP4oP3fYLt1U8mwHq-v0Us8p8-wdYoNl-TxDVaU3jNElk_UilbbaUp HRybmkU-Fl6EYO5dIjvD6eG9VEHz9VsykSv9i_sPtLfIa0ATg0Sn-rFv&sig5AHI EtbR0nM5vHi0LsY8QB0WBCaLy199yJw.

7. See Lizel Steenkamp, 'Political hyenas in feeding frenzy – Vavi', *Beeld*, 26 August 2010: http://m.news24.com/news24/SouthAfrica/Politics/Political-hyenas-in-feeding-frenzy-20100826.

8. For the DMR's full letter, dated 24 January 2011, see http://www.moneyweb.co.za/ mw/action/media/downloadFile?media_fileid=10049.

9. Cynthia Carroll's full speech, made on 4 December 2012, can be found at http://www.moneyweb.co.za/moneyweb-mining/building-the-future--south-africa-and-mining.

CHAPTER 9

1. *Time* magazine, 30 December 2002 – 6 January 2003.
2. Based on notes taken by the author during and after conversations with Brett Kebble, 1996 through 2005.
3. [2007] SCA 26 (RSA).
4. The full Phoenix judgment – Minister of Social Development and Others v Phoenix Cash & Carry Pmb CC (189/06, 244/06) [2007] ZASCA 26; [2007] SCA 26 (RSA); [2007] 3 All SA 115 (SCA) (27 March 2007) – can be found at http://www.saflii.org/za/cases/ZASCA/2007/26.html.
5. Verbatim public testimony, given under oath by Mark Parker at the Rand Commission on 10 April 2002.
6. See Francois Ebersohn and Hilary Joffe, 'Mboweni takes banks to task over rand testimony', *Business Day*, 8 May 2002. Mboweni gave his remarks during an appearance before the Executive Management Institute of Southern Africa the night before. His formal speech can be found at http://www.centralbanking.com/ central-banking/speech/1428883/speech-tito-mboweni-rb-south-africa-may. Mboweni's remarks related to the Rand Commission were not part of his formal speech.
7. Thabo Mbeki's comments on specific sectors of the community were part of his discourse; see http://en.wikipedia.org/wiki/Thabo_Mbeki and http://www.guardian.co.uk/world/2004/oct/05/southafrica.rorycarroll.
8. See 'Upper Echelon podcast: Russell Loubser – CEO, JSE', *Moneyweb*, 19 October 2011: http://www.moneyweb.co.za/moneyweb-upper-echelon/upper-echelon-podcast-russell-loubser--ceo-jse.

EPILOGUE

1. See http://www.bloomberg.com/news/2013-01-31/germany-willnever-let-ecb-shut-deutsche-bank.html.
2. See 'Rothschild provides a full range of financial advisory services from our office in Johannesburg, as well as servicing Africa's French speaking regions from Paris': http://www.rothschild.com/south-africa/. See also http://www.miningmx .com/pls/cms/mmx_rain.profile_detail?p_nid=90.
3. For biographical details on Jürgen E. Schrempp, see http://en.wikipedia.org/wiki/ J%C3%BCrgen_E._Schrempp.
4. See Alexander Eichler, 'CFTC head Gary Gensler on Libor scandal: "We're all losers"', *Huffington Post*, 13 July 2012: http://www.huffingtonpost.com/2012/07/ 13/gary-gensler-libor_n_1672197.html.
5. See 'CFTC orders Barclays to pay $200 million penalty for attempted manipulation of and false reporting concerning LIBOR and Euribor benchmark interest rates', dated 27 June 2012: http://www.cftc.gov/PressRoom/ PressReleases/pr6289-12.
6. See 'The turmoil at Barclays: First-mover disadvantage: Bob Diamond, Barclays

and regulators are all battling to save their reputations', *The Economist*, 7 July 2012: http://www.economist.com/node/21558300.

7. See 'The LIBOR scandal: The rotten heart of finance: A scandal over key interest rates is about to go global', *The Economist*, 7 July 2012: http://www.economist.com/node/21558281.

8. The article in the *Sunday Times Business Times* was published on 14 July 2012, and subsequently appeared on ABSA's website: http://www.absa.co.za/Absacoza/Media-Centre/Press-Statements/Ramos-fights-on-all-fronts.

9. See Alexander Eichler, 'CFTC head Gary Gensler on Libor Scandal: "We're all losers"'.

10. See 'Sasol concludes R1,45 billion Tshwarisano BEE deal', dated 30 June 2006: http://www.sasol.com/media-centre/media-releases/sasol-concludes-r145-billion-tshwarisano-bee-deal.

11. See Barry Sergeant, 'Inglorious justice', *Moneyweb*, 26 November 2009: http://www.moneyweb.co.za/moneyweb-soapbox/inglorious-justice.

12. See Barry Sergeant, 'Maduna's can of worms: A top civil servant accuses the minister of justice of using state apparatus for his own personal interests and agendas', *Moneyweb*, 6 October 2003: http://www.moneyweb.co.za/moneyweb-historical-news-news/madunas-can-of-worms?sn=Daily%20news%20detail.

13. See Barry Sergeant, 'The night Tshishonga was "fired": A chilling night-time telephone call during high summer', *Moneyweb*, 6 October 2003: http://www.moneyweb.co.za/moneyweb-historical-news-news/the-night-tshishonga-was-fired?sn=Daily%20news%20detail.

14. See Barry Sergeant, 'Pickled in Pretoria: Vusi Pikoli, national director of the National Prosecuting Authority, which houses the Scorpions, is in a pickle. Has there been a cover up of fraud and corruption in the liquidations sector?' *Moneyweb*, 9 February 2005: http://www.moneyweb.co.za/moneyweb-historical-news-news/pickled-in-pretoria?sn=Daily%20news%20detail. This article was also published in full on the same date in *The Citizen*.

15. A full account of Mike Tshishonga's experiences can be found in *Whistleblower: The Mike Tshishonga Story* by Lesedi Kuenda (Johannesburg: Abunda Publishing, 2011).

16. The letter of removal sent to Enver 'Motala' was dated 5 September 2011 and was signed by Deputy Master Christine Rossouw, an employee of the Department of Justice and Constitutional Development. The letter ran to nine pages, and was circulated to a number of interested parties, including a specialist attorney who forwarded it to the author. The matter was widely reported at the time; see, for example, http://www.iol.co.za/business/business-news/master-kicks-motala-off-panel-1.1133229?ot=inmsa.ArticlePrintPageLayout.ot.

17. See 'Simelane appointment is "aberration"', *Independent Online*, 7 December 2009: http://www.iol.co.za/news/politics/simelane-appointment-is-aberration-1.466933.

18. See Ernest Mabuza, 'Justice boss faces Ginwala fallout', *Business Day*, 10 December 2008: http://www.armsdeal-vpo.co.za/articles13/justice.html.

19. See 'Sasol Limited's response to finding by European Commission', published by Sasol on 1 October 2008: http://www.sasol.com/media-centre/media-releases/sasol-limiteds-response-finding-european-commission.

20. See page 81 of Sasol's Form 20-F, dated 28 September 2010, filed with the Washington-based Securities and Exchange Commission: http://www.sasol.com/sites/default/files/publications/integrated_reports/downloads/2010.pdf.

21. See 'Manuel wants new auditing laws', *News 24*, 20 February 2002: http://www.news24.com/xArchive/Archive/Manuel-wants-new-auditing-laws-20020220.

22. See pubic release by the Securities and Exchange Commission, dated 15 July 2010, 'Goldman Sachs to pay record $550 million to settle SEC charges related to subprime mortgage CDO: Firm acknowledges CDO marketing materials were incomplete and should have revealed Paulson's role': http://www.sec.gov/news/press/2010/2010-123.htm.

23. The *Global Competitiveness Report 2012–2013*, published by the Geneva-based World Economic Forum, can be found at http://reports.weforum.org/global-competitiveness-report-2012-2013/#=.

24. The letter is from an undated newspaper clipping handed to the author by Kevin Wakeford.

POSTSCRIPT

1. See http://www.justiceonline.org/commentary/fbi-files-ows.html.

2. See Wikipedia, http://en.wikipedia.org/wiki/Black_Wednesday.

3. See http://www.euromoneyplc.com/.

4. See pages 234–235.

5. See the Bloomberg article by journalists Liam Vaughan, Gavin Finch and Ambereen Choudhury at: http://www.bloomberg.com/news/2013-06-11/traders-said-to-rig-currency-rates-to-profit-off-clients.html.

6. See http://www.wmcompany.com/pdfs/026808.pdf.

7. The WM/Reuters rates are published hourly for 160 currencies and half-hourly for 21 more heavily traded currencies such as the British pound and the South African rand.

8. See http://www.ftse.com/. FTSE calculates over 120 000 end-of-day and real-time indices covering more than 80 countries and all major asset classes.

9. See http://www.msci.com/. MSCI advertises itself as a 'leading provider of investment decision support tools to around 7 500 clients worldwide, ranging from large pension plans to boutique hedge funds'.

10. See http://www.morningstar.com/.

11. See http://www.statestreet.com/.

12. See http://thomsonreuters.com/

Index

God does not fear Man

By the same author

Brett Kebble: The Inside Story

There is nothing man can do, no evil on a holocaust scale than can make God tremble or fear the action of man. God is greater than the ...

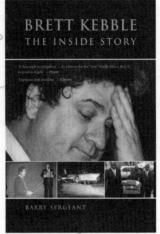

In September 2005, corporate South Africa was rocked by the violent murder of mining maverick Brett Kebble. In life, he was known as a billionaire patron of the arts, compassionate philanthropist, champion of black economic empowerment, urbane raconteur and generous host.

But within six months of his death, Kebble was exposed as the architect of one of the biggest and most convoluted frauds seen by any stock exchange in the world, a flawed genius who lied and cheated and stole so cunningly that even astute auditors were fooled.

By the time he died, Kebble was both broke and jobless. His legacy was a maze of convoluted transactions that would take forensic investigators months, perhaps years, to untangle. The trail would lead from one of the African continent's oldest and most venerable mining houses to more than 100 shell companies; from the diamond fields of Angola to the new black elite in democratic South Africa's upmarket suburbs.

But in the wake of Kebble's death, far darker secrets than his unorthodox and downright criminal transactions would also come to light. Many of them are revealed for the first time in this hard-hitting A-B-C of Brett Kebble's brilliant but terminally crooked business career.

ISBNs: 978 1 77007 306 7 (print) | 978 1 77022 290 8 (ePub) | 978 1 77022 291 5 (PDF)